RESPONSE TO REVOLUTION

RESPONSE TO

REVOLUTION

The United States and the
Cuban Revolution, 1959–1961

RICHARD E. WELCH, JR.

The University of North Carolina Press

Chapel Hill and London

© 1985 The University of North Carolina Press

All rights reserved

Manufactured in the United States of America

Library of Congress Cataloging in Publication Data

Welch, Richard E.

    Response to revolution.

    Bibliography: p.

    Includes index.

    1. United States—Foreign relations—Cuba.   2. Cuba—
Foreign relations—United States.   3. Cuba—History—
Revolution, 1959.   4. United States—Foreign relations—
1953–1961.   I. Title.

E183.8.C9W34 1985   327.7307291   84-25604

ISBN 0-8078-1613-2

ISBN 0-8078-4136-6 (pbk.)

The excerpt from Lawrence Ferlinghetti,
One Thousand Fearful Words for Fidel Castro
is reprinted by permission of New Directions
Publishing Corporation.

For
Christina Marquand Welch
and
Christina Therese Strauss

Contents

Acknowledgments

I am indebted to all the libraries and institutions cited in the bibliography and particularly to the staffs of the Harvard University and Columbia University libraries; the Hoover Institution on War, Revolution and Peace; the John F. Kennedy Library; the New York Public Library; and the libraries of the U.S. Department of State and the Organization of American States.

I also thank the two anonymous readers of the manuscript for their thoughtful suggestions.

I wish to express my appreciation to the President and Board of Trustees of Lafayette College and its Committee on Advanced Study and Research for grants of time and money. I am equally indebted to the secretary of the Lafayette History Department. Hilda Cooper has mastered the technology of the word processor while remaining alert to inconsistencies of spelling and grammar.

My greatest obligation, of course, is to CMW.

Richard E. Welch, Jr.
Lafayette College
Easton, Pennsylvania

THE REVOLUTION

Chapter One

Chronology, Myths, and Phases

The Cuban Revolution directed by Fidel Castro transformed the political organization, economy, and class structure of Cuba. As the most radical social revolution in Latin American history it has inspired widespread sympathy and bitter denunciation. Many of its interpreters have displayed a strong ideological bias; as a result its origins and evolution are wrapped in controversy, exaggeration, and myth. One can best approach the controversies and myths by way of the comparatively solid ground of a summary chronicle, tracing the early development of Castroism and the first three years of the Cuban Revolution.[1]

In the early hours of 1 January 1959 the Cuban dictator President Fulgencio Batista fled the country. Some forty-eight hours later the victorious rebels of the 26th of July Movement claimed control of Havana. These events, representing the culmination of a political struggle that had begun soon after Batista regained power in a coup d'etat of 1952, marked the end of the guerrilla war led by Fidel Castro. Castro enters Cuban history on 26 July 1953, the date of his ill-fated attack on the Moncada Barracks in Santiago, Cuba. "Castroism" may be dated from his famous "History Will Absolve Me!" speech, initially delivered at his trial in October 1953 and subsequently enlarged and amended during his imprisonment on the Isle of Pines. This speech made no effort to describe a detailed blueprint for social or economic reformation. It offered an indictment of Batista tyranny, a justification for armed violence, and a program of political reforms similar to those advocated by the Ortodoxo party, which then claimed Castro's formal allegiance. Castro was content to place himself within the general framework of Cuban left-wing politics and the revolutionary tradition of José Marti.

The beneficiary of one of Batista's periodic general pardons, Castro was released from prison and sailed for Mexico in May 1955.

Two months later, he formally proclaimed the 26th of July Movement. Within a year he had cut ties with the Ortodoxo party and other anti-Batista movements, and announced that Cuban salvation would be achieved through armed insurrection and the leadership of Fidel Castro. With some eighty followers, Castro then embarked in the leaky tub *Granma* for the Oriente coast in eastern Cuba. Ambushed by a detachment of Batista's soldiers, his "army" was reduced to a dozen men who found refuge in the jungle fastness of the Sierra Maestra. From this mountain redoubt Castro issued a call to arms in November 1956 and proclaimed the "Political-Social Manifesto from the Sierra Maestra" on 12 July 1957.

This manifesto was the only formal program signed by Castro before he came to power, and it offers the best illustration of Castroism in its guerrilla phase. Its tone was nationalistic, reformist, and vaguely socialistic, and its goals were free elections, constitutional government, agrarian reform, increased industrialization, and the exclusion of all forms of foreign intervention. Its demands found their origin in the past history of Cuban left-wing democratic, nationalist movements. The originality of the 26th of July Movement lay not in its ideas, but in its armed resistance tactics, its military command structure, the mystique of its leader, and its determination not to accept compromises that could endanger the independence of the movement. In December 1957 Castro censured a "Pact of Unity" fashioned by various anti-Batista representatives in Miami for its failure to prohibit compromise with any post-Batista military junta and its failure to denounce foreign intervention. After Batista was driven from Cuba, it should be the heroes of the Sierra Maestra who would maintain public order, reorganize the army, and establish a provisional government.

Castro had given warning to other elements of the anti-Batista opposition, and with the early days of 1959 he made good his claim to primacy for the *barbudos* (the "bearded ones"). Army generals, comparatively untainted by association with Batista, who hoped to fashion a mixed military-civilian junta quickly were cowed into submission and members of the Civil Resistance and the student underground (the Directorio Revolucionario) who expected to share power with Castro's guerrilla army soon were outmaneuvered. By 8 January 1959 when Castro completed his triumphal progress across the island of Cuba and entered Havana, the city was under the sole control of the 26th of July Movement and its soldiers. Castro's personal appointee, Manuel Urrutia, was installed as president and the regular army purged and melded with the *barbudos* to give Castro control of the armed forces. The next month saw two hundred leading Batistianos tried by revolutionary tribunals and executed, and on 7 February the new government vested all legislative powers in a council of ministers. A week later Castro replaced Miró Cardona as prime minister and for the first time assumed an official post of leadership in the provisional government.

In March, the new government decreed a 50 percent reduction in all rents, denounced the United States for the aid it had given the Batista dictatorship, and "intervened" the Cuban Telephone Company, a monopoly owned by private U.S. capital. In May, Fidel signed an agrarian reform bill in La Plata, the former rebel capital in the Sierra Maestra. A compromise between the competing agrarian reform ideas of land redistribution and national planning, the law of 17 May 1959 was more sweeping than the agrarian reform decree approved by the rebel chieftain in 1958, but it provided for monetary compensation in the form of twenty-year bonds at 4.5 percent interest. The advocates of state operation of the agrarian sector were appeased by the encouragement given agricultural cooperatives and the establishment of the state-run National Institute of Agrarian Reform.

June saw the first of several ministerial shuffles that reflected sharpening disagreement between the evolving moderate and radical factions of the provisional government. With the forced resignation of Urrutia as president in July and his replacement by Osvaldo Dorticós, the moderate faction suffered public defeat and Castro's position as Maximum Leader was emphasized. The moderates were those who continued to believe that social reform was possible under a regulated, mixed economy and a constitutional political system, and who expressed increasing fear at what they saw as the twin dangers of communist influence and totalitarian politics. Their leadership was impaired in the fall of 1959 when Major Hubert Matos was arrested and imprisoned and Major Camilo Cienfuegos died in an airplane accident. Matos and Cienfuegos had been rebel officers during the civil war and were figures of considerable popularity within the 26th of July Movement. With their eclipse, the influence of Raúl Castro and Ché Guevara increased and Fidel came to view the moderates as counterrevolutionaries.[2] By the late fall of 1959, the Cuban Revolution was still ideologically ambivalent, but anticommunism was officially denounced and the revolutionary regime became more centralized and more intolerant of dissent.[3] Among the new wave of emigrés were many original supporters of Fidel Castro and his 26th of July Movement.

The year 1960 was proclaimed the Year of Agrarian Reform. It began with denunciations of the United States for its conspiratorial encouragement of bombing raids by Cuban refugees and with an invitation to Soviet First Deputy Premier Anastas I. Mikoyan to open a Soviet trade exhibition in Havana. Mikoyan's visit was followed, on 13 February 1960, by the signing of trade and economic aid agreements under which the Soviet Union agreed to buy one million tons of Cuban sugar over each of the next five years and extend Cuba $100 million credit for the purchase of industrial equipment. Similar agreements would follow with other members of the Eastern bloc nations.

On 4 March 1960 the French ship *La Coubre*, engaged in unloading a shipment of arms, exploded under mysterious circumstances and Castro immediately blamed the Central Intelligence Agency. Two months later Cuba formally reestablished diplomatic relations with the Soviet Union, and when the Eisenhower administration in July canceled the balance of Cuba's 1960 sugar quota, Khrushchev promised that Russia would increase its sugar purchase by an equivalent amount.

Accompanying the deterioration of Cuban–U.S. relations in 1960 and the development of trade between Cuba and the Soviet bloc were a series of measures increasing the authority of the central government over organized labor, agricultural production, and private property. The Agrarian Reform Act of May 1959 was implemented in a fashion that brought 50 percent of Cuban lands under the direct management of the Agrarian Institute and favored state farms over the communally owned cooperatives. Foreign ownership of land was prohibited and in the summer and fall of 1960 several acts were passed confiscating privately owned enterprises, both foreign and domestic. By October 1960, the "economic heights" had been nationalized and many smaller enterprises as well.[4] Cuba was not yet a socialist country but under the victorious radical faction of the revolutionary government it was already anticapitalist. U.S. oil companies in Cuba, which had refused a governmental order to refine Russian petroleum imports, were nationalized; compensation for confiscated U.S. investments was made dependent on continued sugar sales to the United States; members of the Cuban Communist party, the Partido Socialista Popular (PSP), were admitted to middle-level positions in various government ministries and agencies; and Cuba signed a five-year trade agreement with the People's Republic of China.

Summer and fall of 1960 also saw rising antagonism by the Castro regime toward the Organization of American States (OAS). When the OAS approved the Declaration of San José on 29 August, proclaiming that extracontinental intervention endangered the security and solidarity of the Americas, Castro denounced the OAS as a tool of U.S. economic diplomacy. In his Declaration of Havana, he denied that the Soviet Union had any interventionist designs in the Western Hemisphere while announcing the intention of Cuba to continue to seek Soviet assistance. Castro excoriated the United States at a special meeting of the United Nations General Assembly in September, and the Cuban government subsequently increased its orders for military equipment from Czechoslovakia and other communist countries. When the United States embargoed all exports to Cuba, except for nonsubsidized foodstuffs and medical supplies, the Cuban government expropriated the last of the major enterprises owned wholly or partially by U.S. citizens. As 1960 ended, Cuba and the Soviet Union signed a joint communiqué whereby Cuba expressed support for the foreign policy of the Soviet Union and its allies and applauded their encouragement of economic development in the Third World.

The year 1961 would see an abortive U.S.-backed military invasion of Cuba, the formal proclamation of Cuban socialism, and Fidel Castro's pledge of adherence to a *fidelista* version of Marxism-Leninism. That year was designated the Year of Education, and on New Year's Day thousands of young Cubans left Havana to begin a grass-roots campaign to eliminate illiteracy in rural Cuba. Their success, if exaggerated, was remarkable and capped a series of earlier reform efforts by the revolutionary regime in the areas of housing construction, racial equality, and improved health and sanitary services for the *campesinos* and rural poor. In foreign eyes, these social welfare achievements were overshadowed by diplomatic and ideological developments.

When Castro on 2 January demanded that the U.S. embassy in Havana be reduced from eighty-seven to eleven officials within forty-eight hours, the Eisenhower administration promptly terminated all diplomatic and consular relations with Cuba. This decision was supported by the incoming administration of John F. Kennedy, which fixed the Cuban sugar quota at zero for 1961, issued a White Paper denouncing Castro for his betrayal of the Cuban Revolution, and gave the green light to an armed force of Cuban exiles who had been trained by CIA personnel at a secret base in Guatemala. The exile brigade landed at Playa Girón in the Bay of Pigs on 17 April 1961 and was quickly defeated and imprisoned by the Cuban military under the personal direction of Fidel Castro. After the failure of the Bay of Pigs invasion, Russia was emboldened to forge a more formal alliance with Cuba, and Castro proclaimed Cuba a socialist nation and promised a new socialist constitution. In July 1961 Castro announced the formation of the Organizaciones Revolucionarias Integradas (ORI), which would integrate the 26th of July Movement with the PSP and serve as precursor of a United Party of the Socialist Revolution. Castro defended single-party government as necessary to the continued momentum of a socialist revolution that would provide work, education, equality, and lifelong economic security for all citizens. Agricultural and industrial workers represented the Cuban people, and their approval of Cuban socialism made political elections irrelevant. The new Cuba had no use for parasitic bourgeois capitalism.[5]

By the year's end the United States had declared a total embargo on all trade with Cuba, the USSR had bestowed the Lenin Peace Prize on Fidel, Cuba had announced a four-year industrialization plan, and Castro had proclaimed "I am a Marxist-Leninist." Cuba was a socialist state possessed of a government nationalist and communist, totalitarian and populist.

Its radical evolution and political ambiguities assured that the Cuban Revolution would be the subject of controversy and widely contrasting interpretations. Around those controversies would grow the lichen of legend and myth. For if the early chronology of Castroism and the Cuban Revolution can be summarized with little difficulty, the relationship between events, the motivation of the revolutionary leaders, and questions of responsibility for the rapid transformation of the revolution have been the subject of continuing dispute and exaggeration. Any description of the Cuban Revolution in its early years must supplement chronological summary with an analysis of these myths and controversies.

One of the first myths was carefully cultivated by the leaders of the 26th of July Movement. This myth suggested that it was Castro and the *barbudos* alone who brought down Batista. They alone did the fighting and sacrificed their blood in the cause of liberation. This assertion was propagated in the United States by some of Castro's champions and was frequently associated with the legend that Castro's army was composed of *campesinos* and that his success was the result of a popular peasant rebellion. In point of fact, the war against Batista was fought by sections of all classes—peasant soldiers, middle-class intellectuals, university students, professional and business groups, and urban workers engaged in active and passive resistance.[6] Castro's comparatively small army of bearded guerrillas fought well and courageously, but Batista was brought down by a wide spectrum of opponents and by the dictator's own failures.

The Cuban Revolution, like all revolutions, finds an essential part of its origin in the decay of the existing regime. The corruption, violence, and illegitimacy of the Batista government undermined its support with the urban bourgeoisie. The Cuban economy in 1957–58 exhibited "high-level stagnation," and Batista gradually lost the allegiance of the politically aware segments of the civilian population. Structural weaknesses in the Cuban economy went uncorrected and official terrorism inspired a general sense of civic outrage. One does not deny the historical importance of Fidel Castro or his skill as a guerrilla leader and propagandist by insisting that Batista contributed largely to his own defeat. The economic problems of Cuban society and the eroding coherence of Cuban political organization paved the way for Castro's victory.[7] Castro's political skill was exhibited not in driving Batista into exile but in capitalizing on the confusion and weakness of other anti-Batista organizations and gaining unitary control of the new government within a fortnight after Batista's flight.

Another myth sees Batista and Castro as cause and effect: Castro the revolutionary as the creation of Batista the dictator. As with many myths, there is a small core of truth. Castro perceived Batista as a personal enemy as well as an obstacle to the redemption of Cuban society and sovereignty. But Batista did not make a revolutionary of Fidel Castro. The Batista dictatorship helped a member of the Ortodoxo party find the path of radical political expression necessary to his needs and temperament, and imprisonment by that dictatorship helped inspire an increasing impatience with the Ortodoxos and a determination to pursue a separate course of action. Yet Batista can no more be credited with Castro's self-image as a charismatic leader than he can be blamed for Castro's subsequent determination to sustain revolutionary momentum by means of an alliance with the Cuban communists. Batista inspired the 26th of July Movement; he did not father the nationalistic revolutionary temper of Fidel Castro or the latter's determination to reign as well as to lead.

A more significant and widely held myth holds that Fidel Castro was a communist from the beginning of his career as a Cuban revolutionary. This report was spread by some of Castro's opponents in Cuba and many of his enemies in the United States, including members of the Senate Internal Security Subcommittee. In its most extreme form, Castro was not only a communist by the date of his attack on the Moncada Barracks but was earlier employed by the Soviet Union as a communist agent in Mexico, when he was but twenty-one years old.[8]

Here is a myth that is not an exaggeration but a lie. Castro at twenty-one was a left-leaning student who disliked authority and had feelings of guilt and suspicion toward his own class, the Cuban bourgeoisie. He was a revolutionary in search of a revolution, but he was not a communist. By temperament a *caudillo*, and by the definitions of U.S. political history never a democrat, Castro only became a Marxist sometime between fall 1960 and fall 1961.

Castro himself is partially responsible for the myths surrounding his conversion to Marxist ideology. During a long speech on 2 December 1961 he declared himself a Marxist-Leninist and in parts of that rambling oration seemed to imply that he had long been sympathetic to socialist doctrine. These portions were inaccurately translated in early press reports and subsequently taken out of context by his enemies in the United States. It became a part of anti-Castro mythology that Castro acknowledged he had been a Marxist-Leninist for many years and had purposely concealed his communist identification the better to increase his support and confound his foes.[9] Actually the chief theme of this confused and self-exculpatory address was that although he had always been a socialist intuitively, he was initially in thralldom to bourgeois values. Only by hard study and several stages had he come to a full appreciation of the superior wisdom of Marx and Lenin and the value of their teaching for the reorganization of Cuban society. *Now* he understood that Marxism was "the most correct, most scientific, the only true theory, the only true revolutionary theory."[10]

In later speeches he would make little reference to his days of "bourgeois thralldom," and those forays in autobiographical revisionism have assisted antagonistic interpreters determined to oversimplify the relationship of Castroism and communism. In the process these interpreters have granted Castro an unearned measure of ideological stability. The Castro of the 1950s was a man who thought mostly with his instinct and a man who worried little about doctrinal or ideological consistency. He was prepared at different times to make use of various slogans and appeals, showed a definite aversion to institutionalization of thought or program, and was inspired as much by the cult of action as by any political philosophy. His political program in the 1950s was composed of several disparate, even warring elements: Ortodoxo-style democratic reformism, apolitical nihilism, and an amorphous agrarian socialism. Essentially an activist, Castro was a political opportunist by necessity and sought to make a virtue of his lack of doctrinaire ideology.

From the beginning elements of continuity and consistency existed, but they centered about temperament and antagonisms, not doctrine. There was the will to dominate, a sense of messianic mission, a fervid patriotism, and a hatred of foreign domination over the culture and economy of Cuba. Fidel Castro was the first *fidelista,* and he saw himself as savior of Cuban sovereignty and the Cuban soul. He came to power with visions of radical reform and with a keen distrust of the United States and the power of U.S. capital, but he did not come to power with a Marxist program or ideology. His reading of Cuban history and his personal need for battle had already determined that he would be an enemy of U.S. diplomatic influence and foreign investment, but he became a Marxist by gradual and distinct stages, first for pragmatic reasons and only later from self-induced ideological convictions. Those who insist that "Castro was always a communist" deny the complexity as well as the historical development of the Cuban Revolution.

The same may be said, if less certainly, of the various theories that proclaim Castro "the betrayer of the Cuban Revolution." The best known of these theories is that authored by the journalist-historian Theodore Draper and adopted by Arthur M. Schlesinger, Jr. in the White Paper on Cuba he drafted for the Kennedy Administration in April 1961. According to Draper, Castro was not a communist when he came to power but by the end of 1959 he had determined to join forces with the Cuban communists as a means of retaining and enhancing his personal power. By calculated design he perverted a social democratic revolution into a communist, totalitarian dictatorship, transforming a movement that promised needed reform into a conspiracy that destroyed individual liberty and made Cuba a Soviet satellite. Under Castro's direction the revolution promised by the 26th of July Movement was aborted and betrayed.[11]

Draper is certainly correct in emphasizing that Castro's initial program called for representative democracy as well as social reform and made no demands for the nationalization of land and industry. His chronology, however, oversimplifies the stages of the revolution and accelerates Castro's gradual and erratic journey toward Marxism-Leninism. Moreover, Draper implies a measure of evil intent that is at best unproven. It is probable that Castro initially believed that he could achieve social–economic change and eliminate foreign interference by a revolution respectful of civil liberties and constitutional procedures and only later determined—as the result of a series of domestic and external developments—that one-party dictatorship and the support of Cuban communists and the Soviet Union were necessary to assure the fulfillment and momentum of a radical social revolution. What is at issue here is not the accuracy of Castro's evolving estimate of the requirements for radical social revolution but the question of conspiratorial design.

The initial program of the 26th of July Movement was sufficiently ambiguous so that some of Castro's early followers were bound to feel betrayed however the revolution developed. That development was in the direction of increasing radicalization, and it was the moderate revolutionaries who lost influence, suffered economic injury, and felt betrayed. The Cuban Revolution did not originate as a clear-cut bourgeois revolution or peasant uprising or proletarian revolution, but as an amorphous set of reformist goals calculated to appeal to various groups and classes. Perceptions and expectations varied and for some supporters a sense of betrayal was inevitable.

It requires little effort to list a score of promises that Castro made and broke, but consequences are not proof of intent. Castro's goal was a transformation of Cuban society and the identification of social revolution in Cuba with the movement and person of Fidel Castro. Democratic methods and instruments were rejected and totalitarian ones adopted over the course of 1959–61, but Castro claimed that these changes were made necessary by the opposition of reactionaries at home and abroad and were required to ensure the integrity and progress of the revolution. Political pluralism was impractical for a fundamental restructuring of Cuban society; constitutional restraints must give way to the authority of the state and its revolutionary vanguard. True *fidelistas* would follow their leader, to the Left.

Some historians have claimed that Castro undertook one revolution and finding it insufficient for a restructuring of Cuban society proceeded to make another of socialist and totalitarian design.[12] It seems more likely that there was a single revolution of several phases, whose methods and instrumentalities underwent a radical change that Castro had neither promised nor planned. An indigenous Latin American revolution "went communist" by gradual and perceptible stages.[13] If in the process it was distorted, it was not necessarily betrayed.

It is difficult to exaggerate the importance of analyzing the Cuban Revolution as a historical development of several distinct phases. What is true of Fidel Castro and his revolution at one stage is not necessarily true at another. The Cuban Revolution evolved from a variant of democratic reformism to a variant of communism, and its radicalization is best understood when its early years are divided into three separate periods. These periods cannot be given specific dates, but a logical three-part chronological division identifies as phase one, January–October 1959; phase two, November 1959–December 1960; and phase three, 1961 and spring 1962. Historians differ over the labels to be given these three phases. For the historian who sees Castro's adoption of communism as the main theme of the Cuban Revolution, phase one might be labeled "from anticommunism to anti-anticommunism"; phase two, "from anti-anticommunism to procommunism"; and phase three, "from procommunism to communist."[14] The transformation of the Cuban Revolution during Castro's first forty months in power was, however, more than a question of changing political doctrine; the process of radicalization altered the political, economic, and social structure of the island. The three phases might better be labeled "the polarization of the 26th of July Movement"; "the socialization of the Cuban economy"; and "the establishment of a *fidelista* communist state."

January–October 1959: Polarization of 26th of July Movement

In its first ten months the Castro regime underwent both political and economic transformation, but it was in the political area that the more significant developments occurred. During this period there evolved a sharpening division between moderates and radicals within the 26th of July Movement. For most of the period Castro zigzagged between the two factions, serving as a balance wheel of sorts, but by October 1959 he clearly identified with the radicals.[15] The rift between the moderates and the radicals concerned the rights of private property and the role of free enterprise, but also involved such questions as the desirability of elections, the function of political parties, and the relationship of the provisional government to the Cuban Communist party (the PSP).

The unexpectedly complete collapse of the Batista regime and the emigration of leading Batistianos had rendered leaderless and impotent the conservative Right. Rather to its surprise, the new revolutionary leadership found that initially it faced no organized opposition. This fact encouraged it to proceed more swiftly with agrarian reform and other social-economic measures and to ignore earlier promises about elections and the Constitution of 1940. Centers of dissent then developed within the ranks of the *fidelistas*, which in turn polarized the 26th of July Movement, triggered the first purges, and served as impetus for the radicalization of Castro and his revolution. The development of opposition fueled Castro's antagonism toward the Cuban bourgeoisie, encouraged a renewed emphasis on the role of the Cuban peasants as prime supporters and beneficiaries of the revolution, and brought anticommunism into disrepute as the false cry of traitorous obstructionists.

The first "obstructionists" to be defeated were those who might be called the right-wing moderates. Advocates of a mixed economy and regulated capitalism, they favored modest land redistribution and continued private enterprise in the agricultural sector. They also favored the encouragement of U.S. public and private capital. They were disappointed by Castro's refusal to ask for economic aid during his visit to Washington, D.C. in April 1959; they were disgruntled by the terms of the Agrarian Reform Act of May 1959 (wishing nothing more radical than the terms of the Sierra Maestra decree of October 1958); and they were angered by the forced resignation of President Manuel Urrutia in July 1959, which they attributed to the dictatorial ambitions of Castro. By July 1959 these right-wing moderates had been expelled from the movement and many fled to the United States.

Other self-assessed moderates, more centrist in view, assumed a posture of opposition less from devotion to private enterprise than from fears of communist influence and infiltration.[16] Such early Castro supporters as Hubert Matos and Camilo Cienfuegos were angered by the growing influence of Ché Guevara and Raúl Castro and by the appointment of members of the PSP to the new bureaucracy. They disapproved of Castro's anti-American speech at the UN in September 1959 and were disappointed by Castro's refusal to appoint old *barbudos* companions to top political and military posts. Matos and Cienfuegos plotted to use the remodeled armed forces as a counter to Guevara's influence and to compel Castro to reestablish the anticommunist position of the 26th of July Movement. By the end of October 1959 they, too, had been eliminated.

By that date, not only anticommunism but reformism was in disrepute within the central leadership of the provisional government.

The division of the 26th of July Movement had destroyed Castro's confidence in the movement as a sufficient agent for correcting social and economic ills. Castro was prepared to welcome support from members of the PSP as "truly revolutionary" allies and was determined to proceed with accelerated pace in the task of transforming Cuba's political economy and social structure. This would be largely accomplished in the revolution's next phase.

November 1959–December 1960: Socialization of Cuban Economy

Emphasis during the second period would be primarily on economic decrees and changes, but in the process of promoting the nationalization of mines, utilities, sugar companies, oil refineries, and over 50 percent of Cuban land, the Castro regime also assured further political polarization. The revolution assumed an increasingly class character, and class antagonism became class conflict. Deciding that a democratic government using voluntaristic instruments was insufficient to the task of restructuring the social-economic system, the revolutionary elite promoted political as well as economic centralization. Egalitarian goals demanded expanding authority for the revolutionary government over all economic sectors and institutions. Only a combination of political centralization and socialist planning could eliminate social injustice and every vestige of a colonialist economy.[17]

This phase opened with a new shake-up of the government ministries and an appearance by Castro at the general convention of the major Cuban labor organization (Congress of the Revolutionary Confederation of Labor). At the convention, Castro demanded that PSP members, who were less than 10 percent of the membership, be given 50 percent of the posts on the Confederation council. Resistance by David Salvador and other anticommunist union leaders produced a compromise solution, but by January 1960 the leading anticommunists were purged from the council and by March 1960 Salvador was forced to resign his post. The reorganization of labor under PSP leadership was a clear indication that Castro had determined to use the apparat of the Cuban Communist party as a means for committing organized labor to his regime and program.

While the Cuban bourgeoisie was converted into the domestic enemy, organized labor was to be allied with the *campesinos* as the source of working-class support for the revolutionary government and its evolving socialization of the Cuban economy.[18]

The spring of 1960 witnessed the *La Coubre* explosion and heightened charges of collusion between U.S. agents and domestic subversives. There was extensive censorship of the press and further restrictions on the rights of political organization and dissent. By summer more PSP members were installed in lower-echelon government positions and preparations were being made for initiating a new series of economic decrees that would emphasize state economic planning. With the fall of 1960 came the expropriation of major industries and expanded direction and control by the central government over means of production. Private enterprise was now openly proclaimed an obstacle to the momentum of the revolution as well as to Cuban economic development. The Agrarian Reform Law was administered and revised to restrict land distribution in the form of small freeholds and to encourage the enlistment of peasant farmers in the cooperatives and state farms.[19] By December, the second Organic Law of the Ministry of Labor gave strengthened powers to that body to regulate the wages and assignment of urban labor, and another decree, establishing the Higher Council of Universities, climaxed efforts by the government to limit the autonomy of institutions of higher education and the freedom of student organizations.[20]

By the end of 1960 there was no longer any doubt that Castro had become convinced that in socialization of the Cuban economy lay the best path to effecting a revolution that would end Cuban reliance on U.S. capital and secure justice for the working classes.[21] Taking advantage of the absence of a unified, progressive national bourgeoisie, Castro had proceeded to give the revolution a decided class character. It was a revolution for the working classes and a revolution that would be directed and controlled by a revolutionary elite.[22] Leaders of the PSP were now a part of that elite, but the decision to attack private property and capitalist institutions was made by Castro and the radical wing of the 26th of July Movement, not by the Cuban Communist party.

Although Castro did not formally characterize the Cuban Revolution as a socialist revolution before spring 1961, the "economic heights" of the Cuban economy and most of the larger industrial and agricultural enterprises had been nationalized by the end of 1960. Cuba was not a communist state, however, in December 1960. It would become a communist state, of a special type, over the next sixteen months.

January 1961–April 1962: Establishment of a Fidelista Communist State

The year 1961 was a key year in the evolution of the political style and institutions of communist Cuba. Not only did socialization of the economy accelerate but the Castro regime was increasingly identified with the communist bloc nations, statist controls began to approach totalitarianism, and the formal establishment of a single-party political system combined the remnants of the 26th of July Movement with the PSP.

Castro did not announce the merger of the 26th of July Movement and the PSP until 26 July 1961, but during the previous winter and spring PSP members had become part of the revolutionary political command and in April Castro publicly declared the socialist character of the Cuban Revolution. In his speech of 26 July Castro announced that the ORI would serve as the vehicle of the worker–peasant alliance, and the authority of the one-party state and its leadership was illustrated in a new Law of Labor Organization. On 2 December 1961 Castro delivered his famous speech announcing the identification of the revolution and its leadership with the faith of Marxism-Leninism. Cuba would be a communist state, but communism in Cuba would be joined to the *fidelista* mystique. That fact was made clear to all when in the following March Castro organized a purge of certain of the old communist leaders of the PSP, including its foremost ideologue Aníbal Escalante, thereby asserting Castro's personal leadership of the apparat of the Cuban communists.[23]

In the final analysis, Castro joined forces with the Cuban communists and adopted the doctrines of Marxism-Leninism more from pragmatic than from ideological considerations. The communists would serve as the core of a one-party revolutionary dictatorship and help assure revolutionary momentum; revolutionary socialism would serve as a vehicle for guaranteeing economic development, as demonstrated by the example of the Soviet Union. Once persuaded that Marxist socialism was applicable to the needs of Cuba and compatible with the continued authority of the Maximum Leader, Castro then convinced himself of its doctrinal truth.[24]

The role of Fidel Castro in each of these early phases of the Cuban Revolution has been emphasized because one of the most important elements of continuity in its evolution was the uninterrupted leadership of Fidel. Some students have called Castro the Kerensky and the Lenin of the Cuban Revolution. One might better say he was its Mirabeau and Robespierre. Castro and the revolution moved leftward in unison and at no point was Castro's leadership and control seriously threatened. A broad-based, reformist revolution became by stages a radical, socialist revolution yet it remained throughout a Cuban, Castro-directed revolution. This was a remarkable feat, and it furnishes one explanation for the unique character of Cuban communism as well as the special nature of the Cuban Revolution.[25]

Fidelista communism was guilty of numerous doctrinal heresies. It minimized the importance of Marx's economic stages and implied that these stages could be telescoped and socialism achieved by way of a fast-paced revolution that relied more on the psychic transformation of man than on the achievement of certain levels of monopoly capitalism and proletarian oppression. It stressed what Guevara would call "the New Man" and put its faith in moral rather than in material incentives. But, most importantly, it insisted on combining communist dogma with *fidelista* charisma, favoring charismatic over bureaucratic sanctions. Castro served as legitimizing symbol for the Cuban Revolution, and never more so than when the revolution moved to the stage of a socialist economy and one-party authoritarian government.[26] The paternalistic relationship of Castro to the Cuban working classes assured majority support for the new social order, as Castro linked communism with Cuban nationalism and gave Cuban communism a rural guerrilla mystique.

No other twentieth-century revolution in Latin America produced a leader who maintained the continuous command of Fidel

Castro. For that reason, and others, no Latin American revolution achieved the tempo or breadth of the Cuban Revolution, which effected a more radical social transformation than did earlier social revolutionary movements in Mexico or Bolivia. Cuba was, of course, less handicapped by the power of landed oligarchies or the vestiges of neofeudalism, and had already experienced considerable capitalist economic development, but the comparative social-economic transformations effected by the revolutionary movements in Cuba, Mexico, and Bolivia can only be understood by considering distinctions of leadership as well as national history.

When comparing the Cuban Revolution with communist revolutions in Europe, the most marked difference is that in Cuba the revolution was not the product of a communist clique or externally directed coup and was not beholden to the Red Army. The Cuban Revolution was directed leftward by the radical faction of the 26th of July Movement. Castro subsequently lost faith in the movement as a political vehicle and turned to the Cuban communists, but the latter were his instruments and not his masters. The revolution in Cuba was a radical, national revolution that only by stages "went communist," and in this fact resides not only much of its special character but an important clue in explaining why its leftward course was accomplished with comparatively little opposition or bloodshed.[27]

Certainly it is true that the encouragement and asylum given by the United States to anti-Castro emigrés assisted Castro in ridding himself of opponents without the necessity for bloody purges. But U.S. immigration policy is not the primary explanation for Castro's ability to effect a comparatively peaceful social revolution. Because his revolution began as an independent nationalist movement and because he was able at each stage to identify the revolution with Cuban patriotism and his own messianic leadership, Castro was able to transform Cuba into a communist state with at the very least the passive support of the majority of the Cuban masses. A political opportunist, Castro was also a Cuban patriot and charismatic leader—communism in Cuba would be both totalitarian and popular.

Castro's revolution did not follow some inexorable internal logic or great master plan. It did move always leftward and in the process not only gained identification with "the Communist world" but discovered its own ideology. That ideology was a special Cuban blend of *fidelismo* and Marxism-Leninism.

So far this analysis of the early evolution of the Cuban Revolution and its various phases has emphasized domestic events and causes, which are most important in explaining the leftward course of the revolution. Of nearly equal significance, however, are the foreign policy problems and aspirations of the Cuban revolutionaries.[28] No study of the transformation of Castro's goals can ignore the influence on the Cuban Revolution of the United States and the USSR. Significant interaction existed between Castro's domestic policies and his foreign policy. The most obvious example concerns Castro's need for Soviet aid and his adoption of socialism.[29]

In a manner similar to his decision to seek the support of the PSP, Castro by the early months of 1960 decided to seek the aid of the Soviet Union. Castro first sought Soviet trade and later military supplies and still later identification with the Warsaw Pact nations as a means of sustaining his social revolution while counteracting real and anticipated injury from the United States. Initially he believed neutralism in the Cold War would be sufficient to the needs of Cuban self-determination; subsequently he opted for an alliance with the Soviet Union. That alliance would create a new form of dependence, but Castro and his fellow radicals were convinced it was a different and more malleable form of dependence.[30] The Soviet Union, for its part, was less the pursuer than the pursued. Concerned with sustaining the "spirit of Camp David" and fearful that overt Russian support might lessen the appeal of Castroism in Latin America and inspire U.S. military intervention in Cuba, Khrushchev was wary of linking Russian prestige with a bearded Robin Hood whose revolution stood outside communist discipline and control. Khrushchev could see advantage in encouraging Caribbean revolutionaries to take a posture of defiance toward the United States; an America distracted by developments in its immediate sphere of influence was less likely to cause problems for the Soviet Union in other regions. But Khrushchev would tread cautiously as long as Castro's success appeared uncertain.

It was thus Castro who was the initiator at each stage in the evolving relationship of Cuba and the Soviet Union. It was the self-assessed needs of revolutionary Cuba rather than the diplomatic ambitions of the Soviet Union that would draw the Cuban Revolution into the power conflicts of the Cold War. That involvement in turn further polarized supporters and opponents of the revolution in Cuba and affected the future course of the Cuban Revolution.[31] Indeed, some historians, most notably Andrés Suárez, insist that Castro's conversion to communism was primarily determined by foreign policy considerations, and the transformation of Cuba into a communist state primarily the result of Castro's decision that he needed the support of the other nuclear power.[32] Such a judgment exaggerates and oversimplifies. Suárez is correct, however, in emphasizing Castro's emerging conviction that as a "national democratic" ally he could not be sure of Soviet support. That conviction, together with domestic requirements for sustaining revolutionary momentum, encouraged his conversion to socialism. Castro needed to increase his bargaining leverage with Moscow and saw the advantage of confronting the Soviets not only with a "national-liberationist" revolution but a revolution of socialist design and allegiance.[33]

Cuba could lessen its isolation by inspiring a wave of revolutionary activity in Latin America or by gaining support from the communist bloc. By 1960 it was clear that there would be no wave of imitative revolutions in the Caribbean basin. Henceforth Castro would seek to strengthen Cuban ties with the USSR and other communist bloc nations and he would use the PSP at home as witness and propagandist for the evolving identification of his revolution with socialist goals and programs.[34] Concurrently, Castro became convinced that the socialist path offered the most likely route for Cuban economic development and the desired transformation of Cuban society. The need to obtain greater material and diplomatic commitments from the Soviet Union did not itself persuade Castro of the rightfulness of Marxist socialism for Cuba, but it did accelerate his conversion.

Similarly, the escalating animosity between Fidel's regime and the United States encouraged both the radicalization of the Cuban Revolution and Castro's search for Soviet support. Antagonism between Havana and Washington had direct impact on Castro's Russian policy. That policy incited U.S. economic and diplomatic sanctions, which in turn drove Castro to seek additional assistance from members of the Warsaw Pact. The reenforcing effect of external and internal pressures helps to explain Castro's election of a totalitarian, socialist framework for maintaining and expanding the Cuban Revolution:

The United States did not force Fidel Castro to adopt socialism or a revolutionary dictatorship or an alliance with the Soviet Union. American policy encouraged those developments, however, and was influential in determining the chronology of the stages of the revolution. Initially bewildered and erratically uncooperative, U.S. policy became more and more antagonistic. By 1961 antagonism had become open enmity. Castro capitalized on that enmity to speed the formation of a communist state at home and to forge closer links abroad with a Russian government now eager to promote a Soviet presence in the Caribbean.

The question of the relationship of the U.S. government to the Cuban Revolution requires further analysis. It frequently has been charged than an unwilling Castro was driven into the arms of communism and the Soviet Union by the calculated hostility of American policy makers.[35] This interpretation is perhaps not as inaccurate as the countermyth to the effect that the United States wished to be a cooperative Big Brother to the Cuban Revolution and was rebuffed times without number before being forced to recognize the Revolution as an implacable enemy,[36] but it has proven more lasting. Initially, of course, this interpretation received support from Cuban revolutionaries as well as Castro sympathizers in the United States. Once Castro declared Cuba a socialist republic and announced his conversion to Marxism-Leninism, there was no further suggestion by the revolutionaries of Havana that U.S. policy, however evil its intent, had been the primary cause of Castro's alignment with the Cuban communists and the Eastern bloc nations. The applicability of Marxism to the Cuban situation provided sufficient cause. Many Castro sympathizers in the United States, however, continued to insist that American enmity gave Castro no choice but to seek alliance with the PSP and Moscow.

America's Cuban policy was neither intelligent nor successful. It was not, however, the primary cause of the radical course of the Cuban Revolution or of Castro's convergence with the Soviet Union and Marxism.

Whatever the ideological bent of policy makers in Washington, it was virtually certain that there would be some degree of confrontation between the United States and the revolutionaries in Havana.[37] Had Castro consented to a gradualist, democratic social revolution, that confrontation might have been limited and sporadic, but Castro came to power with vaguely anticapitalist and strongly antiimperialist convictions and the large U.S. investment in the Cuban economy was a natural target. Significant change in the system of economic ownership and distribution required that U.S. private capital be expelled from its strategic position. Once the radical faction of the 26th of July Movement had decided in summer 1959 that the weakness of their internal opposition made possible an accelerated pace for social-economic change, they did not expect accommodation with Washington and saw advantage in displaying Cuban independence by severing diplomatic and economic ties with the United States. Accommodation would mean compromise and compromise would limit the objectives of the revolution. U.S. policy at several points helped the radical faction of the 26th of July Movement, but U.S. policy did not create that faction or its goals for the social-economic transformation of Cuba. It diminishes the importance of the Cuban Revolution and confuses the chronology of its evolutionary stages to view its radicalization as the product of actions done or left undone by the administrations of Dwight Eisenhower and John Kennedy.

For the cross-fertilization of animosity that developed in 1959–61, both nations were responsible. The initiative was taken as often by Havana as by Washington. Castro found U.S. antagonism a useful rallying cry for revolutionaries at home as well as an effective argument for support from abroad. Conciliation of the United States would not only undermine his authority among radical revolutionaries in Cuba but destroy his diplomatic leverage with Soviet bloc nations and lessen his appeal for potential revolutionaries in Latin America.

It is possible to accept two seemingly contradictory propositions: (1) Castro's revolution probably would have turned leftward whatever the United States did or did not do. (2) Although U.S. policy did not force Castro to establish a revolutionary dictatorship, a socialized economy, or a communist state, it did have very real influence on the evolution of the Cuban Revolution. Actions by the United States do not furnish the primary explanation for the course of the Cuban Revolution but they facilitated its radical transformation.[38]

One must make distinctions between the magnitude of U.S. influence on Castro's evolving association with the PSP, with the USSR, and with the ideology of Marxism-Leninism. American policy was probably most influential in determining the tempo and direction of Castro's Russian policy. On the other hand, it appears to have been least influential in Castro's decision to proclaim an identification with Marxist doctrine and was of only indirect influence on Castro's decision to acquire the support of the Cuban communists. When Castro elected to seek the support of Russia and the Communist bloc nations, his decision was determined in part by injuries received and anticipated from the United States. Quite possibly Castro's need for defense supplies and economic subsidy would have required an alliance with Russia at some point, but U.S. economic sanctions hastened the evolution and timing of the Cuban–Russian alliance.

More complicated is the story of U.S. influence on the hopes and failure of Castro's domestic opponents. Some of the earliest of those opponents were Cuban entrepreneurs closely connected with U.S. property investment in Cuba, and the issue of property protection was a major concern for self-styled "moderates" among the professional classes as well as large landowners and successful businessmen. The fears of Cuban and American capitalists were mutually reenforcing; both were quick to suspect communist infiltration of the new revolutionary regime. As the PSP received growing recognition from the Castro government, they concluded that the PSP was taking over the revolution.

Castro denounced the anticommunist rhetoric of Urrutia and Matos as the propaganda of suborned spokesmen of U.S. economic imperialism. Fidel successfully linked domestic dissenters with foreign enemies and in the process identified dissent with treason. Dissenters were fifth columnists, plotting in behalf of monopoly capitalists in the United States. His charges were exaggerated but effective in rallying support for the leftward drift of his revolution. Furthermore, they appeared to receive support from a U.S. immigration policy that welcomed Cuban refugees without restrictions or quotas. The availability of asylum in Miami did not create the successive waves of emigration but it was a source of encouragement.[39] While some opponents of Castro stayed in Cuba and hoped that intensifying American pressure would force a shift to the Right, other opponents fled Cuba and hoped to organize in the United States a counterrevolution backed by American arms and money.

The most important effect of U.S. Cuban policy was not in determining the program of the revolutionary elite but in helping Castro convince the Cuban people of the necessity of turning the revolution ever leftward. U.S. policy helped Castro persuade the Cuban masses that the United States was the enemy of the Cuban Revolution and that security for the revolution lay in nationalization of the economy and association with the brotherhood of socialist nations. Indeed, U.S. policy had effects diametrically opposite to its intentions, by furthering the centralization of the Cuban political system, facilitating the power of the Cuban revolutionary elite, and speeding the formation of the Cuban–Russian alliance.

To say that U.S. policy determined the evolution of the Cuban Revolution in 1959–61 is to perpetuate a myth; to say that U.S. policy had the unintended effect of accelerating that evolution in several important ways is accurate. Any study of U.S. response to the Cuban Revolution must begin then with an analysis of official diplomatic response, which, like the early history of the Cuban Revolution, is best analyzed by chronological stages. The next four chapters cover the evolution of U.S. Cuban policy from the oscillation of the Eisenhower administration to the aftermath of the Bay of Pigs invasion.

THE OFFICIAL RESPONSE

Chapter Two

The Failure of Ambassador Bonsal

Eisenhower Cuban Policy, January 1959–
February 1960

The United States was the first country to recognize the government of Fidel Castro. On 6 January 1959 the State Department sent a formal note of recognition and proclaimed "the sincere goodwill of the Government and people of the United States toward the new Government and people of Cuba." A fortnight later, the Department announced that the career diplomat Philip Bonsal would be the new U.S. ambassador to Havana.

The selection of Bonsal was intended to demonstrate that the United States, whatever its worries over Castro's political susceptibilities and inexperience, was prepared to wish for the best. The best would be a Cuban government that would combine necessary political reform with respectful attention to long-standing diplomatic and economic ties with the United States. Bonsal's successful ambassadorial tour in Bolivia, where he had gained the goodwill of the left-of-center government, should convince Castro that the new ambassador was no enemy of change. He was untainted with any identification with the Batista dictatorship, spoke fluent Spanish, and would be a wise counselor to a government that wished to effect New Deal-style liberal reforms.

Bonsal arrived in Havana on 1 March with high hopes for cordial relations with the Cuban revolutionaries. He had no doubt that he would be more popular and more helpful to the advancement of Cuban democracy than his predecessor, Earl E. T. Smith.

Smith, a Palm Beach financier and political appointee, had served as U.S. ambassador from March 1957 to December 1958, when the civil war against Batista raced to its climax. Though less enamored

of Batista than *his* predecessor, Arthur Gardiner, Smith was a classic example of the wrong man in the wrong place at the wrong
time. Pridefully conscious of his position as a self-made million-
aire, Smith was also the prideful amateur suspicious of diplomatic
professionals and bureaucrats. He saw his role as that of the guard-
ian of American influence and American business interests in
Cuba. Revolutionaries were agents of disorder and from the first he
was ready to believe the worst of Castro.

By the summer of 1958 Smith had lost faith in Batista's ability
to serve as a satisfactory instrument for ending insurrection, but
he hoped that Batista could be persuaded to cooperate with conservative and professional elements in arranging a peaceful succes-
sion that would exclude any participation by Castro and his 26th of
July Movement. Smith had not approved Washington's decision in
March/April to cut off arms supplies to Batista; the action encouraged the Sierra Maestra guerrillas while lessening the influence of
the United States on the Batista government. He was irritated by
Washington's declarations of nonintervention in Cuban affairs and
by a policy that seemed content to drift with events. Smith had
urged Batista to allow the presidential election of November 1958
to be held as scheduled, and though displeased that the election
was overtly rigged in behalf of a Batista puppet, Dr. Rivero Agüero,
Smith requested the State Department to give Agüero its full political and military support. Smith went to Washington on 23 November to urge an end to a policy of nonintervention that could only
help Castro and risk a situation of political paralysis conducive to
the evil designs of the Cuban communists. He was informed by
William Wieland, director of the Office of Caribbean and Mexican
Affairs, and Roy R. Rubottom, assistant secretary of state for Latin
American Affairs, that the circumstances of Agüero's election denied any possibility that "respected civil and military elements"
would give him support or that he could end the civil war and form
an effective government. Smith returned to Havana and on 15 December was instructed by the State Department to request a personal interview with Batista and inform the Cuban president that
the United States favored his early resignation so that certain un-
identified groups in Cuba might have the opportunity to "salvage
the rapidly deteriorating situation." Smith found the task distasteful and was disappointed by Batista's subsequent decision to flee

the country. For a brief forty-eight-hour period after Batista's flight, Smith held out hopes that Colonel Barquín and a military-civilian junta might prevent Castro's ascension to power, but on 6 January with a sense of personal defeat and grievance he forwarded to the new government and its provisional president Manuel Urrutia formal notification of U.S. recognition.[1]

Smith's sense of grievance was directed as much toward the bureaucrats of the fourth floor of the Department of State headquarters in Washington as toward Fidel Castro. The passage of time heightened his sense of injustice, and Smith became a favorite witness of right-wing senators who sought to demonstrate that Marxist-oriented "liberal intellectuals" in the Department of State had sold Batista down the river, as earlier they had undermined free enterprise capitalism and Chiang Kai-shek in China. By the time he wrote his account of the "Castro Communist Revolution," Smith was ready to charge that Castro sympathizers in the Havana embassy and in the State Department were personally responsible for Castro's assumption of power and the subsequent victory of communism in Cuba. He elaborated a conspiracy theory that indicted credulous newsmen, such as Herbert L. Matthews of the *New York Times*, Batista-hating embassy officials, and left-leaning bureaucrats. Among the latter the archvillains were Wieland and Rubottom. As a result of their stupidity, or worse, Washington had failed to heed Smith's warnings that the victory of Castro would represent a victory for international communism.[2]

Though Smith would not present his full indictment until 1962, certain senatorial and press critics of the State Department were noisily evident by the summer of 1959. The State Department would respond to their charges erratically and ineffectively. The Department sought to appease the Senate Subcommittee on Internal Security while denouncing its press releases as "inaccurate and misleading."[3] The Department's response to Castro's charges of American military collaboration with the Batista regime was more consistent, although factually incomplete.

In his early days in power Castro combined assurances of democratic intent with denunciations of the collaboration of the U.S. military with the fallen dictator. On 15 January 1959 the State Department issued a blanket denial of the charges, protesting the "widespread lack of understanding of what United States policy toward Cuba has been." It pointed to the arms cutoff to Batista in the spring of 1958 as proof that the United States had sought "to avoid all possible involvement in Cuba's internal conflict." The presence in Cuba of a U.S. military mission had been authorized by the government of Dr. Carlos Prío Socarrás back in 1950; no mission personnel had been present in "zones of operation"; Batista had received no U.S. arms by way of Nicaragua.[4] The U.S. explanation was accurate in its specific details, but it did not speak to the broader implications of Castro's charge. The last months of the Cuban civil war had not seen the United States giving military support to Batista's army, but there had been sporadic and ineffective efforts to prevent a political victory for the 26th of July Movement. The claim of the State Department that its policy "has been strictly one of nonintervention in Cuban domestic affairs" stretched the truth.

In November 1958 the CIA, with the approval of the Department of State, had made contact with Justo Carrillo and some anti-Castro rebels known as the Montecristi group; on 9 December 1958 William D. Pawley (a wealthy businessman and diplomatic troubleshooter) had been sent on a secret mission to Havana, with vague instructions to discover how Batista might be induced to surrender power to a caretaker government both anti-Batista and anti-Castro in character; and in the State Department several meetings were held in the last weeks of 1958 at which possibilities of U.S. encouragement of a "third force solution" were reviewed in meandering fashion.[5] These activities did not represent a concerted anti-Castro strategy nor were they "overt intervention," but Castro's belief that the 26th of July Movement owed little to the goodwill of the United States was justified.

U.S. efforts to deter or limit the political success of Fidel Castro were indecisive and stillborn.[6] The pace of military events in Oriente Province, and the surprisingly swift collapse of the political props of the Batista regime following the desertion of its leader, make them appear feckless at best. They provide, however, a part of the diplomatic burden inherited by Philip Bonsal. The history of the last months of 1958 along with the history of the preceding sixty years made doubtful if not impossible a fresh beginning in Cuban–American relations.

Although dubious about the probable future course of the Cuban Revolution, the State Department was prepared by the end of the first week of January 1959 to acknowledge a fait accompli and recognize Castro's effective control of the Cuban government. Acting Secretary of State Christian Herter was consoled by reports that Castro had reiterated his commitment to the Cuban Constitution of 1940 and its restoration.[7] Dwight David Eisenhower, who had displayed comparatively little interest in Latin American and Caribbean developments, informed a news conference at the end of January that he hoped the new Cuban government "will be truly representative of the Cuban people" and "will achieve the ability to reflect their views, their aspirations, and . . . help their progress."[8]

Castro was determined to demonstrate that the new government would operate independently of the dictates of the United States, and Bonsal's early efforts to arrange a personal meeting were unavailing. Bonsal believed that his first priority was to assuage suspicions and gain the confidence of the Cuban people and their new government. As he later recalled, "I made every effort . . . in talking with newspaper and magazine editors and many other influential citizens to convey the good will of the people and the government of the United States."[9] Bonsal's personality was that of a sophisticated, intelligent, ambitious career professional. He sincerely wished the new government well, yet was totally incapable of understanding the temperament of Fidel Castro. Bonsal prized control and was constitutionally allergic to the melodramatic. He would labor earnestly to gain the confidence of the young revolutionaries of the 26th of July Movement and he would persistently fail. His failure was made probable by the long identification of the United States with conservative and subservient Cuban regimes, and it was made more certain by the personality differences of Philip Bonsal and Fidel Castro.

Charges by Herbert Matthews that Bonsal, a descendant of Gouverneur Morris, was too "aristocratic" and by Karl Meyer and Tad Szulc that Bonsal was too anxious "to avoid exposure and conflict" were wide of the mark.[10] Bonsal was neither reactionary nor timid. Rather he was a man of goodwill who put great reliance on doing things in an orderly way, by regular channels. Diplomacy should be characterized not by emotion and oratory but by rational analysis and intelligent compromise. All governments should evaluate foreign policy options by weighing advantages and disadvantages in a cost/benefit analysis. The Cuban government must recognize that it needed the aid and support of the United States and so come round to welcoming the proffered friendship and guidance of the United States.

Bonsal approved the selection in March of Ernesto Dihigo y López as the new Cuban ambassador to Washington. He judged Dihigo a moderate and hoped his advice would neutralize the anti-American rhetoric of Ché Guevara and Raúl Castro. Bonsal was equally pleased with Eisenhower's formal "reply" when Dihigo presented his credentials. After assuring the Cuban ambassador that "our nation has not forgotten its own revolutionary origin," Eisenhower noted "with deep satisfaction" Dihigo's assurances that the changes "being wrought by the recent revolution in Cuba" reflected the desire of the Cuban people "for freedom and for the effective exercise of representative democracy."[11] Bonsal, however, was an intelligent man as well as a diplomat who thought it wise policy to put the best face on things. He certainly was aware in the spring of 1959 that Eisenhower and Castro would find it difficult to agree on a definition of "representative democracy"; consequently, Bonsal entertained doubts about the probable success of Castro's visit to the United States in mid-April.

Castro's invitation came not from the Eisenhower administration but from the American Society of Newspaper Editors. He was invited to address the National Press Club in Washington on 17 April. Fidel's acceptance surprised and irritated Eisenhower as well as Christian Herter, about to be nominated as John Foster Dulles's successor as Secretary of State. Eisenhower in late March had received word from the CIA that "the Castro regime was moving more and more towards an outright dictatorship." He decided that Castro's visit should receive no presidential blessing. Eisenhower would go to Augusta, Georgia to play golf and leave to Herter and Vice-President Richard Nixon the task of meeting informally with Castro to hear his requests and try to discover his true intentions respecting communism, constitutional democracy, and Cuban relations with the United States.[12]

Nixon wrote Eisenhower a long memorandum of his conversation with Castro. The abbreviated version he later made public emphasized the vulnerability of a credulous Fidel to the designs of international communism.[13] In many ways the more interesting reaction was that of Herter, however. Herter first reported to Ike in Augusta, where he informed him that he found Castro "a most interesting individual, very much like a child in many ways" and "quite immature regarding problems of government." The appearance of "Castro's bearded wild-eyed bodyguard" was "one of the most startling sights" that the proper Bostonian had ever seen.[14] A few days later, Herter wrote a more detailed evaluation. He cautioned that "the Castro who came to Washington was a man on his best behavior"; indications that Cuba "would remain in the western camp" must be regarded as "uncertain." Despite Castro's efforts to conciliate the American public, there was "little probability that Castro has altered the essentially radical course of the revolution." The United States had best continue a wait-and-see policy and should evaluate Castro's "decisions on specific matters before assuming a more optimistic view than heretofore about the possibility of developing a constructive relationship with him and his government."[15]

Herter, Nixon, and Bonsal were all surprised that Castro did not take the opportunity of his Washington visit to ask for U.S. economic bounty. The balance of evidence indicates that the Eisenhower administration in the spring of 1959 was prepared at least to discuss economic assistance to the revolutionary government of Cuba. Indeed, there was an expectation that a request from Castro for a long-term aid package would open the way to discussions about the political direction of the Cuban government and Castro's attitude toward foreign property investment in Cuba.[16] In early April Castro had indicated to some Cuban treasury officials that he was considering a request for U.S. economic aid, but shortly before he embarked for Washington he had decided that such a request might endanger the independence and momentum of the revolution. The United States might seek a political veto on the extent of revolutionary change, and even the appearance of collaboration with the Yankee superpower could impair his popularity with revolutionaries at home and abroad.[17] Whatever Castro's reasons, the fact is that he decided against making a request for U.S. capital and technical assistance *before* he arrived in Washington. Those who damn the Eisenhower administration for its failure to "seize the opportunity" and win the favor of the Cuban revolutionaries by a

Caribbean equivalent of the Marshall Plan not only ignore the probable response of Congress but the refusal of Castro to play the role
of an Ernest Bevin or Georges Bidault.

Bonsal was disappointed that the Eisenhower administration did
not give Castro a more official welcome or flatter his ego with the
trappings of an interview in the Oval Office. He realized, however,
that the drumhead trials of several hundred Batistianos in January/
February had turned many congressmen and newscasters against
the new Cuban government. Moreover, he had recently experienced
at a conference in San Salvador an example of the suspicions of
some of his diplomatic colleagues. At this conference of U.S. am-
bassadors to Caribbean and Central American nations, Robert C.
Hill, ambassador to Mexico, had branded Castro a communist and
urged a get-tough policy against the Cuban revolutionary government. Bonsal had made a detailed presentation urging a continued
policy of "patience and forbearance." Castro, he declared, was not a
communist and a get-tough policy could only benefit the Cuban
communists by destroying all hopes of repairing Cuban–American
relations. Bonsal described Castro's broad popular support in Cuba
and the sympathy he had aroused in much of Latin America, and
insisted that Cuba had needed a revolution. He continued to hope
that once Castro had implemented certain reforms he would cease
his verbal attacks on the United States and the OAS and "return to
the family of Latin American nations." Castro must be persuaded
that the best hope for Cuba lay in renewed alliance with the American security system.[18]

Bonsal advocated the path of persuasion when faced with the first
major test of his ambassadorship: the Cuban Agrarian Reform Law
of May 1959. The United States should be understanding of the
need for land reform in Cuba while insisting on assured compensation for American citizens who owned some of the largest sugar
estates and ranches on the island.[19] Bonsal probably did not personally object to the proviso that payment would be made in long-term
bonds to be issued at some subsequent date by the Cuban government. He sympathized with the economic problems of the Cuban
Treasury Department and doubted its ability to offer cash on the
barrelhead. The State Department, more conscious of burgeoning
anti-Castro sentiment in Congress and sensitive to charges that it
was "soft on Castro," was less sympathetic about the cash flow

problems of Fidel's regime. The note Bonsal was instructed to give the Cuban minister of state on 11 June sought to give warning without giving undue offense.

The United States acknowledged that under international law any nation had the right to expropriate private property within its jurisdiction for public purposes. That right, however, was coupled with the obligation to offer "prompt, adequate, and effective compensation." U.S. citizens who had acquired property in Cuba over many years had done so in full obedience to Cuban statutes and constitutions. The latter, including the Constitution of 1940 which the new government was pledged to redeem, had provided that for expropriated property "there must be prior payment of the proper indemnification in cash, in the amount judicially determined." The recent agrarian reform law gave the government of the United States "serious concern" as to the adequacy of compensation that would be given U.S. citizens. It hoped that its concern would be mitigated by free and frank discussion, and regretted that to date "the Government of Cuba has found no opportunity to hear the views of those United States investors in Cuba whose interests would appear to be adversely affected."[20]

The Cuban government never saw reason to request their views, and Bonsal as well as the State Department came to see "agrarian reform" as little more than a cover for confiscation. The Cuban government issued none of its promised long-term bonds and many of the subsequent interventions of foreign-owned agricultural property took place outside the terms and sanctions of the Agrarian Reform Law. By November, Bonsal was losing faith in the likelihood or utility of free and frank discussion with Fidel Castro. This was the result of many factors, however, some more important than the "illegal" implementation of the Agrarian Reform Law. Among those factors was Castro's increasing disrespect for the OAS.

Bonsal, like most American diplomats with primary experience in the Latin American area, considered the OAS a major U.S. diplomatic achievement and an important part of the national security system. Castro's attacks on the organization as a creature of Washington and an instrument for preserving U.S. hegemony in the Western Hemisphere were judged unwarranted. Bonsal remained convinced that Castro was neither a communist nor an agent for communist subversion in the Caribbean, but he had no wish to see

Castroism expand and believed Castro was encouraging insurrectionary activity in several Caribbean nations. Latin American dictatorships, such as those in the Dominican Republic and Nicaragua, were an anachronism, but it was contrary to the Act of Chapultepec and the Rio Treaty for one country to seek to instigate insurrection against the legal government of a neighboring state. Bonsal was hopeful that the upcoming meeting of the foreign ministers of the American republics would address the problem of Cuban allegiance to the hemispheric security system.

The Eisenhower administration had seized the opportunity of charges by the Dominican Republic of two abortive invasions of its territory by rebel forces allegedly trained in Cuba to prod the Council of the OAS to schedule a meeting of American foreign ministers in Santiago, Chile, in mid-August.[21] Eisenhower had informed a press conference that the Caribbean area was "in a state of unrest" and that the United States hoped the meeting in Santiago would review the situation and propose corrective action.[22]

For the Eisenhower administration, the Santiago conference was a disappointment. Secretary Herter wished to obtain a collective warning to Cuba in exchange for an embargo against the unpopular Trujillo regime in the Dominican Republic, but the Declaration of Santiago, a bland and windy document, avoided specific reference to Cuba.

In his address to the plenary session, Herter had proclaimed that adherence to the doctrine of nonintervention and "maximum cooperation" for "the effective achievement of democratic principles" were essential to the purposes of the inter-American system, and that system constituted "one of the bulwarks of freedom" in a world threatened by the expansionist designs of international communism. Herter wanted the conference to issue a statement that would make clear that the OAS was concerned with communist subversion and infiltration as well as Pan-American amity. The OAS should support both the prohibitions of an expanded version of the Monroe Doctrine and the promises of the Good Neighbor Policy.[23]

Some of the delegates at Santiago saw a measure of contradiction in Herter's dual demand and were aware of the popularity of Castro and his revolution with a wide spectrum of left-of-center groups in Latin America. The Declaration of Santiago offered no criticism of

Cuba or *fidelista* propaganda. It spoke in broad terms of the importance of human rights and "the exercise of representative democracy" for the effective harmony of the American republics. Antidemocratic regimes were proclaimed a violation of the principles on which the OAS was founded and "a danger to united and peaceful relationships in the hemisphere." Herter subsequently would attempt to interpret these professions as a warning to Castro to eschew dictatorial methods and totalitarian associates and would point to the "strengthened" Inter-American Peace Committee, but the Eisenhower administration had lost faith in the OAS as an instrument for inhibiting the leftward trend of the Cuban Revolution.[24]

By the fall of 1959 Bonsal referred disapprovingly to that trend and to the submergence of the moderate faction of the 26th of July Movement. He informed Herbert Matthews that the Cuban communists hoped to encourage the radical faction to institute hasty and ill-considered reforms the better to produce a condition of confusion and anarchy.[25] As Castro declared anticommunism to be the subterfuge of enemies of the revolution, Bonsal found access to the revolutionary government increasingly difficult. He tried to explain that the readiness of certain American journalists and congressmen to label Castro a communist puppet did not represent the official policy of the United States, but the Havana newspaper *Revolucíon* became increasingly shrill in its denunciations of the U.S. "grand conspiracy" to thwart efforts by the revolutionary government to achieve economic independence and social justice.[26] Bonsal found himself caught between instructions from Washington to warn Castro of communist subversion and the deepening conviction of Castro and his more influential advisers that charges of communist infiltration were simply a rhetorical cover for vested interests that would restrict the revolution to milk-and-water reforms.

Bonsal's difficulties were heightened in October by the imprisonment of Hubert Matos, which certified the victory of the radical faction, and by Fidel's charges that the United States was encouraging Cuban defectors to bomb Cuban civilians. The latter charge was inspired by a "raid" conducted by a Cuban defector, Major Pedro Díaz Lanz on 21 October. According to Castro's account, Díaz, operating from an airfield in Florida, dropped several bombs on Havana that inflicted heavy civilian casualties, and the U.S. government was guilty of purposeful complicity in this aerial invasion. According to Washington, Díaz dropped anti-Castro leaflets, not bombs, and the injuries to Havana residents were the result of ill-directed antiaircraft fire. Washington insisted that it was unable to police all the small airfields in Florida and, though it regretted the unauthorized departure of Major Díaz, was guiltless of any wrong-doing. Bonsal was instructed to deliver a long statement to President Dorticós, defending the United States against the "utterly unfounded" charges of the Cuban government and voicing concern about the deterioration of the "traditional friendship" of the two nations.

In the judgment of the State Department, Cuban distrust and hostility were without warrant, for U.S. conduct had been friendly and correct at all times. The United States had been careful to observe a policy of nonintervention in the internal affairs of Cuba, and had earnestly sought to prevent illegal acts by its residents, "including citizens of Cuba who have sought refuge in Florida." On their own initiative, U.S. officials had authorized an intense investigation of "the reported flight over Havana on October 21 of an aircraft which dropped leaflets containing political propaganda." The current prohibition of arms sales to Cuba was part of a general policy adopted by the United States for the Caribbean region to discourage military shipments "likely to contribute to an increase of tension in the area." The government had as a matter of course made this policy known to its friends and allies in Europe, who "fully retained the right to make their own decision."

As an advocate of social and economic progress throughout the hemisphere, the United States had an obligation to call attention to "the antidemocratic, subversive activities of Communists in the service of foreign totalitarianism." Communism, "with its avowed purpose of imposing authoritarian rule and denying freedom of speech, religion, and assembly," stood in direct opposition to "the principles on which the American Republics and other free nations of the world are founded." Warnings against the "subversive activities of Communists" represented not an intrusion into the domestic affairs of Cuba but an obligation to the Free World and to the hemispheric security system of the Americas. The United States earnestly hoped that the government of Cuba would carefully review its policy and attitude toward the United States. For its part, the United States stood ready to use all normal diplomatic channels to correct misunderstandings and restore the traditional friendship of the two nations.[27]

Bonsal considered the statement firm but temperate. He must have had some qualms about the protestation that U.S. efforts to restrict arms sales were "not directed against the Government of Cuba," but he agreed with the State Department that the deterioration of Cuban–American relations was the responsibility primarily of Fidel and his anti-American advisers.[28] In contrast to Herter and Eisenhower, however, Bonsal had studied Cuban history and understood the long association of Cuban nationalism with anti-Yanqui sentiment. Eisenhower, on the contrary, seemed honestly puzzled at the animus shown by Fidel Castro. Confident of the forbearance of his administration's Cuban policy, he convinced himself that the Cuban leaders were either numbskulls or Red-tainted scoundrels. He told a news conference that he was downright puzzled by the conduct of the Castro government:

> I do feel . . . here is a country that you would believe, on the basis of our history, would be one of our real friends. . . . the trade concessions we have made, and the very close relationships that have existed . . . make it a puzzling matter to figure out just exactly why the Cubans and the Cuban government would be so unhappy when, after all, their principal market is right here. . . . I don't know exactly what the difficulty is.[29]

Seeing no explanation in logic for Cuban behavior, Eisenhower came gradually to the conclusion that CIA reports of increasing communist influence must be correct. As he told another news conference in early November, "The Communists like to fish in troubled waters, and there are certainly troubled waters there."[30]

The Department of State was divided in the closing days of 1959 on the question of the extent of communist influence in Cuba, but it was united in its belief that the spread of Castroism would endanger U.S. influence and effective economic development in Latin America. There was now a perceptible increase in the attention given Latin America by the Eisenhower administration. Reversing an earlier position, the White House expressed a willingness to see the United States participate in an inter-American development bank; it indicated an interest in programs aimed at stabilizing the price of certain Latin American agricultural exports; it appointed a National Advisory Committee on Inter-American Affairs to advise the secretary of state on the "long-range problems" of U.S.–Latin American relations. These measures were accompanied by unconvincing statements that they had no connection with the activities and propaganda of Fidel Castro.

Differences between Washington and Havana appeared irreconcilable. The Eisenhower administration found the radical revolutionary designs of the Castro regime increasingly distasteful, its Cold War neutralism dangerously provocative, and its acceptance of the assistance of the Cuban communists an open invitation to the machinations of international communism. Bonsal's hopes for a last-minute rescue of Cuban–American relations were doomed to disappointment; nevertheless he would attempt that rescue when called back to Washington on 21 January 1960 for consultation and a review of U.S. Cuban policy.

In Washington the tug and pull among Eisenhower's advisers on Latin American affairs climaxed on 25 January in a White House meeting of Bonsal with Herter, Rubottom, and the president. Eisenhower indicated that he was receiving advice to break all diplomatic and economic relations with Cuba. Reluctant to go to these lengths, he thought "the best course of action" would be for the OAS to go "down the line for us" and put some restraints on Castro. When Rubottom said that it would be difficult to get the fourteen votes necessary for any type of OAS action, Eisenhower replied that some of our OAS partners appeared to be "fair-weather friends." He suggested that a U.S. quarantine of Cuba could bring hunger and economic hardship to the island and inspire the people "to throw Castro out." He quickly backed away from this suggestion, however, when Bonsal argued that the United States "should not punish the whole Cuban people for the acts of one abnormal man." Eisenhower made clear that his chief concern was the extent of communist activities in Cuba, and Bonsal offered the opinion that though Guevara seemed to be under communist influence, Castro did not intend to turn Cuba into a communist state. The

United States should stand its ground but not invite a rupture; it must not give substance to Castro's false charges by precipitate or punitive actions.[31]

Bonsal presented the draft of a statement on U.S. Cuban policy. With minor revision, that draft provided the substance of the much-publicized statement issued by Eisenhower on 26 January 1960. Its tone was firm but conciliatory, and it represented a definite if brief success for the views and counsel of Philip Bonsal.

Eisenhower's "restatement of our policy toward Cuba" embraced six major points:

1. The United States remained committed to a policy of nonintervention in the domestic affairs of other countries in accordance with long-standing treaty obligations.
2. The United States was doing all in its power to prevent the use of its territory for illegal acts against Cuba, and in this respect compared favorably with Cuba whose government had failed to prevent the departure of "a number of invasions directed against other countries."
3. The United States was seriously concerned by the unfounded accusatations of Prime Minister Castro and other Cuban officials. Those attacks created "the illusion of aggressive acts and conspiratorial activities aimed at the Cuban Government" and this could only obstruct "the development in the real interest of the two peoples, of relations of understanding and confidence."
4. The United States recognized the right of the Cuban government and people to undertake social, economic, and political reforms which, "with due regard for their obligations under international law," they judged desirable.
5. The United States hoped that differences of opinion between the two governments would be resolved through diplomatic negotiations. In the event, however, that disagreements between the two governments should persist, it was the intention of the United States to seek solutions through "appropriate international procedures."
6. The U.S. government had confidence in the ability of the Cuban people "to recognize and defeat the intrigues of interna-

tional communism which are aimed at destroying democratic institutions in Cuba and the traditional and mutually beneficial friendship between the Cuban and American peoples."[32]

On the same day that Eisenhower issued this statement, the Argentine ambassador to Cuba was encouraged by the U.S. embassy in Havana to approach Castro unofficially with a first-step proposal for improving Cuban–American relations. Under this plan, Castro was to agree to cease his campaign of television and press attacks on the United States, welcome Bonsal back to Cuba with all courtesy, and allow Bonsal and Cuban foreign minister Roa to begin discussing American grievances and the possibility of U.S. economic assistance.[33]

Bonsal returned to Havana but Castro did not respond favorably either to Eisenhower's statement or to the compromise plan of Ambassador Julio Amoedo of Argentina. Both were judged propaganda ploys designed to conceal America's true intentions. In February Castro welcomed Mikoyan to a Soviet trade fair in Havana and began negotiations for Russian aid. A few weeks later he charged the United States with responsibility for the explosion that damaged the French ship *La Coubre* as it unloaded arms at the docks of Havana.

Castro's curt dismissal of the administration's self-assessed peace offering would itself probably have been sufficient for Eisenhower subsequently to reject Bonsal's counsel of continued patience, but it was Mikoyan's visit that made rejection certain. The activities of Cuban communists were a worry; solicitation of Russian communists was insupportable. As Bonsal later mournfully observed, the policy outlined in the statement of 26 January "lasted but a few weeks."[34]

The reaction of Latin America to any overt U.S. interference in Cuba was a major concern of the State Department. It was easier to reject Bonsal's advice of continued forbearance than to decide what policy could effectively hurt the revolutionary regime in Havana without endangering the new emphasis on inter-American cooperation. It was nonetheless prudent to lay the groundwork for possible future economic sanctions against Cuba. At a press conference on 18 February Secretary Herter suggested that "the question of economic retaliation" was under review. The United States would alter the preferred position of Cuban sugar in the American market only with the greatest reluctance, but might find it necessary to propose a revision of the Sugar Importation Act.[35]

Upon his return from a quick four-country trip to South America, Eisenhower made no mention of economic retaliation or sugar quotas, and in a Washington Day address laid emphasis upon the virtues of U.S. policy in Latin America while deploring the manner in which it was often misinterpreted by our Latin American friends. The United States was prepared to cooperate in "sound development schemes" and would strive to promote mutual security and the triumph of human liberty throughout the hemisphere.[36] A few weeks later, Eisenhower received a report from Allen Dulles, head of the CIA, suggesting that Castro now posed as great a danger to "mutual security" as had Jacobo Arbenz of Guatemala. Arbenz had been effectively dispatched in 1954 when the United States had armed and trained a force of anticommunist Guatemalan rebels under Colonel Armas Castillo. Anti-Castro refugees could be used to the same purpose.

In the early days of March 1960 Eisenhower had yet to commit himself either to economic sanctions or to covert military operations but both were under serious consideration. He was convinced that Castro was the self-declared enemy of hemispheric security and the United States. There would be no further proposals along lines suggested by the statement of 26 January or the mediation plan of Ambassador Amoedo. Bonsal's tour of duty would continue for another eight months, but by early March he acknowledged a sense of defeat. Efforts to gain direction of events in Cuba by a policy of verbal strictures and self-proclaimed restraint were viewed as a failure in Washington. The details of a new policy were still uncertain, but it would be a policy that marked a victory for "hard-liners" and ignored the advice of the U.S. embassy in Havana.

Bonsal later would suggest that the Eisenhower administration made a mistake in not pursuing for a longer period the policy outlined in the 26 January statement—offering pledges of nonintervention and proposing negotiation through regular diplomatic channels while supporting the spoliation claims of U.S. citizens. Had this policy of "moderation and restraint" been continued, it could have "slowed down the Soviet involvement in the Cuban economy" and made it more difficult for Castro to persuade the Cuban masses that the United States was an enemy of social revolution. It might, indeed, have created "favorable conditions for local opposition to crystallize." Bonsal was too honest a man, however, to claim that had the United States followed his advice undeviatingly, Cuba would have rejected socialism, made no overtures to Russia, and re-welded its ties to the OAS. He appreciated that Cuban domestic needs and developments were more crucial to the leftward turn of the revolution than was U.S. policy. In the final analysis, he defended his counsel for "moderation and restraint" not on the grounds that it guaranteed Castro's alignment with the diplomatic objectives of the United States but because it provided the best guarantee that, whatever the course of the Cuban Revolution, the United States would retain the sympathy of responsible elements in Latin America. They would admire U.S. patience and see Castro's diatribes as the efforts of a demagogue trying to make political capital of his own fantasies.[37]

S. Cole Blasier, one of the most perceptive students of Eisenhower's Cuban diplomacy, though sympathetic to the lamentations of Bonsal, notes the inconsistencies in the implementation of the American policy of "forbearance." Blasier maintains that by the end of January 1960 relations had worsened to a point at which a pledge of nonintervention and a call for Castro to embrace the ways of traditional diplomacy offered little hope of success. Some members of the Eisenhower administration were fearful of Castro's objectives from the beginning, and the relationship of U.S. investment and the Cuban propertied classes inevitably made Castro suspicious of U.S. intentions. The U.S. government and American business interests possessed the greatest potential to thwart the Cuban Revolution and presented a natural enemy for the radical faction of the 26th of July Movement. For Blasier, Castro's suspicion of U.S. intentions was not illogical; it was, however, exaggerated and based more on injuries anticipated than those received.[38]

There had been a large degree of self-delusion in the belief of certain U.S. officials in January 1959 that the Cuban Revolution would be democratic, gradualist, and respectful of American advice, a combination of Jeffersonian principles and New Deal reform. Subsequent disillusion with the revolution was, in part, the result of false hopes and an ethnocentric version of Cuban history and Cuban–American relations. The primary reason, however, for the deterioration of Cuban–U.S. relations between January 1959 and March 1960 was neither the ethnocentricity nor the suspicions of Washington but the evolving needs of the Cuban Revolution as assessed by Fidel Castro. The initiative in Cuban–American relations in these fourteen months lay more with Castro than Eisenhower.

Eisenhower's policy was not without its errors. Officials placed undue emphasis on cash compensation for U.S. citizens whose property was expropriated by the Agrarian Reform Law and displayed insufficient sympathy with the financial problems of the Cuban Treasury Department. The Eisenhower administration could have offered economic assistance to the Castro regime and not waited for begging requests that never came. It was negligent in patrolling the Florida airfields and policing the activities of Cuban refugees. The United States was guilty of trying to pressure certain of its European allies not to sell arms to Castro's Cuba and of magnifying Cuban efforts to inspire rebel invasions against reactionary regimes in the Caribbean. Finally, the United States exaggerated communist influence in Cuba and anticipated Cuban alignment with the Soviet Union by almost a year.

It is doubtful, however, if these errors singly or collectively altered the course of the Cuban Revolution or fundamentally determined the domestic and foreign policies of the Cuban government between January 1959 and March 1960. Possibly they accelerated in a limited way the radicalization of the revolution; probably they deepened the conviction of the radical faction of the 26th of July Movement that the United States was the enemy of any fundamental restructuring of Cuban society; certainly they made easier the efforts of Castro to sustain revolutionary unity and momentum by rallying the masses against a foreign enemy and its domestic hirelings. But the fact remains that Havana more than Washington shaped the course of Cuban–American relations in this fourteen-month period, when American policy was characterized more by ambivalence and confusion than aggressive intent.

The same cannot be said of Cuban–American relations in the last ten months of the Eisenhower administration. In March 1960, U.S. Cuban policy took a distinct turn. If Castro had felt threatened before that date, over the next year his fears and propaganda found substantiation in the designs and actions of U.S. diplomacy.

Chapter Three

The Victory of Richard Nixon

Eisenhower Diplomacy, March 1960–

January 1961

By midsummer 1959, Vice-President Richard M. Nixon was convinced that Castro was a danger as well as a nuisance. He began to urge President Eisenhower and Secretary of State Herter to take a more belligerent stance toward revolutionary Cuba and to consider ways to undermine the Castro regime. Influenced by the analyses of Robert Hill and Earl Smith, and by conversations with William Pawley and J. Edgar Hoover, Nixon concluded that Castro was a willing agent of the Cuban communists and the international communist conspiracy. He became increasingly impatient with the recommendations of Ambassador Bonsal for continued forbearance and a balanced response, and persuaded himself that from the very first he had spotted Castro as an instrument for the introduction of communism into the Caribbean region.[1]

Nixon assumed the leadership of a loosely knit group of hard-liners within the Eisenhower administration and with March 1960 could claim a large measure of victory. In that month, Eisenhower authorized the CIA to recruit and train selected Cuban refugees for possible future guerrilla operations in Cuba and requested congressional authority to alter Cuba's sugar quota. Months earlier, Nixon had suggested that the method found for eliminating Arbenz and the threat of a Red Guatemala in 1954 could provide the model for eliminating Castro, and had publicly announced in January 1960 that Cuba's "enmity to the United States" furnished sufficient cause for distributing the Cuban sugar quota among other nations.[2]

Eisenhower's decision to accept the recommendation of the CIA to arm and train Cuban exiles was neither coerced or precipitate. As early as December 1959 the CIA had begun to interview possible recruits among the Cuban exile community in Florida and to plan for the selection and training of an instructor cadre. During the winter of 1960 Guatemala was chosen as a possible staging ground for their training if and when presidential authorization for a counterrevolutionary force was received.[3] A series of events in February and early March persuaded Eisenhower to give his approval. Castro's trade agreements with the USSR and other East European countries and Castro's charge of U.S. complicity in the explosion of the arms ship *La Coubre* on 4 March were the most important of these developments.[4]

Allen Dulles formally presented the CIA proposal to the president on 14 March and Eisenhower approved it three days later. His decision was motivated primarily by his conviction that Castro was determined to make the Caribbean a new theater of the Cold War. Eisenhower was not unmindful of the property loss of American investors in Cuba and considered Castro's implementation of the Agrarian Reform Law dishonest and extortionary, but antipathy to communism and concern for U.S. hegemony in the Caribbean dictated his decision. Within the Washington bureaucracy the hardliners had more effective political allies than did the spokesmen for moderation, and those allies had the president's ear by the spring of 1960.[5] Eisenhower had become convinced by the arguments of Nixon, Admiral Arleigh Burke, and Senators Styles Bridges and Kenneth Wherry that the alarmist memorandums of the CIA were more to be trusted than the back-and-fill reports of the intelligence section of the State Department. Though Cuba's ties with the Soviets were presently economic in nature, economic ties could lead to military alliance. Castro's threat to the national security of the United States lay in the future advantage he might afford the international communist movement.

Eisenhower, however, does not appear to have entertained any great sense of urgency respecting the covert military operation. He seems to have considered it potentially reversible, and, rather unaccountably, would by late June be asking his aide Gordon Gray to refresh his memory about the plan he had authorized fourteen weeks earlier.[6] There is no evidence that Eisenhower considered the possibility that Cuban intelligence would uncover the project and that this discovery might prove politically advantageous to the procommunist faction within the Cuban government. No more does Eisenhower appear to have considered the difficulty of disbanding the exile force were its operational use to be subsequently vetoed.[7]

Whatever Eisenhower's inattention to the details or consequences of his decision to authorize the training of Cuban exiles, the CIA moved forward with expedition. Not only was the training cadre appointed and arms secured under various covers, but the CIA proceeded to build a fifty-kilowatt radio station on Swan Island, 110 miles off the coast of Honduras. This station was designed as a medium for anti-Castro propaganda throughout the Caribbean region and with the thought it might prove useful in any operation to support anti-Castro guerrillas in Cuba.

In April/May, the Department of State sharpened its anti-Castro rhetoric. Castro's public repudiation of Cuba's obligation under the Rio Treaty and the formal reestablishment of diplomatic relations between Havana and Moscow inspired a flurry of press releases, and Eisenhower took advantage of a letter from the Chilean Student Federation, calling upon the United States to mend its quarrel with Cuba, to denounce Castro's betrayal of the initial goals of the Cuban Revolution. In June/July, the Eisenhower administration embarked on a policy of economic sanctions against Cuba designed to erode Castro's popularity with the Cuban people and encourage his removal.

On 6 July Eisenhower ordered a 700,000-ton cut in Cuba's 1960 sugar quota of 3,120,000 tons. As Cuba had already shipped over 2,300,000 tons of sugar to the United States since 1 January, this executive order effectively barred the further importation of Cuban sugar. Eisenhower informed the press that this action was not a reprisal against the Cuban government, but rather a response to the need of the American people for a regular and assured supply of imported sugar. Recent sugar sales agreements by Cuba with East European nations made the availability of Cuban sugar uncertain and it was necessary to rearrange the quotas of the sugar-exporting nations the better to assure the needs of the American consumer.[8] The explanation rang hollow. The decision to eliminate the balance of the Cuban sugar quota for 1960 was motivated by a desire to put pressure on the Cuban government to change its ways or risk economic collapse, and it was a decision made in mid-March, during the same week Eisenhower authorized the training of Cuban exiles for possible future guerrilla action in Cuba.

Eisenhower had announced in March that he would ask Congress for a revision of the 1948 Sugar Act that would give him standby authority to alter national quotas, and this request was aggressively pursued by Secretary Herter in hearings of the Senate and House agricultural committees in June. There was a brief attack on the proposal by farm bloc congressmen who feared it might disturb current subsidy and price stabilization programs for domestic producers, and the Democratic chairman of the House Agriculture Committee was so bold as to make reference to "overt economic aggression," but closed-door testimony by Secretary Herter cut short the debate. On 3 July Congress voted to give the president discretion to reduce the import quota for Cuban sugar to any level he considered to be in the U.S. interest.[9]

In Havana and at the UN, spokesmen for the Cuban government denounced Eisenhower's order of 6 July as an example of economic warfare and illegal interference in Cuban domestic affairs. Probably, however, Castro was not displeased. The left wing of the Cuban revolutionary regime had for some months been criticizing the dependency of Cuba's main export on the U.S. market and insisting that the premium price paid for Cuban sugar was designed as protection for high-cost U.S. producers and as a bribe for assuring preferential entry of U.S. goods in the Cuban market. Castro knew, however, that it would not be easy to find substitute markets quickly and that a period of depression for the Cuban sugar economy might follow. Better then to let the United States take the initiative in rupturing the traditional market arrangements for Cuban sugar exports. Eisenhower obliged.

As the Eisenhower administration might have expected, Castro secured from the Soviets a promise to increase their sugar imports to equal the American cut, and during August and September Castro authorized seizures of U.S. investments in manufacturing, commerce, finance, and transportation.[10] Combined with earlier nationalization of U.S.-owned properties in agriculture and mining, these expropriations effectively eliminated U.S. property ownership in Cuba.

Ambassador Bonsal had predicted such a result were the Cuban sugar quota to be eliminated, as had such U.S. Latin American scholars as Robert J. Alexander and Arthur P. Whitaker.[11] Their opinions, however, were deemed irrelevant by the Eisenhower administration. Programs of technical assistance to Cuba in the fields of agriculture and civil aviation were abruptly terminated, and on 8 July the United States announced that it was freezing the assets of Cuban citizens in the United States. Some weeks earlier, the Eisenhower administration had attempted to do economic damage to the Castro regime by restricting its choice of petroleum imports.

A Cuban–Soviet agreement of February 1960 had provided for the import of a large quantity of Russian crude oil, and in May the Cuban government demanded that U.S. and British-owned refineries process this oil and reduce their imports from Venezuela. After consulting with Washington, Texaco and other American companies refused. Between 29 June and 2 July the refineries of Texaco, Esso, and the Shell Petroleum Company were nationalized and placed under the control of the Cuban Petroleum Institute. The Cuban government denied the claim of the American companies that the technology of their plants was not equipped to handle low-grade Soviet petroleum and took their refusal as a direct challenge to Cuban commercial and foreign exchange policies.

When Secretary of the Treasury Robert Anderson advised the American oil companies to refuse to refine Russian crude oil and stand firm against Castro's threats, the Eisenhower administration was presumably acting on two highly optimistic assumptions: (1) that Castro was only bluffing and would not retaliate by expropriating the refineries; (2) that if Castro did expropriate the refineries the American companies would be able to stop the export of Venezuelan oil to Cuba and put pressure on independent tanker fleets not to lease their vessels for the transport of oil from the communist nations to Cuba. The first assumption demonstrated the continuing failure of the State Department to distinguish Castro from Cuban leaders of the past and give sufficient recognition to his messianic temperament and fervent nationalism. The second assumption demonstrated erroneous calculations respecting the size of the Russian tanker fleet and the identification of independent tankers with the interests and dictates of the Western alliance.

As with the sugar quota cut, this U.S. effort to coerce the Cuban government into good behavior boomeranged. The Soviets increased their oil shipments to meet Cuban requirements, the nationalized plants experienced no technological difficulties refining Russian crude, and there were no bottlenecks in tanker transport. The result, indeed, was the seeming validation of Castro's orientation toward a socialist economy and economic alliance with the Soviet Union.

U.S. efforts at economic coercion in the summer of 1960 produced results antithetical to the goals of U.S. foreign policy. They strengthened rather than weakened Castro's political authority; they made it easier for the Russians to accept the application of their Cuban suitor; they enhanced the importance of communist supplies and markets for the Cuban revolutionary regime. The United States overreacted to the failure of its earlier efforts to influence the Cuban Revolution by a policy of verbal strictures, and the Cuban and Russian response to the more aggressive policy pursued by the United States in the spring/summer of 1960 virtually destroyed the possibility of reconciliation between Cuba and the United States.

Ambassador Bonsal is obviously a prejudiced witness to the effects of policies urged by his critics, but his later evaluation of those policies is persuasive:

The United States government measures . . . went far beyond the retaliation warranted by the injuries American citizens and interests had up to that time suffered at Castro's hands. Such retaliation should have been roughly proportionate to those injuries rather than evidence of an intention to overthrow the regime through an exercise of superior force. . . . [A] measured American response might have appeared well deserved to an increasing number of Cubans, thus strengthening Cuban opposition to the regime instead of, as was the case, greatly stimulating revolutionary fervor.[12]

Eisenhower, though disappointed that efforts to inflict damage on the Cuban economy had failed to disturb the political authority of Castro in Cuba, blamed the failure not on U.S. policy but Russian interference. Exhibit number 1 was Khrushchev's speech before the All-Russian Teachers' Congress in Moscow, 9 July 1960. In that speech, Khrushchev accused the United States of planning an economic blockade of Cuba at the behest of "American monopolies," and pledged that Fidel Castro would not lack support in his "struggle for freedom and national independence." Particularly inflammatory was Khrushchev's warning that the United States was itself not immune from attack:

> Figuratively speaking, in case of need, Soviet artillerymen can support the Cuban people with their rocket fire if the aggressive forces in the Pentagon dare to launch an intervention against Cuba. And let them not forget in the Pentagon that, as the latest tests have shown, we have rockets capable of landing directly in a precalculated square at a distance of 13,000 km. This, if you will, is a warning to those who would like to settle international issues by force and not by reason.[13]

The Eisenhower administration seized this statement as proof of the necessity for a get-tough-with-Castro policy, and was quick to respond. Only hours after the State Department had received and translated the Khrushchev speech, a statement was issued in the name of the president:

> The statement which has just been made by Mr. Khrushchev in which he promises full support to the Castro regime in Cuba is revealing in two respects. It underscores the close ties that have developed between the Soviet and Cuban Governments. It also shows the clear intention to establish Cuba in a role serving Soviet purposes in this hemisphere. . . . I affirm in the most emphatic terms that the United States will not be deterred from its responsibilities by the threats Mr. Khrushchev is making. Nor will the United States, in conformity with its treaty obligations, permit the establishment of a regime dominated by international communism in the Western Hemisphere.[14]

Eisenhower's statement established the themes that would dominate official explication of U.S. Cuban diplomacy for the balance of his administration, whether in meetings of the UN and the OAS or press conferences of the president and secretary of state. In a matter of weeks a well-orchestrated series of speeches and releases made it clear that the Eisenhower administration saw no hope of an improvement in Cuban-American relations so long as Castro was in power. Further, it was determined to demonstrate here and abroad that Castro's enmity toward the United States and the hemispheric security system was the result not of American actions but the expanding influence of communists in Havana aided and abetted by the Soviet Union. In the UN, Ambassador Henry Cabot Lodge proclaimed that the Monroe Doctrine was "fully alive and will be vigorously defended by the United States."[15] Press releases of the State Department sought to emphasize the obligation of the United States to do its duty by the OAS and to proclaim the falsehood of Russian charges of American aggression against the Cuban government. The OAS Charter was designed to protect the independent status of the American states against the "extension to this hemisphere of a despotic political system," and the Rio Treaty of 1947 specifically provided for "common action to protect the hemisphere against the interventionist and aggressive designs of international communism." As for the charge of U.S. aggression, it was a "straw man," a malicious attempt to draw attention away from Soviet imperialism by projecting "a nonexistent menace of U.S. aggression against Cuba."[16]

Whether the denial of "aggression" was a lie is a question of definition. A case can be made that the punitive features of U.S. policy in the summer of 1960 were primarily a response to the increasingly anti-American posture of the Castro regime. But repeated assertions that the United States had "no aggressive purposes against Cuba" found no believers in Havana, and Secretary Herter's declaration: "I have never talked with the President about military intervention in Cuba, nor have we here in the Department made any such plans or preparations" was only technically true.[17] There is no evidence that Herter knew of the CIA training camp in Guatemala or the landing of several CIA-trained guerrilla bands in Cuba in the summer of 1960, but Herter's veracity was debtor to his ignorance.[18]

Eisenhower made no denials for the record, and appears to have offered, in private conversations, fluctuating estimates of the probable effectiveness of anti-Castro guerrillas and American economic sanctions.[19] He wavered as well in his attitude toward the utility of the hemispheric security machinery of the OAS and the political value of economic assistance to Latin America.[20]

The major effort of the Eisenhower administration in behalf of a hemispheric approach to the Cuban problem came with the conference of foreign ministers in San José, Costa Rica, in late August.

Eisenhower's advisers agreed that consideration should be given to public opinion in Latin America, but they divided on which would be the more harmful Latin American reaction: a conviction that the United States was a bully seeking a veto power on the Cuban Revolution or a belief that the United States was a pushover for radical revolutionaries, willing to permit the property of its citizens to be expropriated and its government vilified with impunity.[21] Nixon saw the latter as the primary danger and the failure of our OAS partners to provide adequate support at San José made his opinion increasingly popular in the Eisenhower administration.

The OAS meeting in San José was technically two meetings: the Sixth and Seventh Meetings of Consultation of the Foreign Ministers of the American Republics, with a day's recess between them to mark their separation. The first meeting concentrated on the problem of the Dominican Republic and the charge that it was guilty of subversive acts against the government of Venezuela and was implicated in an unsuccessful plot to assassinate its president. The second meeting had as its main business "the extra-continental menace to hemispheric solidarity, security and democracy." It was Herter's assignment to dispatch quickly the Dominican issue, while preventing action that would require the member states to sever all political and economic relations with Trujillo, and then urge the ministers to take action against Cuba as an instrument of Soviet and Chinese intervention in the Western Hemisphere.[22]

The United States agreed to certain sanctions against the Dominican Republic, and failed to receive what it considered a sufficient quid pro quo. Herter's charges of Cuban aggression and communist infiltration did not convince a necessary majority of the foreign ministers. Some continued to believe that the Cuban problem was primarily a bilateral disagreement between Cuba and the United States, and others found it convenient to profess such a belief. The Declaration of San José was somewhat stronger than the Santiago statement of the previous year but it fell short of satisfying the Eisenhower administration. Herter had sought a document proclaiming Cuba guilty of an offense against the whole hemisphere; the declaration condemned in the abstract the intervention of any extracontinental power but made no specific mention of Cuba, the Soviet Union, or Communist China.[23]

At San José, Herter denounced extracontinental intervention by

Communist China as well as the Soviet Union, but this reference to the dual nature of the communist threat better demonstrated a new public relations tactic than a sudden conviction that the government of Mao Tse-tung posed a danger equal to that of the Soviet Union. The State Department was not unconcerned by intelligence reports of Chinese agents in Cuba, but the chief enemy remained "the international communist conspiracy" directed by the Kremlin. When reporting to the president on the San José conference, Herter not only complained of the unfortunate "skepticism" of our Latin American neighbors, but blamed Mikoyan's visit to Havana in February for the obduracy of the Cubans and their failure to respond to U.S. warnings.[24]

Having twice sought the assistance of the OAS with unsatisfactory results, the Eisenhower administration in its closing months concentrated on compiling a record of its relations with Cuba that would make clear the aggressive intent of Castro and provide justification for any future actions by the United States.

In compiling the record of Castro's sins, the Eisenhower administration operated under a double injunction: to prove to its domestic critics that it had not been weak and credulous in its dealings with Castro; to demonstrate to world opinion that it had been admirably moderate in its response to Cuban provocations and only reluctantly had become persuaded that the demands of American safety and honor required that patience be succeeded by measured retaliation. The best way to reconcile these contrary requirements was to emphasize that the Cuban Revolution was a revolution that had been perverted. The Cubans had been promised in January 1959 a democratic, reformist revolution and the United States had naturally wished it well; now in the fall of 1960 it was clear that the Castro regime sought not social justice but a totalitarian dictatorship, in imitation of its Marxist allies, and the United States was obliged to recognize its enmity.[25]

Accompanying these efforts to make clear the wisdom and consistency of U.S. Cuban policy were efforts to tighten the economic screws on Castro. American citizens were directed not to travel to Cuba "except for compelling reasons," nations receiving U.S. aid were advised not to buy Cuban sugar with U.S. funds, and complicated efforts were made to deny Cuba credit to import spare parts from the United States or its allies. The Senate voted to cut mutual security appropriations to any country that supplied military or economic assistance to Cuba, and on 19 October the Eisenhower administration, acting under the authority of the Export Control Act, took the major step of prohibiting all exports to Cuba, except medical supplies and nonsubsidized food products—exceptions that were soon canceled. Though Cuba's declining dollar reserves and the refusal of the Cuban government to release funds for payments to American creditors had already sharply limited the extent of U.S.–Cuban trade, this executive order was nonetheless a purposeful escalation of economic warfare against the Cuban government. The State Department announcement spoke of the requirement to protect U.S. exporters from further discrimination and injury, but there was comparatively little effort to conceal the fact that the Eisenhower administration hoped that the inability of the Castro regime to import U.S. equipment and spare parts would cause costly shutdowns and disrupt the manufacturing sector. Even if such disruption did not stimulate general opposition to Castro it might have "an encouraging effect on the dissident groups now becoming active in Cuba." There was, moreover, the unstated assumption that an economic embargo of Cuba would dissuade other Latin American nations from following Castro's path.[26]

U.S. economic warfare was closely linked with warnings about Castro's armament program and its communist sources. These warnings reflected honest concern about Castro's insurrectionary intentions in the Caribbean and a calculated effort to justify the administration's program of economic coercion. The campaign against Cuba's military buildup officially began on 28 October with a note from John C. Dreier to the secretary general of the OAS detailing the increase of Cuban armaments, claiming that it was occurring "with the notorious assistance of extraterritorial powers" and represented an augmented capacity to give "arms support to the spread of . . . revolution in other parts of the Americas." Releases from the State Department confirmed this claim, citing "a number of sources which are considered to be reliable."[27]

Cuban–American relations in the Eisenhower years now moved toward the almost inevitable climax of the severance of diplomatic relations. On 2 December the Eisenhower administration allocated one million dollars from executive contingency funds for Cuban refugee relief, and took the opportunity to draw parallels between the Cuban exiles of 1960 and earlier migrations to freedom and asylum in America.[28] Two weeks earlier the United States, without preliminary consultation with the OAS, had announced that surface and air units of the U.S. Navy were being positioned off the shores of Nicaragua and Guatemala to help those countries "prevent intervention on the part of Communist-directed elements in their internal affairs." The Cuban government denounced the move as further evidence of a planned U.S. attack.[29]

On 31 December the Cubans formally requested a meeting of the UN Security Council to meet the danger of an imminent U.S. invasion in violation of the sovereignty of a member state. Raúl Roa, the Cuban foreign minister, claimed that the Cuban government had in its possession evidence of a sinister conspiracy "conceived by the Central Intelligence Agency, in close collaboration with the Pentagon and the United States monopolies adversely affected by the public welfare legislation promulgated by the Cuban revolution and with the open co-operation of Cuban war criminals who have sought refuge in the United States." On 4 January 1961, U.S. Representative Wadsworth offered a lengthy reply to the Cuban charges, but a day earlier the Eisenhower administration had announced that it was terminating diplomatic and consular relations with Cuba. The Cubans had demanded that the U.S. embassy in Havana be reduced from 87 to 11 persons within forty-eight hours, probably hoping that this would incite the United States to assume the onus of initiating the break. Once again the Eisenhower administration obliged.[30]

In his statement of 3 January announcing the severance of diplomatic relations with Cuba, Eisenhower informed the American people that the actions and demands of the Cuban political leadership gave him no choice:

There is a limit to what the United States in self-respect can endure. That limit has now been reached. Our friendship for the Cuban people is not affected. It is my hope and my conviction that in the not-too-distant future it will be possible for the historic friendship between us once again to find its reflection in normal relations of every sort. Meanwhile, our sympathy goes out to the people of Cuba now suffering under the yoke of a dictator.[31]

Philip Bonsal, recently reassigned to a liaison post with the OAS, considered Eisenhower's action precipitate and regretted it. Richard Nixon considered it overdue and applauded it. It reconfirmed Nixon's victory and was the logical culmination of Eisenhower's get-tough-with-Castro policy that began the preceding March. Though there was an antagonistic interaction between Cuba and the United States throughout the years 1959–60, the early spring of 1960 had seen a shift in the balance of initiative and response. Previously, Cuba was more the initiator of events and Castro the more guilty of overreaction; from March 1960 it was more often the United States and Dwight David Eisenhower.

Eisenhower's conversion to a posture increasingly hostile to the new Cuban revolutionary regime was not the product of anticommunist paranoia. Rather it was the result of a conviction that were the Castro regime to continue in power in Cuba, it would represent an escalating threat to U.S. national security in a Cold War world. Neither Abilene, Kansas, nor the U.S. Army had prepared Eisenhower for Fidel Castro, and it was natural that he would feel a sense of personal distaste for an unkempt, bearded radical offering criticisms of the United States and the history of Cuban–American relations. Neither Eisenhower's ethnocentric bias nor his limited knowledge of Cuban history was the most decisive factor, however; it was Castro's overtures to the Soviet Union.[32] Those overtures were of recent date and Cuban–Soviet ties few in number, but a good military strategist did not allow the enemy within the gates before moving to the attack. Nor did a wise politician fail to take cognizance of the increasing anti-Castro sentiment in Congress and the press. By spring 1960 Eisenhower had become convinced that there was no hope of an acceptable and honorable compromise solution with the radical revolutionaries of Havana. U.S. diplomatic objectives as well as considerations of political prudence made the removal of Castro a necessary policy goal.

The Latin American policy of the Eisenhower administration had four major diplomatic objectives: to keep the Caribbean area quiet and peaceful, to keep communist and Soviet influence out of the Western Hemisphere, to sustain U.S. hegemony in the Caribbean and U.S. diplomatic primacy throughout Latin America, to encourage economic development and social welfare in Latin America by means of U.S. private investment and limited government aid.[33]

Eisenhower did not consider these objectives to be imperialistic or selfish. Progress in Latin America was dependent upon conditions of stability and upon the strength and prosperity of the only great power in the Western Hemisphere. Just as surely, Castroism posed a threat to tranquillity in the Caribbean and the immunity of the hemisphere from extracontinental intrusions and Cold War conflict.

Eisenhower's decision to sponsor a counterrevolutionary force of exiles for possible future guerrilla operations was not the equivalent of authorizing an invasion. It was, however, a far-reaching decision, and one that had influence on the future actions of both Fidel Castro and John F. Kennedy.

There is little doubt that Castro soon knew of the CIA plan to arm a counterrevolutionary force of Cuban exiles, however uncertain he was of its training site and specific objectives. This intelligence obviously strengthened his antipathy to the United States, nourished a belief that the United States was a mortal threat to his regime, and incited further effort to obtain arms from the communist bloc. Castro did not turn to the Cuban communists and to the Soviet Union as a result of reports that the CIA was recruiting Cuban exiles in Miami. Domestic considerations had already encouraged such a course, and Eisenhower's actions did not force the revolutionary leadership in Havana to nationalize the Cuban economy or seek alliance with the Soviet Union. But surely the anti-Castro moves of the Eisenhower administration made the policy advice of Guevara and other members of the revolutionary left appear more logical, and made a procommunist orientation for the Cuban Revolution more probable. Eisenhower assisted Castro in identifying Cuban socialism with Cuban sovereignty and, at the same time, helped assure that left-wing elements in Latin America would retain sympathy for Castroism now that Castro could more convincingly portray himself as a Cuban David struggling against the Yankee Goliath.[34]

The Eisenhower years, 1959–60, were a crucial period in U.S. response to the Cuban Revolution. That these were years of failure for U.S. Cuban policy was not the fault solely of the Eisenhower administration, but the Cuban policy of the Eisenhower years can only be judged a failure. Its legacy was one of defeat and animosity. By January 1961 U.S. private interests had lost investments valued at nearly one billion dollars—a loss larger than American investors had suffered in either the Bolshevik or the Chinese revolutions. By January 1961 the Cuban and American governments viewed one another with bitterness and anger. In Cuban eyes the United States had proved itself an enemy of the revolution; in American eyes the Cuban revolutionaries had purposely perverted a movement for social justice into a new and more dangerous form of dictatorship, one marked by radical Marxism and the expansion of Soviet influence. Indeed, Washington now entertained a dual betrayal thesis. Not only had Castro betrayed the initial promise of the Cuban Revolution but he had betrayed the long-standing relationship of Cuba and the United States. In a manner not dissimilar to the earlier conviction of many Americans that with the victory of Mao, we had "lost" China, many in Washington now felt that as a result of the deceptions and evil designs of the Castro regime, we had "lost" Cuba. Our long-time economic dependency and some-time playground was now our enemy. The transformation was not only intolerable but unnatural.

Cuban–American relations in 1959–60 offer at least two obvious lessons: the cumulative impact of bilateral threats and suspicions, and the importance of analyzing the probable effects of retaliatory measures in advance of their implementation.

By the summer of 1960, the fears and suspicions of Cuba and the United States toward one another had achieved a self-perpetuating momentum. Threats, counterthreats, retaliations, counterretaliations had convinced each country that their worst suspicions of the other were justified and proven.[35] By that point each side had accumulated a long list of grievances. The Cuban government complained of U.S. opposition to agrarian reform and nationalization laws, refusal of American-owned refineries to process Soviet petroleum, elimination of the Cuban sugar quota, failure of the United States to prevent air attacks by Cuban refugees in Florida, special U.S. immigration treatment for Castro's enemies, restrictions on U.S.–Cuban trade, and known and suspected anti-Castro espionage by the CIA. The United States complained of communist infiltration of the Cuban government, Cuban recognition of Communist China, Cuban trade agreements with the Soviet Union, Cuban aid to insurrectionaries in other Caribbean countries, expropriation of the property of U.S. citizens without compensation, suppression of civil liberties, and Castro's defamation of the U.S. government.[36] On both sides was reason for complaint; on both sides exaggeration and the anticipation of injury. Most clearly, there was the self-perpetuating momentum of anger and suspicion. The fever chart of Cuban-American relations rose uninterruptedly, particularly in the last ten months of the Eisenhower administration.

In those months, the United States moved to a more offensive posture. In each instance, one could argue that the United States was acting in retaliation to some charge or action of the Cuban government, but what is indisputable is that the United States failed to analyze in advance the probable effects of its retaliatory measures. In the outcome, measures of economic coercion not only failed to force Castro to reverse course, but they had the effect of augmenting his personal power and accentuating his determination to break free of the diplomatic and economic authority of the United States. One can justly criticize the Eisenhower administration for poor policy analysis. It is, of course, possible that a more careful weighing of policy options might have resulted in decisions identical with those taken in the spring and summer of 1960. It is equally possible that continuation of a policy of irritable forbearance would not have produced any change in the drift of the Cuban government towards radical socialism and dependency on the Soviet Union. It could, however, have altered the balance of blame incurred by each nation for the deterioration of Cuban–American relations.

By the inauguration of John F. Kennedy, Cuban–American relations were at an historic nadir. Many felt they could only improve under the dynamic young president. They were wrong.

Chapter Four

Intervention at the Bay of Pigs

Kennedy Diplomacy, January–April 1961

John F. Kennedy gave comparatively little thought to the region of Latin America before the presidential campaign of 1960. Until then his primary foreign policy interests had been Russian–American relations and the Atlantic Alliance. Sensing the popular concern with Castro's Cuba and the vulnerability of the Eisenhower administration on the score of its Cuban policy, Kennedy began in August 1960 to make repeated references to the communist orientation of the Castro government and the danger faced by America from a threat "ninety miles from our shore."

Among Kennedy's campaign advisers, however, were Chester Bowles, Adolf A. Berle, and Arthur M. Schlesinger, Jr., who urged him to call for a revival of the Good Neighbor Policy and to advocate social-economic development measures that would enhance the political future of progressive elements within the nations of Latin America. Determined to show that his foreign policy would be more forward-looking than that of the tired old men of the Republican party, Kennedy alternated attacks on the weakness of Eisenhower's Cuban policy with prophecies of a new era of understanding and cooperation among the American republics. We should ally ourselves with the forces advocating democratic change, and we must assist the valiant Cubans who had escaped to the United States. The ambivalent nature of the Latin American policy of the Kennedy administration was foreshadowed in Kennedy's campaign speeches in the fall of 1960.

Kennedy appeared more certain that Eisenhower's Cuban policy was worthy of blame than where the blame should be placed. He suggested on one occasion that the primary failure was in not ending support of Batista earlier and more completely, and implied that the Eisenhower administration had missed a golden opportunity by not embracing Castro on his trip to Washington in April 1959 and thereby preventing his subsequent alliance with the communists. At other times, however, Kennedy took an opposite tack and berated the Eisenhower administration for ignoring warnings that Castro's movement was infiltrated by communists and must be kept from power. The Eisenhower administration had failed to enforce the Monroe Doctrine and was responsible for allowing the Iron Curtain to advance "almost to our front yard." It was to be criticized as well for its failure to demonstrate to the peoples of Latin America that we would assist them in their fight against poverty and hunger.[1]

It was only late in the campaign that Kennedy paid homage to the anti-Castro exiles as "the real voice of Cuba," and attacked the administration for its "harassment" of the Cuban emigrés by means of "our Immigration and Justice department authorities." We should attempt to strengthen the anti-Castro forces in exile and in Cuba itself, and lend them all possible moral support. Neither "harassment" nor "moral support" were given specific definition.[2] Nor was Kennedy more precise when during the fourth Kennedy–Nixon debate on 21 October 1960, he advocated U.S. encouragement for Castro's Cuban enemies. Kennedy appeared convinced that it was in the power of the United States to direct the course of change in Cuba and in Latin America. If the right man was elected, presidential leadership would find the solution.

In the months between his election and inauguration, Kennedy established a Task Force, headed by Adolf Berle, with a vague assignment to survey the situation in Latin America and make recommendations for measures deserving immediate implementation by the new administration. Although the Task Force proclaimed the existence of a full-scale Latin American Cold War, its recommendations were comparatively modest: the United States should establish a Latin American political command post and propaganda-information center, support the idea of an inter-American common market, and stabilize the price of certain commodity exports.[3] Berle was rewarded with an appointment to head a second Latin American Task Force.[4]

Berle would have little independent authority, but his new Task Force was a source of suspicion for the Bureau of the American Republics in the State Department and offered further evidence of the organizational confusion that beset the new administration in its efforts to establish a Latin American policy more generous and more aggressive than that of its predecessor. But if there was uncertainty as to means, there was no lack of optimism. A new generation of pragmatic liberals would demonstrate that a new day had dawned for U.S. sponsorship of economic and social progress in the Americas, as they gave proof that communist penetration of the hemisphere while not negotiable, was reversible.

In his inaugural address, Kennedy proposed to "our sister republics" a new alliance for progress that would enable the free governments of the Americas to cast off the chains of poverty.[5] Some seven weeks later, at a White House reception for Latin American diplomats, he offered a Spanish translation of this promise: U.S. participation in an Alianza para el Progreso. The 1960s must see a bold and cooperative effort that would mark the beginning of a new era for the Americas. By the end of the decade, "the living standards of every American family will be on the rise, basic education will be available to all, hunger will be a forgotten experience, the need for massive outside help will have passed, most nations will have entered a period of self-sustained growth, and . . . every American Republic will be the master of its own revolution and its own hope and progress."[6] With the encouragement of government loans and public investment from the United States, the Latin American governments would implement long-range plans for economic development and the promotion of social justice, and their success would bear witness that only freedom and democracy could chart the path of constructive change.[7]

In counterpoint to proposals for a "new ideal of Pan-Americanism" came a series of moves to tighten economic sanctions against Cuba and to publicize the cause of Cuban exiles. The exclusion of Cuban sugar from U.S. marketing allotments was continued, with the proviso that an uncommitted quota would be assigned Cuba "when a government friendly to the United States replaced the Castro regime." Americans were prohibited from traveling to Cuba without special passports because of the inability of the U.S. government to provide "normal protective services," and Secretary of State Dean Rusk offered Kennedy the opinion that a total prohibition of Cuban exports to the United States found legal sanction in the Trading with the Enemy Act. Castro might receive some small political advantage by accusing the United States of economic aggression, but this was less important than the need "to deny the United States market to Cuban exports" and thereby lend encouragement "to those now engaged in resisting the Castro regime."[8]

As the Kennedy administration came closer to authorizing the amphibious invasion at the Bay of Pigs, there was an understandable desire to accentuate the number and the legitimacy of Castro's Cuban enemies. Two weeks after his inauguration, Kennedy issued a press statement promising increased government assistance to Cuban refugees in Florida, "until such time as better circumstances enable them to return to their permanent homes in health, in confidence, and with unimpaired pride."[9] Abraham Ribicoff, as secretary of Health, Education, and Welfare, was encouraged to give "tangible assistance for Cuban scholars and professional leaders who have temporarily fled their country." Their presence unmistakably attested that "an essential part of a free Cuba is now here with us."[10]

Kennedy was careful in the early months of his administration to avoid any public promises of military assistance to the Cubans who someday would leave America's embrace for "their permanent homes." He gave the impression that a rising tide of opposition would cause the Castro regime to collapse from within, and the exiles would then join forces with other progressive elements and create a Cuba democratic, liberty-loving, and sensible. Kennedy did not in fact have much faith in moral force as an agent for historical evolution. He had no doubt that the interests of American policy required the removal of Castro, nor did he have much doubt that this would require U.S. assistance to the Cuban enemies of Fidel.

Kennedy did not reach the decision to authorize the Bay of Pigs landing easily, but it was a decision very much of a piece with the ambivalent ambitions of Kennedy's Cuban speeches during the campaign of 1960. For if Kennedy wished to identify the New Frontier with economic progress in Latin America, he was even more determined to demonstrate that the exemplars of the New Frontier were hard-nosed realists, capable of giving the containment policy a new vigor and success. He would strengthen the Atlantic Alliance and defend West Berlin; he would prevent Soviet domination of Laos; and he would end the menace of a communist regime in Cuba. Kennedy would not give his opponents at home or abroad reason to question his courage. He must not appear less resolute in his opposition to a communist Cuba than the old men of the Eisenhower administration. Eisenhower's authorization order of March 1960 combined with the machismo requirements of the New Frontiersmen to make probable, if not inevitable, the Bay of Pigs invasion.[11]

Before the presidential election of 1960, the CIA plan for utilizing Cuban refugees in a covert operation against Castro had undergone a significant change. No longer were they to be used as small bands of guerrillas infiltrated into Cuba; rather they were to be used as a strike force, a pocket army, in a beachhead assault. By December 1960, foreign experts in guerrilla tactics had been dismissed and by January 1961, training at the secret camps in Guatemala was directed by a team of U.S. instructors skilled in the tactics of amphibious assault.[12] The Cuban exile force already numbered more than 500 men, and they were given to understand that they would receive air and artillery support as well as transportation by the U.S. government whenever it authorized an invasion somewhere on the southern coast of Cuba. Kennedy first heard of the secret training camp in Guatemala in the course of a briefing visit by Allen Dulles in Palm Beach some weeks after the election, and soon after his inauguration he ordered his national security adviser, McGeorge Bundy, to initiate a review of the project in cooperation with Richard Bissell, head of CIA covert operations.

Kennedy held the first formal review session on U.S. Cuban policy on 8 February. It was a rather diverse group of Old Hands and New Hands that met in the Oval Office: Dean Rusk, Adolf Berle, Thomas Mann, Charles Bohlen, Robert McNamara, Paul Nitze, William Bundy, Haydn Williams, Allen Dulles, Richard Bissell, Tracy Barnes, and McGeorge Bundy.[13] Few of these men possessed expert knowledge of Caribbean America and still fewer were students of Cuba and social revolution, but they did represent the bureaucratic power fulcrums of State, Defense, CIA, and the executive office. From the first there was a noticeable difference between the views of the CIA and Defense and the views of the State Department. This division was represented by the conflicting judgments of Richard Bissell, the father of U-2 surveillance, and Thomas Mann, recently appointed as assistant secretary for Inter-American Affairs.

In a memorandum preparing Kennedy for the meeting, ̦
Bundy informed the president that Defense and CIA "̦
enthusiastic about the invasion." They believed an invasi̦
establish a permanent beachhead, incite popular support from the
Cuban population, and assure a "full-fledged civil war in which we
could then back the anti-Castro forces openly." Bundy predicted
that the State Department would take "a much cooler view," point-
ing out the "political consequences" of a proxy invasion in the UN
and in Latin America. Mann would urge "careful and extended diplomatic discussions with other American states, looking toward an
increasing diplomatic isolation of Cuba" before embarking on "an
invasion adventure."[14]

Kennedy expressed neither moral nor diplomatic objections to
"an invasion adventure" at the meeting of 8 February but set matters in a holding pattern. He authorized "the encouragement of a
junta and a revolutionary council" among the Florida refugee community and the exploration of "alternative plans for action by anti-
Castro Cubans," but decided that "no other actions beyond that
authorized earlier" would be taken pending further study.[15]

Kennedy was soon the recipient of a series of reports urging the
necessity of an immediate effort to topple the Castro regime. Sherman Kent, chairman of the Board of National Estimates of the CIA,
provided Kennedy with two memorandums addressed to the question "Is Time on Our Side in Cuba?" The answer was an unqualified No. Castro's position was growing stronger. He was arming the
Cuban militia and training "security forces" to assure his mastery
"over daily life in Cuba." Though he was experiencing some economic difficulties as a result of U.S. sanctions, it was doubtful that
they would generate enough opposition to jeopardize his political
control. Nor need Castro worry about "effective international action against Cuba." The member nations of the OAS were divided
and such countries as Brazil, Chile, and Mexico indicated "reluctance or unwillingness to participate in collective action on the
Cuba problem."[16]

From the CIA's Current Intelligence Weekly reports, Kennedy received warnings that Castro was stepping up his attacks against
domestic opponents and that counterrevolutionaries in Cuba were
anxiously awaiting evidence of outside military support. The Cuban counterrevolutionary underground was itself unable to per-

form the task of toppling Fidel. It could play an important auxiliary role, but it lacked organizational unity, and was not sufficiently "security conscious" to direct a military operation.[17] There was ambiguity in the intelligence reports of the CIA about the strength and importance of the Cuban underground. Some reports concentrated on the weakness of the Cuban underground; others stressed the increased activities of guerrillas in the Escambray Mountains and Oriente Province. Oriente Province was "seething with hate," the Cuban army and militia were filled with potential defectors, and Castro was increasingly forced to rely on the Rebel Youth Association.[18]

Unlike the State Department's Bureau of Intelligence and Research, the CIA wasted no time in deliberating whether Castro was a communist or only a "willing fellow-traveler" who had given communism the opportunity to penetrate the Caribbean.[19] Castro was to be labeled a communist without qualification; communists were infiltrating the key positions of his government; the Kremlin planned to use Castro's Cuba as a base for plotting pro-Soviet revolutionary coups in Latin America. An assault landing by the Freedom Brigade would inspire anti-Castro demonstrations throughout the island and give the United States and other American nations justification for recognizing the Cuban Revolutionary Council as the provisional government of a free Cuba. It would not be difficult to conceal U.S. support for the invasion by transporting the brigade in privately leased vessels, attributing bombing raids to defectors from the Cuban air force,[20] and keeping U.S. advisers off the beach during the landing operation.

Proponents of an invasion invariably noted the geopolitical importance of Cuba. Naval historian Alfred T. Mahan had written that "Cuba is surely the key to the Gulf of Mexico as Gibraltar is to the Mediterranean," and his warning was still relevant in an era of nuclear weapons and communist conspiracy.[21] Cuba was, moreover, an "infection" that threatened the health of the hemispheric security system. Hopes that the Alliance for Progress could promote social and economic reform in Latin America would prove abortive if Cuban communist propaganda and subversion were not stopped at the source. As an agent of Soviet imperialism in the Western Hemisphere, Castro represented an immediate menace. The failure of South American governments to recognize that fact required bold unilateral action by the United States. Kennedy consequently should approve military action by exiled opponents of the Cuban regime.

While deliberating the CIA proposal, Kennedy did not make any concerted effort to elicit arguments against the operation, and those of his advisers who considered it unwise or illegal were tardy in articulating their objections and enjoyed little standing in the military and intelligence communities. Thomas Mann, Chester Bowles, Abram Chayes, and Arthur Schlesinger raised objections, but those objections were limited by team loyalty, restricted information, and a peripheral position in the decision-making process.[22] Senator J. William Fulbright was the most forthright opponent of an American-sponsored invasion of Cuba, but his advice was solicited very late and only once.[23] Of the doubters, Mann alone was a continuing member of the Cuba Group, and his opposition was restricted by his conviction that Cuba was a communist satellite and by the apparent neutrality and owlish silence of his superior officer, Secretary of State Dean Rusk.

Concerned to show that they, too, were diplomatic realists, untainted by moralism or naiveté, the doubters (with the exception of Fulbright) made no effort to condemn the invasion proposal as false to the values of a democratic society. Their objections centered on the difficulty of hiding the extent of U.S. involvement, the probable adverse reaction of our European and Latin American allies, and the likelihood that the United States would be charged with violating its treaty commitments not to intervene in the internal affairs of another American republic. It was to our national interest to extol the rule of law and stand forth as a champion of legitimacy and respect for the sovereignty of all nations. The latter consideration was best expressed by Abram Chayes, the legal adviser of the Department of State, in a memorandum to Arthur Schlesinger.

The United States has solemnly undertaken an obligation to forswear the unilateral use of force in the Western Hemisphere. The Act of Bogotá, establishing the Organization of States, is unequivocal on this point. . . . We are a leader in and beneficiary of a network of treaties around the world. Upon them we depend not only for the mobilization of our power but for the pursuit of our most important world purposes. An essential premise of our policy is, therefore, that these treaty obligations should be recognized by all as binding in law and conscience.[24]

The advisers of John F. Kennedy were divided on the wisdom of a proxy invasion of Castro's Cuba, but the division was an unequal one. Advocates were more numerous and more confident of their position. Opponents were few and appeared uncertain whether to urge that the operation be scrapped or only delayed. It is unlikely that Kennedy desired an argument among his advisers over the substance of U.S. Cuban policy or the role of covert operations in the diplomatic practice of a liberal democracy. It is certain that there was no such argument. Kennedy did not make his decision in a vacuum but rather in an organizational context that made inevitable his approval. The Old Hands were in place and prepared; the Kennedy men were divided and uncertain. Old Hands and New Hands were united in their conviction that Castro posed a threat to national security, that Cuba was a Cold War issue, that the essential objective of U.S. policy was the frustration of the designs of international communism. All saw themselves as proponents of an active foreign policy; none wished to be considered a weak sister.[25] Finally, they shared a desire to match and surpass the anticommunist labors of past administrations. They had criticized Eisenhower's foreign policy as unimaginative yet Eisenhower supposedly had succeeded in saving Guatemala from communism. Any parallel between Guatemala in 1954 and Cuba in 1961 was seriously flawed, but the analogy had a will-o'-the-wisp attraction for John F. Kennedy and his advisers.

Partisan politics is seldom absent from diplomatic decision making and Kennedy was well aware that were he to cancel an operation that the Eisenhower administration had begun, it was likely that the cancellation would soon be "leaked" and furnish a source of Republican criticism. There were political risks in authorizing the proxy invasion—its failure could besmirch the carefully cultivated image of a new administration of superior efficiency—but there would be serious political disadvantage were the American public to hear that Kennedy had "cancelled something that Eisenhower'd set entrain which would have liberated Cuba."[26]

It would appear that Kennedy was more quickly convinced of the disadvantageous consequences of canceling the operation than persuaded by CIA promises that the role of the United States could be easily hidden. Kennedy gave the green light only by stages and at each stage insisted, with some self-deception, that he still kept open the option of rejection. A crucial stage in the decision-making process was reached with Kennedy's directive of 11 March.

On that date Kennedy made a commitment to the Miami Front as well as to the Freedom Brigade. The CIA was directed to "assist patriotic Cubans in forming a new and strong political organization." In connection with this effort, "a maximum amount of publicity buildup" should be given the leaders of the organization, "especially those who may be active participants in a military campaign of liberation." Kennedy gave no final approval to Bissell's scenario for an amphibious assault, declaring that "the best possible plan from the point of view of combined military, political and psychological considerations, has not yet been presented," but the National Security Action Memorandum concluded, "The President expects to authorize U.S. support for an appropriate number of patriotic Cubans to return to their homeland."[27]

Bissell was disappointed by the president's hesitation, but Kennedy had approached the point of no return with the formation of the U.S.-approved Revolutionary Council. Operational details were subject to further debate, but as Bissell brought forth further evidence of prospective deliveries of Soviet bloc arms to Havana and the training of Cuban pilots behind the Iron Curtain, the advantages of delay appeared to evaporate. Once again the argument was made that time was on the side of Castro. With more time he would be equipped with Russian MIGs and an air arm that could endanger the success of the operation; with further postponement the morale of the Cuban freedom fighters would suffer and the prospective rainy season make difficult the establishment of an impregnable beachhead.

By late March, the CIA was selling Operation Zapata as an all-purpose plan. It would provide a beachhead that would give cover to U.S. recognition of a provisional government. It would ignite a national revolt that would topple the Castro regime. It would, at the very minimum, serve to supply and reenforce the anti-Castro guerrilla underground.[28] Kennedy would not give the go-ahead for another fortnight but this final delay was primarily designed to give the State Department the opportunity to remind foreign governments and domestic opinion of the sins of Castro.

The opening gun was a White Paper on Cuba authored by Arthur M. Schlesinger, Jr. and issued with orchestrated fanfare on 3 April. Schlesinger had received the assignment on 11 March and within a week had prepared a rough draft. Aware that the president wished a document that could justify the recognition of a rival Cuban government—in the event that the invasion force succeeded in gaining a secure beachhead—Schlesinger was also determined to produce a document that would persuade the Democratic Left in Latin America of the threat of Castroism to national independence and hemispheric security.[29] Useful to that purpose was the thesis recently propounded by the journalist-historian Theodore Draper, which took issue with both pro-Castro apologists who blamed U.S. policy for the radicalization of the Cuban Revolution and commentators on the Right who insisted that the 26th of July Movement had been from its inception a communist trick.[30] Schlesinger agreed with Draper that the tragedy of Cuba was that *after coming to power* Castro had betrayed the initial promise of the Cuban Revolution when he turned to the Cuban communists for his chief source of support. This was an interpretation that allowed the United States to censure Castro while expressing support for the goals of social justice and democratic reform. The United States did not wish the return of Batista tyranny; its objective was the redemption and implementation of the initial promise of the Cuban Revolution.[31]

The White Paper underwent many drafts but its theme remained constant: the United States was on the side of social and economic reforms and the Castro regime was to be condemned for delivering the Cuban Revolution "into the hands of powers alien to the hemisphere" and transforming that revolution into an instrument for subversive intervention. A movement "to enlarge Cuban democracy and freedom" had been perverted into a mechanism "for the seizure by international communism of a base and bridgehead in the Americas." In its final form, Schlesinger's White Paper was divided into four sections: "The Betrayal of the Cuban Revolution," "The Establishment of the Communist Bridgehead," "The Delivery of the Revolution to the Sino-Soviet Bloc," "The Assault on the Hemisphere." The paper's subtitles made clear its argument.

Schlesinger's analysis of Cuban developments was expectedly one-sided, but neither its organization nor its prose can be faulted. It remains the best-written exposition of the U.S. indictment against Castro. Schlesinger exaggerated the control of Partido Socialista Popular over Cuban "centers of power," the development of Cuba into "a modern totalitarian state," and Castro's ambition to convert all Latin America to the Cuban model; he appeared ready to use as synonyms the Sino-Soviet bloc, international communism, and the USSR; he was less than truthful in his assertion that "Dr. Castro was in fact cordially received when he visited the United States in the spring of 1959," but the Cuba White Paper was a skillful blend of propaganda and historical analysis. It demonstrated Schlesinger's belief that anticommunist liberals must furnish "the Vital Center" in Latin American affairs as well as in U.S. politics. He achieved at points a kind of Wilsonian eloquence:

> The people of Cuba remain our brothers. We acknowledge past omissions and errors in our relationship to them. The United States, along with other nations of the hemisphere, express a profound determination to assure future democratic governments in Cuba full and positive support in their effort to help the Cuban people achieve freedom, democracy and social justice. . . . For freedom is the common destiny of our hemisphere—freedom *from* domestic tyranny and foreign intervention, *from* hunger and poverty and illiteracy, *for* each person and nation in the Americas to realize the high potentialities of life in the twentieth century.

Had such an appeal been issued in 1958 and directed to the Cuba of Batista, it would have received widespread support from spokesmen of the Latin American Democratic Left. Issued in April 1961 it brought a mixed response; for it appeared to presage a greater measure of U.S. support for anti-Castro exiles: "We call once again on the Castro regime to sever its links with the international Communist movement . . . and to restore the integrity of the Cuban Revolution. If this call is unheeded, we are confident that the Cuban people, with their passion for liberty, will continue to strive for a free Cuba."[32]

The White Paper received respectful attention from a large majority of the American press, and was accepted as a fair-minded appraisal of the danger of Castroism to hemispheric security and "the authentic and autonomous revolution of the Americas."[33] A few dissenting views were to be heard. The *American Legion Magazine* criticized the White Paper's failure to underscore the economic losses of U.S. investors in Cuba, while *Mainstream* denounced the document as a shoddy effort to prepare public opinion for a new episode in imperialist gunboat diplomacy, but Schlesinger had little reason to complain of journalistic response.[34] Nor did the Kennedy administration have cause for complaint when it decided to give Operation Zapata the green light.

The American public would receive news of the Cuban invasion on 17 April with a general sense of surprise and with an apparent readiness to attribute the operation to the spontaneous efforts of Cuban refugees determined to recover their homeland. This reaction was in fair part the result of the cooperativeness and lethargy of the American press. Rumors of a secret training camp in Guatemala had circulated over the previous weeks, but few newspapers took public heed of these rumors or were prepared to embarrass the administration by precipitate disclosure.[35] Editors were predisposed to believe that the exiles were inspired solely by a love of freedom and enjoyed wide-scale underground support in their native Cuba. That predisposition was fostered by the press releases of two public relations firms subsidized by the Cuban Revolutionary Council with CIA funds. Lem Jones Associates, Inc. in New York and Abrams, Osborne and Associates in Miami were hired to provide publicity for the Revolutionary Council, its democratic credentials, and its identification with the Cuban people.

Only in two instances had the Kennedy administration felt the need to call forth the argument of "national security" in an effort to assure self-censorship by the press. The first of these efforts concerned the *New Republic* and an article by Karl Meyer on the connection of the CIA with the Miami refugees. Before publishing this piece Gilbert Harrison, owner of the *New Republic*, sent galleys to Arthur Schlesinger. After consulting with Kennedy, Schlesinger requested that the article not be released. Harrison complied. The

New York Times proved equally obliging. When Tad Szulc filed a story describing CIA recruitment efforts and indications of a probable invasion of Cuba in the near future, Turner Catledge, managing editor, held up the article while asking the advice of the head of the *Times* Washington bureau, James Reston. Reston advised against publication and the Szulc article was rewritten in a fashion to delete all allusions to the CIA and possible U.S. involvement.[36] It is not certain that Reston acted at the request of the White House, but his counsel that publication could prove damaging to national policy would have received presidential approval.

At a press conference on 12 April Kennedy had informed his audience that the administration had no plans to intervene in Cuba with U.S. armed forces, would try to prevent involvement by U.S. citizens in the efforts of Cuban freedom fighters to restore democracy in Cuba, and would not allow Cuban refugees to use U.S. ports for launching an invasion.[37] The assembled reporters accepted these assurances at face value and did not press the president with embarrassing questions. Reston wrote a column in which he suggested that the president had failed to answer the "difficult question" of whether the United States was prepared to provide the refugees "with all the money and arms necessary to launch the invasion, not from American ports and airfields, but from somewhere else." But though he was ready to remind the administration of its nonintervention pledge under the Charter of the Organization of the American States, Reston made no mention of the CIA or of the information obtained by his colleague Szulc. There were certain matters the president "could not very well discuss in public."[38]

Few subjects have been more often and tendentiously described than the invasion of Brigade 2506[39] at Playa Girón, and no purpose would be served by offering a detailed recital of the tactical misadventures of an operation that has been characterized with justice as "a perfect failure."[40] The legality of the invasion remains a matter of controversy as does the assignment of blame for its failure, but its chronology has long been a matter of public record.

On Saturday, 15 April (D-Day minus 2), three B-26 bombers piloted by American-trained Cuban refugees left an airfield in Nicaragua with orders to render ineffective Castro's small air force. The planes had been painted with Cuban markings in an attempt to attribute the raids to defectors from Castro's air force.[41] Bombs were dropped on three Cuban airfields with comparatively little damage to Castro's handful of T-33 trainers but with considerable effect on the state of readiness of the Cuban government. The 200,000-man militia was put on full alert and Castro began to round up all suspected "fifth columnists." In New York, Dr. Raúl Roa informed the UN that the anticipated American invasion of Cuba had begun and demanded action by the Security Council. Ambassador Adlai Stevenson declared the Cuban charge a lie: it was a B-26 of the Cuban air force which bombed the Havana airfield before the "defecting" Captain Zuñiga had flown to asylum in Florida.

A second air raid scheduled for the early morning of D-Day was canceled by order of President Kennedy at the request of Secretary Rusk. Rusk saw the Zuñiga cover story lose credibility and received reports of Stevenson's suspicion that he had been duped. Concerned with "the international noise level" at the UN, Rusk urged that further air strikes must appear to originate from the airstrip at Playa Girón; they must follow and not precede the establishment of a beachhead. Receiving news of the cancellation from McGeorge Bundy on Sunday evening, Richard Bissell and General Charles P. Cabell, CIA deputy director, went to Rusk's office and argued lengthily for the scheduled second strike. They failed to demonstrate its necessity for the success of the operation and a last-minute call from Rusk to Kennedy sustained the cancellation order.

The brigade arrived at Red Beach in the Bay of Pigs in the early dawn of Monday, 17 April in an ill-assorted flotilla whose decrepit character would presumably ensure nonidentification with the U.S. Navy. Confusion and mischance marked its history from the beginning. Cuban militia units were alerted within minutes of the first landing; a paratroop detachment failed to blow up the causeways leading to the beachhead areas; the *Houston* was set aflame by a lucky hit by one of Castro's pilots before it could unload its ammunition cargo; the *Río Escondido* suffered a similar fate with the brigade communication van and fuel supplies still aboard. All companies of the brigade were finally put ashore and their CIA-selected commander, Pepe San Román, penetrated a few miles along the main road through the Zapata swamps, but the effort to establish a secure beachhead was unsuccessful. Hampered by shortage of ammunition and the lack of radio communication, harassed by the skillfully deployed Cuban air force that retained control of the air, the brigade was pounded by Castro's tanks and enveloped by the Cuban militia.[42] By Tuesday afternoon the invaders were in retreat; by Wednesday afternoon they were defeated. A few escaped to the American ships hovering on the horizon and some attempted to find refuge in the Zapata swamps, but most surrendered and began a prison captivity that would last for twenty months. Less than seventy-two hours after the first of the "freedom fighters" landed at Red Beach, Castro announced the total defeat of "the mercenary army." There had been no internal uprising in support of the invaders; Castro's effective control of Cuba had been demonstrated and strengthened.

In the last hours of the brigade's desperate struggle to avoid being pushed back into the sea, Kennedy had flirted with the idea of a limited introduction of U.S. air power. At an emergency midnight meeting at the White House, Tuesday, 18 April, Kennedy, at the urging of Bissell and Admiral Burke, had authorized a flight of six unmarked jets from the carrier *Essex* to fly cover for a scheduled B-26 bombing attack from Nicaragua the next morning. The U.S. jets were not to attack Castro's planes except in defense of the brigade bombers. The distinction was vague but in the outcome irrelevant. Because of a delay in the transmission of Kennedy's authorization, the jets arrived over the beach at Playa Girón an hour after the B-26 bombers had turned back to Nicaragua. It was but the last of a series of blunders that guaranteed an operation based on false assumptions would culminate in unalloyed failure.

To his credit, Kennedy did not attempt to compound error by heeding the advice of Admiral Burke to save the operation by an overt commitment of U.S. military power. Despite Kennedy's repeated warning that American participation would be limited to "recruiting, financing, equipping, training, and counseling" the Cuban opponents of Castro, certain proponents of Operation Zapata, as well as the Cuban Revolutionary Council in Miami, had expected the introduction of U.S. armed force in the event of a threatened collapse of the invasion. Kennedy disappointed them and thereby prevented a humiliating defeat from achieving the status of a diplomatic disaster.

Kennedy's first private reaction to the disaster at the Bay of Pigs, as reported by his special counsel Theodore Sorensen, was to ask "How could I have been so stupid to let them go ahead?" It is but one of several questions pertinent to an evaluation of an operation that promised national disadvantage in success as well as in failure.[43]

Some analysts of the Bay of Pigs debacle would place all blame on the CIA: the CIA transformed a plan to supply reenforcements to Cuban guerrillas into a World War II-type amphibious operation and in the process sought to replace the State Department as formulator of U.S. Cuban policy and misled the new president. The indictment contains a measure of truth, but it is too simple and too easy.

There can be little disagreement that an amphibious invasion by 1,400 men was too large a task for a clandestine service whose primary mission was spying. As the project evolved, it had taken on an increasing complexity of function. The CIA station chief in Guatemala City, for example, became an undercover construction boss as he supervised the building of barracks at Helvetia and an airfield at nearby Ratalhulen. CIA agents in charge of training the invasion force had little or no communication with CIA agents instructing small bands of counterrevolutionaries inside Cuba. By the fall of 1960, if not earlier, the project had become too big for a covert operation, but the CIA refused to recognize the fact. It is not unusual for bureaucratic organizations to identify control with duty. Richard Bissell, for his part, associated personal control over the operation with its secrecy and success. Bissell hungered for neither power nor fame, but he saw himself as the essential man, the most dedicated, the most efficient, the most capable.

The arrogance of Richard Bissell found justification in personal capacity; the same cannot be said of many of the lower-echelon CIA agents who were given the task of organizing the Cuban exiles and establishing liaison with the leaders of a future provisional government. Not all were as ill-chosen as Gerry Droller, who under the pseudonym of "Frank Bender" tried to compensate for his ignorance of Spanish and Latin America by adopting the pose of a proconsul,[44] but many displayed an ethnocentric indifference for the sensitivities of the exiles and an irritable impatience when they failed to fall into line. They misinterpreted important political divisions within the exile community and—in disregard of administration policy—were quite prepared to recruit Batistianos. More generally, they directed most of their funds toward the older and more conservative exile leaders, discriminating against such reform-minded emigrés as Manuel Ray, suspected advocates of "Castroism without Castro."

The relationship between the CIA and the exiles was an unhealthy one on both sides.[45] If CIA agents saw the exiles as American dependents, some of the older exile leaders appeared ready to adopt that status. Such men as Miró Cardona and Antonio de Varona had grown up in a Cuba that saw the United States as final arbiter of Cuban politics and prosperity, and while they protested the refusal of their CIA contacts to keep them more fully informed, they concurrently sought CIA approval and largess. The failure of the Bay of Pigs operation was not of their making, but the quality of leadership of the Revolutionary Council made highly unlikely Bissell's promised uprising.

Integral to the planning strategy of the CIA was its determination to sustain the fiction that the invasion was a Cuban operation that had no official connection with the U.S. government. Secrecy and deception became ends in themselves: the clumsy code word was "nonattribution." The goal of nonattribution inspired a series of tactical decisions that made more certain the debacle of 17–19 April. Under the compulsion of hiding U.S. involvement, Nicaragua was chosen as the location for the secret air base; obsolete B-26 bombers were selected because they had become common currency in international arms sales; fighter escorts were forbidden in the preliminary bombing raid because they could not be attributed to Cuban defectors; antiquated ships were obtained on private lease and U.S. naval vessels ordered to guide their lumbering progress at a discreet distance. Emphasis on secrecy and disguise restricted the number of persons who could be consulted for information and advice. The outstanding examples of ill-considered exclusion were certain members of the intelligence community in Washington and the U.S. embassy at the UN. In Washington neither the CIA's deputy director for intelligence Robert Amory, Jr. nor the Research and Intelligence Bureau of the State Department was privy to the Cuban invasion plan. In New York, Adlai Stevenson was kept completely in the dark and as a result was trapped into parroting falsehoods that did much to destroy the credibility of an American trusted and respected in European and Third World capitals. In the process the Kennedy administration recklessly risked one of its more valuable diplomatic assets.[46]

The disadvantage of confining policy review to the already committed is obvious. What has generated controversy is the question of assessing individual blame. Whatever the errors of the CIA, it did not act without presidential authorization nor did it provide more than two members of the White House Cuba Group. It was President Kennedy who gave Bissell and the CIA the green light; it was the chairman of the Joint Chiefs of Staff who allowed Kennedy to believe that Operation Zapata had their approval. How much responsibility should be born by the president and his military advisers for the debacle at the Bay of Pigs?

This question was implicitly addressed by the Taylor Commission, an ad hoc group established by Kennedy on 22 April 1961 to examine the causes of the failure at Bay of Pigs and make recommendations for military and paramilitary policy based on that examination. Its chairman was General Maxwell Taylor and its other members were the president's brother, Attorney General Robert F. Kennedy, CIA Director Allen Dulles, and Chief of Naval Operations Admiral Arleigh Burke. It held twenty meetings between 22 April and 25 May and heard testimony from over fifty witnesses. A "sanitized" copy of that testimony and of Taylor's summary report letter to the president has been declassified,[47] which provides, if not a satisfactory explanation of the origins and failure of the Cuban invasion, considerable insight into the intramural struggle over the apportionment of blame. Witnesses from the executive branch sought to exonerate the president and pointed to the inaccurate information provided by the CIA and the approval given Operation Zapata by the Joint Chiefs. CIA representatives focused on Castro's control of the air and the importance of the cancellation of "the second strike." Marine General David M. Shoup and other representatives of the military denied that they had ever formally approved the operation and suggested, at least by implication, that the operation had been run by the White House and ruined by the nervous nellies at State.

Robert Kennedy was the most aggressive interrogator on the Taylor panel, and it would appear that he was as concerned to exculpate his brother as to trace the evolution of the Cuban expeditionary force. His questions were directed at two objectives: (1) to get the

CIA to admit that it had expected that the invasion would serve as catalyst for a mass uprising and to extract from the military an admission that the beachhead plan only made sense when tied to the expectation of civilian insurrection, and (2) to get the CIA to acknowledge that it had offered assurances that in the event of failure to establish a secure beachhead, the brigade could take "the guerrilla option" and retreat into the mountains. An auxiliary objective was to demonstrate that the president had been handicapped by a lack of accurate intelligence and by the "reticence" of his military and civilian advisers. Testimony by Secretary Rusk and Secretary McNamara supported these contentions but McGeorge Bundy was presumably a less successful witness. That at least would be one explanation for Bundy's subsequent request on 4 May to substitute for his oral testimony a written memorandum. In that memorandum, he maintained that the success of the invasion was always understood to be dependent on the internal Cuban reaction and reiterated Rusk's judgment that Cabell and Bissell had failed to make clear that they considered the D-Day air strike to be crucial to the operation. Had they done so, it was Bundy's belief that the president would have reversed his cancellation order.

Efforts of self-justification by Kennedy's civilian counselors were easily matched by the Joint Chiefs of Staff, as they sought to demonstrate that though they had offered advice they had not granted approval. Something close to endorsement had been given to the CIA's initial proposal, Operation Trinidad—a landing on the southern coast of Cuba some one hundred miles east of the Bay of Pigs and considerably closer to the Escambray Mountains—but that proposal had been vetoed by the president because its airstrip was too small to provide a cover or base for the B-26 bombers. They had not been sufficiently consulted on the shift from Trinidad to Zapata, and they had not been consulted at all on the cancellation of the second air strike. General Lyman Lemnitzer attributed the collapse of the invasion to the failure to control air space over the beachhead, and recommended that in the future all military operations be under the direct command of the Pentagon.

Witnesses from the CIA understandably preferred to emphasize the justification for the invasion rather than its operational details. Bissell offered a concise explanation of why the agency believed that time was running out on the possibility of using Cubans to perform the necessary task of removing Fidel Castro. The brigade was at hand and in a state of readiness. To have delayed the operation would have seriously damaged its morale and caused problems with the president of Guatemala; to have disbanded the brigade would have sent a dangerously wrong message to the anti-Castro underground in Cuba as well as to the exile community. Bissell had no apologies for urging administration approval of Zapata; though, in retrospect, he believed that unnecessary concessions had been made in favor of "disclaimability."

No witness or member of the Taylor Commission raised questions of propriety or morality. There was apparent agreement that the operation's offense was that of failure, and questions of controversy were confined to the cancellation of the second air strike, the accuracy of intelligence reports, the coordination of command, the selection of the landing site, and "the guerrilla option." Only tangentially was the CIA criticized for false assumptions and for its negligence in providing contingency plans in the event of failure.[48]

Nowhere does one see a recognition that a "successful" outcome for Operation Zapata and the proclamation of a rival Cuban government headed by Miró and Varona would have precipitated a long and bloody civil war with a high probability of an open-ended U.S. military intervention. By any cost/benefit analysis, the Cuban invasion of April 1961 was a losing proposition. It was, moreover, strategically stupid, contrary to U.S. treaty commitments, and morally dubious.

The Bay of Pigs invasion has been justly characterized as an operation "too large to remain secret and too small to succeed."[49] But its strategic stupidity has broader compass. The risks entailed were always greater than the advantages promised and those advantages were largely illusory. Any initial "success" would have been followed by policy decisions that offered only a choice of evils. Ellis O. Briggs, a foreign service officer with strong conservative credentials, observed that the failure of the Cuban expeditionary force was "a fortunate (if mortifying) thing for the United States, which otherwise might have been saddled with indefinite occupation of the island." A similar judgment was made by Philip Bonsal in his memoir: "Although the disaster of the Bay of Pigs was . . . deeply humiliating to all Americans and particularly to those who held that the good name of our country had been diminished in the conception and conduct of the operation, I now believe the outcome was the most favorable realistically to be desired, granting the undertaking and the policy that motivated it."[50]

In several OAS resolutions between 1946 and 1958, the United States had explicitly agreed that interference by one American state in the domestic affairs of another was forbidden. For the United States to recruit, equip, train, and direct exile enemies of the legitimate government of Cuba was a violation of the OAS Charter and the Bay of Pigs operation was without justification in international law. Adolf Berle insisted, before and after the event, that the invasion was authorized by the Rio Treaty and its denunciation of extra-hemispheric intervention. At most, however, that treaty authorized collective OAS action. Unless one accepts the assumption that the Castro regime posed a threat to the continued existence of the United States requiring immediate resort to the law of self-defense, the Bay of Pigs invasion was an illegal act.

But does illegality translate into immorality? There is a popular school of thought that would deny that morality has realistic meaning for the decisions of international politics. The United States, however, claimed a higher moral code than that of its antagonists. The United States also prided itself on its observance of the right of national self-determination. By an extreme exercise in wishful thinking, the Kennedy administration could claim that Brigade 2506 represented the aspiration of the Cuban people, but only by ignoring available evidence that the Castro regime was supported by a majority of Cubans and held the fervent loyalty of many. In the final analysis, the Bay of Pigs operation was an act of aggression and was correspondingly susceptible to the charge of immorality.

John F. Kennedy, the martyred president, cannot escape responsibility for the stupidity, illegality, and immorality of the Bay of Pigs invasion. The memorialists of Camelot have sought to make Kennedy the victim of a process set in motion before his inauguration, but their explanation fails to persuade. Kennedy did indeed inherit the brigade and the plan for an amphibious invasion, but his authorization of that invasion was in harmony with promises he had made during the campaign of 1960 to encourage the Cuban exiles. Gutsy action had appeal for John F. Kennedy and Bissell's optimistic assessments were not unwelcome. Philip Bonsal makes the important point that Kennedy's hesitations did not arise from questions of principle but from a concern over "possible errors in the calculations of the experts." Bonsal concludes: "His assumption of full responsibility [after the event] was more than a gesture of generosity and nobility; it was a highly creditable recognition of the truth of the matter."[51]

If Kennedy's admirers resist the conclusion that Bay of Pigs saw Kennedy accept the role of the aggressor, many Latin Americans saw the invasion as a reversion by the United States to the bullying, gunboat diplomacy of an earlier day. Indeed, one of the consequences of the Bay of Pigs operation was that it strengthened the position of Fidel Castro. Castro's success in defeating the invaders enhanced his stature in Latin America and consolidated the power and authority of his regime in Cuba.

Another consequence—one diametrically opposite to the interests and objectives of the United States—was to strengthen the ties between Cuba and the Soviet Union. The Russians saw Castro as a more permanent and important figure and Castro successfully requested increased Soviet aid as a means of combating U.S. enmity. The Soviet Union played no role in Castro's response to the Cuban expeditionary force, but the Russians as well as Castro benefited from the United States's debacle at Playa Girón.[52]

It is not difficult to damn the Bay of Pigs operation. The path is well-marked and well-trod. The event furnishes a test, however, for the student who would display the primary criterion of historical-mindedness: understanding the moods and fears of another era. Judged in the context of the 1980s, the Bay of Pigs invasion appears not only wrong but irrational, a paranoid response to Castro and his popular dictatorship. In the context of 1961, it can be judged wrong but not irrational. Kennedy and Bissell were not alone in the spring of 1961 in seeing the world in Manichaean Iron Curtain terms.[53] Many Americans blamed Castro for removing Cuba from "its natural position" as our dependent-ally and delivering it to the enemy. Unnatural actions provided excuse for retaliatory aggression, or so they believed, and this belief explains the continuity of U.S. Cuban policy from March 1960 through April 1961, and beyond.

Chapter Five

Standoff

Kennedy and Castro after the Bay of Pigs,

April 1961–April 1962

John F. Kennedy more than most presidents expected success and felt betrayed by failure. His immediate reaction to the collapse of the Cuban invasion was a mixture of personal shock and political calculation. He realized the probable impact of the defeat on the domestic popularity and international reputation of his administration; almost immediately he sought to limit damage on both fronts.

Some weeks earlier he had agreed to speak at the annual dinner of the American Society of Newspaper Editors on 20 April. He now took that opportunity to set the guidelines for press reaction to the Bay of Pigs debacle and in the process to direct public anger against the victorious Castro. He would exhibit not contrition but resolve and stand forth not as the apologetic sponsor of an abortive filibustering expedition but as the reincarnation of Winston Churchill during the Battle of Britain.

Some members of his audience must have been aware of an element of irony in the setting. Two years before, almost to the day, the bearded Fidel in his rumpled green fatigues had addressed them from the very same rostrum at the Statler Hilton's main ballroom. Now they listened to Castro's acknowledged enemy as he spoke in martial tones: "If the nations of this hemisphere should fail to meet their commitments against outside Communist penetration, then this government will not hesitate in meeting its primary obligations which are the security of this nation." The attempt of the exiles to recover their homeland was "a struggle of Cuban patriots against a Cuban dictator," and in such a struggle "we could not be expected to hide our sympathies." Unilateral U.S. intervention in Cuba, "in the absence of an external attack upon ourselves or an

87

ally," was contrary to traditions, but "let the record show that our restraint is not inexhaustible." The issue at hand was nothing less than "the survival of freedom in this hemisphere itself," for all of the free nations in the Americas were threatened by "the menace of external Communist intervention and domination in Cuba." On this issue "there can be no middle ground." Kennedy concluded, "As President of the United States, I am determined upon our system's survival and success, regardless of the cost and regardless of the peril."[1]

From the editors, Kennedy received a standing ovation and from their papers more sympathy than censure. There is perhaps a natural tendency for Americans to support a chief executive who is being criticized by Paris intellectuals and Moscow commissars, but the reluctance of a majority of the press to blame the president for the failure at Playa Girón was due as well to Kennedy's skillful handling of the Washington press corps.

Not only did many papers praise Kennedy's 20 April address for its candor and patriotism, but they echoed certain of its themes. Kennedy was correct to inform Khrushchev that the United States had no need for lectures from those who had crushed freedom "on the bloody streets of Budapest." The failure of the exile army to ignite a popular uprising was the result not of Castro's popularity but the repressive power of a police state. Cuba was a potential launching pad for subversive communist activity in the Caribbean. Now was not the time to dwell on the extent or sufficiency of U.S. involvement, but to express our sympathy for the captive freedom fighters.[2]

The supportive response of a majority of the press found confirmation in the public opinion polls, where Kennedy's approval rating showed a surprising increase in the week after the Bay of Pigs disaster,[3] but there were numerous exceptions among the press and public. Neither the *Nation* nor the *Monthly Review* hesitated to attack the Kennedy administration, and there were antiadministration rallies in nine major cities. Walter Lippmann denounced the invasion as illegal, irresponsible, and strategically stupid.[4] Other columnists, however, were more susceptible to the Kennedy treatment. William S. White, after a long interview at Kennedy's Virginia retreat, Glen Ora, wrote sympathetically of the external circumstances that had forced Kennedy to authorize the invasion and then limit the extent of U.S. support. Kennedy's personal friend Stewart Alsop, though critical of the government for attempting to combine "a covert operation" with a pose of "virginal innocence," saw reason to blame not the White House for the failure but the poor advice of military advisers and the undue concern of Adlai Stevenson for world opinion.[5]

Kennedy brushed aside adverse criticism in the editorial columns of the *Nation*, and reserved his irritation for articles inspired by self-justifying sources in the Pentagon or the CIA. He had hoped to limit intramural controversy to the secret testimony collected by the Taylor Commission, and he was angered by an article in *Fortune* that echoed the Pentagon line and blamed the failure of the invasion on last-minute White House alterations that had sabotaged a soundly conceived military operation. Kennedy informed a news conference that "this is the most inaccurate of all the articles that have appeared on Cuba," and he dispatched Maxwell Taylor to *Fortune*'s publisher, Henry Luce, with a seventeen-point critique and rebuttal.[6]

More important than inaccurate journalists, however, were potential critics from the ranks of the Republican opposition. Efforts to limit the damage done the administration at the Bay of Pigs were directed first and foremost at preventing the debacle from becoming a point of partisan attack. Here Kennedy counted heavily on the cooperation of his predecessor and it was forthcoming.

Kennedy telephoned Gettysburg to inform Eisenhower of the details of the failure at the Bay of Pigs, so far as they were known, and invited Richard Nixon to the White House to receive a similar briefing. Eisenhower and Nixon realized that any demand by the Republican minority in Congress for a Pearl Harbor-style investigation would spotlight Eisenhower's order of March 1960 and embarrass the CIA. For his part, Eisenhower felt no animosity toward his successor and had a keen appreciation of the value of bipartisan cooperation for the presidential direction of foreign policy. Nixon disliked and distrusted Kennedy, but he could not criticize him for utilizing an assault force fashioned by his predecessor. It would be three years before Nixon made public his judgment that "soft-liners" in the Kennedy administration had undermined "the original concept of the operation" by "last-minute compromises." In April 1961, Nixon was content to advise Kennedy "to find a proper legal cover" and try again.[7]

The examples of Eisenhower and Nixon inhibited Republican conservatives in the Senate, as did the widespread sentiment that a nation should close ranks in time of diplomatic defeat.[8] Partisanship found expression, however, in the tangled debate over the proposed "prisoner–tractor exchange." In that debate, there was duplicity on the one side and venom on the other, and honor for neither.

John F. Kennedy felt an understandable responsibility for the imprisoned freedom fighters cast into crowded Havana jails after mock public trials. He seized upon a suggestion that Castro might be prepared to release the prisoners in exchange for several hundred tractors needed by the Cuban Agrarian Institute. Presidential adviser Richard Goodwin was instructed to notify Milton Eisenhower, Eleanor Roosevelt, and Walter Reuther that the president wanted them to form a private committee to arrange this exchange. It would receive official blessing, and contributions to the tractor fund would gain Internal Revenue Service sanction as charitable deductions. From the start, Kennedy sought to hide the presidential origins of the Tractors for Freedom Committee—insisting that the administration was "putting forward neither obstacles nor assistance to this wholly private effort"—but initially he was prepared to offer his personal endorsement of its humanitarian purpose: "I hope that all citizens will contribute what they can. If they were our brothers in a totalitarian prison, every American would want to help. I happen to feel deeply that all who fight for freedom—particularly in our Hemisphere—are our brothers."[9]

Then senatorial critics attacked the committee's purpose as an example of cowardly appeasement, and Kennedy fell silent. Republican Senators Karl Mundt, Styles Bridges, Homer Capehart, and Barry Goldwater took the floor of the Senate to berate the State Department for encouraging an effort that could only bring "humiliation and disdain" to our country. The bulldozers would be used to enhance the economic strength and so the military danger of a communist dictator. Senator Everett Dirksen denounced the proposed exchange as a request that "the American people pay blackmail to Fidel Castro." Human lives were not a proper subject for barter, and Kennedy had no right to encourage private citizens to pay Castro an indemnity.[10] Right-wing criticism, administration timidity, and Castro's shifting maneuvers to gain maximum propaganda advantage[11] combined to frustrate the efforts of the Tractors for Freedom Committee; it disbanded in a mood of understandable irritation. Eventually the imprisoned members of Brigade 2506 would be ransomed, but not until the fall of 1962 and at a price more than double the cost of five hundred bulldozers.

The Kennedy administration was primarily concerned with the impact of the failed invasion on press opinion and domestic politics, but it recognized as well the potential for diplomatic embarrassment. It was decided that at the UN General Assembly and the OAS Council, the best defense would be one that alternated professions of innocence with baleful warnings. The United States had not overreacted to the threat posed by communist Cuba; rather its moderation should be applauded and its strictures carefully attended.

At the United Nations, the U.S. delegation had little trouble in sidetracking a Cuban-sponsored resolution condemning U.S. aggression, though its effort to consign all investigation of the Bay of Pigs invasion to the Peace Committee of the OAS failed to receive the necessary majority. The final outcome was not unsatisfactory to the Kennedy administration. The General Assembly passed a resolution exhorting all member states "to take such peaceful action as is open to them to remove existing tension," and then dropped the matter.[12]

The U.S. representatives had insisted throughout the debate that the United States had no aggressive purpose against Cuba. Indeed, they sought to make failure the proof of innocence: "If this was a United States military operation, do you think it would succeed or fail? . . . Perhaps the best evidence of the falsity of the shrill charges of American aggression in Cuba is the melancholy fact that this blow for freedom has not yet succeeded." The members of the General Assembly—particularly the nations in the Western Hemisphere—should not be distracted by the false charges of the Cuban delegate from the central issue: "the penetration of force from outside our hemisphere, dominating a puppet government and providing it with arms, tanks, and fighter aircraft."[13]

Claims of American innocence did not prevent the world press from expressing a widespread conviction that the U.S. had inspired and directed the exile invasion, but the Kennedy administration found the UN debate useful as a practice session for its approach to the OAS and Latin America.[14]

Pro-Cuban demonstrations in Caracas, Mexico City, and Rio de Janeiro were publicly dismissed by the State Department as the work of a small handful of radical students, but by early June the Kennedy administration had mounted a major propaganda offensive designed to counter the adverse effects of the invasion fiasco. Its objectives were to convince the nations of Central and South America that they had more to fear from Cuba than did the United States, that no possibility remained for meaningful negotiations with Fidel Castro, and that the requirements of hemispheric security demanded both a "system of surveillance in the Caribbean" to frustrate the subversive designs of Cuba and a concentrated effort "to move ahead with all urgency on the Alianza para el Progreso."[15]

The origins of the Alliance for Progress can be traced to Brazilian president Kubitschek's Operation Pan-America as well as to the long-term requirements of U.S. trade and investment in Latin America, but the note of urgency characterizing State Department press releases in the summer of 1961 was the result of a determination to turn the attention of Latin America away from the Bay of Pigs and toward the importance of economic development as a safeguard against the contagion of Castroism. Senator Mike Mansfield, a member of the Senate Foreign Relations Committee and a recognized friend of the New Frontier, had warned Kennedy as early as 19 April—the last day of the abortive invasion at Playa Girón—that "if there is a quick and total collapse of the anti-Castro forces," the sensible policy would be to "cut our losses and concentrate action on the Alianza para Progreso as the only visible counterbalance."[16]

Chester Bowles, Adolf Berle, and Richard Goodwin offered similar advice over the next month, and by June the propaganda program for the Alliance was well under way. Cameramen were invited when Kennedy signed an agreement with the president of the Inter-American Development Bank establishing the Social Progress Trust Fund; Secretary Rusk made an awkward appearance on a CBS television program to extol the value of economic and social development as a shield against communist penetration of Latin America; and the State Department bureaucracy was instructed "to push ahead energetically with the Alliance for Progress as a fundamental measure for combatting Sino-Soviet imperialism in the Hemisphere."[17] Adlai Stevenson was sent on a publicized tour of six Latin American capitals, with a mission to enunciate the "sovietization of Cuba" and elicit support for an "inter-American program for social and economic development."

Upon his return Stevenson gave Rusk a detailed report, which, in summary form, received immediate publication. Attempting to combine the roles of Jeremiah and varsity cheerleader, Stevenson aimed his report at the subscribers to the Department of State *Bulletin*. Communism in Latin America was assuming the guise of an indigenous revolutionary movement under the name of "Fidelismo." The people of Latin America must be alerted to its subversive intent, but Latin American officials could not successfully meet this threat by diplomatic weapons alone. "Acts on the home front" were necessary to counter the attraction of communism and "its alter-ego Castroism." Urban slum conditions and "rural insecurity" must be corrected if the poor in the cities and the countryside were to have confidence in the possibility of economic improvement under free institutions. John F. Kennedy had pointed the way with "his proposal for a hemispheric Alliance for Progress to speed social and economic advance."[18]

The publicity campaign for the Alliance reached its natural climax with the meeting at Punta del Este, Uruguay, where on 17 August the representatives of all of the American Republics (except Cuba) signed the Declaration of the Peoples of America and a charter formally establishing the Alliance for Progress. Twelve goals of social and economic development were outlined for the decade of the 1960s. Their achievement would assure the people of the participating countries "maximum levels of well-being, with equal opportunities for all, in democratic societies adopted to their own needs and desires."[19]

The ambitious rhetoric of the Alliance Charter was echoed by John F. Kennedy at San Carlos Palace, Bogotá, Colombia, in December. The guests at a state dinner were informed that on the success of the Alliance rested "the future of human dignity and national independence" in the Western Hemisphere. Alianza para el Progreso was "revolutionary in its dimensions" and stood in diametric opposition to the communist program of class war and mass regimentation. Communism—as demonstrated by the drabness of life in Eastern Europe and widespread hunger in China—promised progress and brought only poverty and the subjection of man to the will of the state. If "the leaders of Latin America, the industrialists and the landowners accepted their new responsibilities," the Alliance would demonstrate anew that only under conditions of freedom could human welfare increase and social justice triumph. If the Alliance failed, "the heritage of centuries of Western civilization" could be "consumed in violence."[20]

The Kennedy administration convinced itself that the Alliance for Progress was the central feature of its Latin American policy, but it was essentially a component of its Cuban policy. After the Bay of Pigs, the Kennedy administration tried to structure an anti-Castro containment policy, and the Alliance was one of its building blocks. Other blocks were political isolation, economic sanctions, and increased attention to the techniques of counterinsurgency. In combination they would supposedly assure the containment—and so the frustration and weakening—of Castro's Cuba.[21]

Failure at the Bay of Pigs did not disillusion the Kennedy administration with the efficacy of armed force; rather it had the effect of encouraging a greater emphasis on counterinsurgency training and paramilitary action. There was no intent to sponsor another proxy army of Cuban exiles, but there was increased determination to assist Latin American governments in antiguerrilla training and achieve improved coordination between the Department of Defense and the CIA in the area of covert operations. Guerrilla movements and so-called wars of national liberation would provide the new test for the United States, in Latin America as well as in Southeast Asia. If the revolutionary virus were to be quarantined, its potential victims must be trained in the techniques of counterinsurgency. The Alliance for Progress would provide long-term immunity against the subversive appeal of Castroism, but for the immediate future the United States must be prepared to expand its intelligence operations and paramilitary capability if it would thwart Castro's expansionist designs. Such a direction had been urged by the Taylor Commission in its 13 June report to the president when it recommended "a national Cold War strategy capable of including paramilitary operations."[22] Kennedy did not accept Taylor's specific suggestion for a new "coordinating agency" for Cold War strategy, but he did revive the Board of Consultants on Foreign Intelligence Activities and transferred all covert military operations above a certain size from CIA to Defense.[23]

The containment of Castro's Cuba also required economic sanctions. Every effort should be made to cripple the Cuban economy and thereby lessen the danger of the spread of *fidelismo*.[24] A program of economic denial would not only reduce the ability of the Castro regime to export subversion, but it would undermine its popular support in Cuba, demonstrate the failure of a socialist economy to stimulate growth or raise the standard of living, and increase the cost to the Soviet Union of maintaining a satellite in the Caribbean. In pursuit of these objectives, the Kennedy administration broadened its ban on Cuban trade and imports and exerted more pressure on its NATO allies to cooperate in denying Cuba machinery, spare parts, and markets.[25]

The anti-Castro containment policy had its political component, too. Cuba must be isolated in the Western Hemisphere. To that end, the United States would publicize the subversive intent of Castro's secret agents in Latin America and thereby persuade the American republics to expel Cuba from the OAS and impose collective sanctions. The goal was clear but its accomplishment proved difficult.

Many Latin American governments were suspicious of the appeal of Castroism for their left-wing opponents, but they were reluctant to accept the elastic interpretation that the United States was determined to give the Rio Treaty of 1947 and the Act of Bogotá of 1948. The Rio Treaty permitted collective action when a member state was subjected to armed attack or when it declared its independence and sovereignty threatened by subversive intervention; the Act of Bogotá declared that "by its anti-democratic nature and its interventionist tendency, the political activity of international communism ... is incompatible with the concept of American freedom."[26] The United States argued that the Sino-Soviet bloc had successfully pursued a policy of subversive intervention in Cuba and, consequently, the Castro government endangered the peace of the Americas. The Rio Treaty and Bogotá resolution authorized collective action against the hemispheric renegade.

Some of the larger Latin American nations—Mexico, Argentina, Brazil among them—believed that such an interpretation could threaten the independent sovereignty of member nations of the

OAS and undermine the principle of nonintervention, which they saw as more essential to hemispheric accord than a collective front against Castro. They did not deny the increasing dependence of Cuba on Soviet aid, but they pointed out that Soviet advisers were in Havana by open invitation and questioned the assumption of the U.S. State Department that the discovery of radical propaganda in the possession of Cuban diplomatic officials was proof that Cuban sovereignty was sacrifice to an international communist conspiracy. To U.S. claims of the right of collective self-defense, they posed the contrary claims of the right of national self-determination.

The State Department labored from May until December to persuade the member nations of the OAS to hold a meeting on the "Cuban danger." With the first days of December it received the assistance of Fidel Castro and the government of Colombia. On 2 December Castro made his famous "I am a Marxist-Leninist" address, and within twenty-four hours Colombia requested a meeting of consultation of the ministers for foreign affairs of the American republics. On 4 December the Council of the OAS passed a resolution "to consider the threats to the peace . . . that might arise from the intervention of extracontinental powers directed toward breaking American solidarity."[27] The meeting was scheduled to open on 22 January at Punta del Este, birthplace of the Charter of the Alliance for Progress.

Washington had been encouraging Colombia to make this request for some time, and Castro's speech appeared to give increased credence to the U.S. position. DeLesseps S. Morrison, U.S. Representative to the Council, laid heavy emphasis on Castro's "confession of intrigue and deception," as he belabored the sins of Cuba. Accepting the validity of the garbled United Press International report of Castro's speech, the United States now abandoned the Draper thesis of a democratic revolution betrayed for the conspiracy thesis of ex-ambassador Earl E. T. Smith. Castro had been "basically influenced by Marxist-Leninist theory" while still a student at Havana University. By this conclusion the government unwittingly did much to undermine the State Department's claim that Soviet intervention was responsible for the current enmity of Cuba for the American System, but logical consistency was deemed less important than an assured majority in the Council. Morrison declared that "Castro's 'guerrilla warfare' was synonymous with Khrushchev's 'wars of national liberation'" and reminded the Council that the OAS had "a grave responsibility to act collectively to protect . . . this hemisphere from any extension of the treachery of *fidelismo*."[28]

That "grave responsibility" was the theme of Dean Rusk's departure statement when he left Washington for Punta del Este on 20 January. The forthcoming meeting of the American foreign ministers was "of paramount importance." It was essential that the ministers "make the policy decision to exclude the Castro regime from participation in the organs and bodies of the inter-American system." No longer could they allow a situation to exist whereby Cuba was privy to the deliberations of the Inter-American Defense Board charged with "planning the defense of the hemisphere against the aggressive designs of international communism."[29] Rusk made no secret of his wish to see Cuba expelled from the OAS and for that organization to impose stringent sanctions on the Cuban enemy. He wanted a general trade embargo and collective enforcement of a ban on arms traffic between Cuba and the rest of the hemisphere. He suspected that he would have to settle for less.

At Punta del Este, the United States gained the long-sought public condemnation of the Castro regime and "exclusion of the present government of Cuba from participation in the inter-American system." It did so only after withdrawing its demand for collective sanctions and only at the cost of increasing disunity within the OAS. The vote on the expulsion of Cuba was 14 to 1 (Cuba dissenting), but six nations abstained. Those nations—Argentina, Bolivia, Brazil, Chile, Ecuador, and Mexico—contained more than half the population of Latin America.

Rusk naturally sought to claim a victory for U.S. diplomacy at Punta del Este and for its policy of Cuban isolation. The Castro regime had been formally recognized as "incompatible with the purposes and principles of the inter-American system."[30] Cuba's isolation, however, was less than complete, so long as several Latin American states continued diplomatic ties with Havana and OAS disapproval was confined to words. The Kennedy administration would give lip service to the importance of collective action after January 1962, but it had lost faith in the OAS as an instrument for promoting its Cuban policy.

Although the proclaimed goal of that policy was the containment of Castroism, the wish to eliminate Fidel Castro continued. After its defeat at the Bay of Pigs, the Kennedy administration saw Castro as its enemy. The New Frontiersmen had inherited a get-rid-of-Castro policy, but they provided the element of personal animus. They had been humiliated by Fidel and they craved the satisfaction of revenge. This fact ruled out any form of dialogue with Havana. Kennedy declared publicly that there could be no negotiation with Cuba so long as it incited subversion in Latin America and was allied with the communist bloc. In fact, he ruled out negotiation so long as Fidel Castro was in power. Suggestions that Castro might be encouraged to become a Caribbean Tito were brushed aside as wishful thinking. The policy of economic denial had the implicit aim of economic strangulation and the creation of conditions of economic misery that would incite domestic insurrection and the destruction of the Castro regime at the hands of the disillusioned Cuban populace.[31] Propaganda broadcasts beamed to Cuba had a similar intention,[32] as did the more secret maneuvers given the code name Operation Mongoose.

At a meeting in late August 1961 members of a new Cuban Task Force and representatives of the CIA had agreed to recommend a policy of selective sabotage of "targets important to the [Cuban] economy," and three months later Kennedy issued a secret order "to use our available assets . . . to help Cuba overthrow the Communist regime." Colonel Edward Lansdale, champion of the Green Berets and supposed expert on counterinsurgency, was appointed to head a program of concerted sabotage, using CIA contacts in Cuba, to be known as Operation Mongoose. It would be supervised by a review committee (the Special Group Augmented) and its tasks were indicated by a comment of Attorney General Robert F. Kennedy: "My idea is to stir things up on the island with espionage, sabotage, general disorder, run and operated by Cubans themselves."[33] There is insufficient evidence to support an evaluation of the extent or success of the operation, but its establishment alone supports the retrospective judgment of Robert McNamara: "We were hysterical about Castro at the time of the Bay of Pigs and thereafter."[34]

Did hysteria and resentment endorse murder as well as espionage? It is known that abortive efforts were made by CIA officials Richard Bissell, William Harvey, and Sheffield Edwards to arrange the assassination of Fidel Castro; what is uncertain is the question of presidential knowledge and approval. That question frequently arose during the deliberations of Senator Frank Church's Select Committee, which held hearings in 1974–75 on the past activities of the U.S. intelligence community and "alleged assassination plots involving foreign leaders." The Church Committee concluded that though the CIA did plan to utilize underworld figures to assassinate Castro as early as the fall of 1960 and made several abortive efforts between the summer of 1961 and the winter of 1963, neither President Eisenhower nor President Kennedy knew of the Castro assassination plot or gave it official sanction.[35]

By the spring of 1962, Robert F. Kennedy was aware, through information furnished him by J. Edgar Hoover and the FBI, that the CIA had at one time approached certain underworld figures with the purpose of hiring gunmen to go to Cuba and kill Castro. It is likely, however, that the attorney general never relayed the information to his brother. In a conversation with Senator George Smathers, John Kennedy had expressly disapproved the notion of arranging the assassination of Fidel Castro. His disapproval was offered not on moral grounds but those of political strategy. Castro's assassination would be blamed on the United States and its president; Castro's successor might be worse than Castro.[36] John Kennedy's Cuban policy embraced covert invasion, sabotage, and espionage, but there is little reason to believe that it included premeditated murder.

Kennedy's Cuban policy after the Bay of Pigs was directed toward the contrary objectives of containing and eliminating Castroism. The instruments of that policy were in place by the winter of 1962, and the remaining twenty-two months of the Kennedy presidency saw little change and little success. Those months found their most terrifying moments in the Cuban Missile Crisis, but that event was essentially a confrontation between Kennedy and Khrushchev. Castro played but a minor role and its outcome had surprisingly little impact on U.S. Cuban policy. From Punta del Este until Dallas, Kennedy's policy aims remained constant: the isolation of Cuba in the Western Hemisphere; the strangulation of the Cuban economy; and the encouragement of "espionage, sabotage, general disorder" in the island of Cuba.

The Kennedy administration shared with its predecessor a determination to topple Castro and bring Cuba back into its "natural alignment" with the United States. Like its predecessor, it pursued policies that had effects exactly opposite to their purposes. Kennedy succeeded in expelling Cuba from the U.S.-dominated American security system, but he failed to weaken the hold of the Castro regime on the Cuban population and saw the developmental model of socialist Cuba gain additional converts within the Latin American Left. Although Russian–Cuban relations were temporarily soured in the aftermath of the Missile Crisis, the Kennedy years saw on balance the increasing reliance of Cuba on the USSR and the Warsaw Pact nations. The Cuban economy suffered a new form of external dependence, but it experienced neither suffocation nor stagnation. Soviet military power in the Caribbean was enhanced and the intrusion of the Cold War into the Caribbean made permanent.

As with the Eisenhower administration, these developments could not be attributed alone to the policies of John F. Kennedy; nor is it certain that alternative policies would have produced different results. It is certain that the response of the Kennedy administration to the Cuban Revolution was a response that compounded danger without compensatory benefit.

THE PUBLIC RESPONSE

Chapter Six

Response of the Political Right

The official U.S. diplomatic response to the Cuban Revolution was in general harmony with the public response: the response of politicians and lobbyists, religious spokesmen and academicians, investors and labor leaders, columnists and editors. There was, expectedly, a wider spectrum of judgments in the public at large than in the executive branch; the opinions of William Buckley and C. Wright Mills were at greater variance than those of Richard Nixon and Philip Bonsal. There was more initial enthusiasm for Fidel Castro in the American press than in the memorandums of the State Department, and a more erratic and diverse evolution toward the conviction that Castro represented a danger to U.S. national security. There was a livelier debate over the Bay of Pigs invasion in the Harvard Yard than in the Senate, and more militancy in the American Legion than the diplomatic corps.

It would appear, however, that administration policy and mainstream public opinion were seldom seriously at odds in their reaction to the revolution in Cuba and the response it demanded of U.S. foreign policy. Public opinion polls indicated that a majority of Americans supported the cancellation of the Cuban sugar quota, the break in diplomatic relations, the expulsion of Cuba from the OAS, the trade embargo. In part this was the result of effective news management and public relations by the Eisenhower and Kennedy administrations, but the press was as much a reflector of popular apprehension as a repository for official propaganda and the relationship of official policy and majority public opinion was a manifestation of pressure exerted by each side in a process of mutual reenforcement.

Opinion polls are not the most satisfactory instrument for quantifying political attitudes and the elusive reality called public opinion. Certainly they do not provide any conclusive figures for the number of Americans concerned with U.S. Cuban policy or the percentage of Americans who at any single point in the years 1959–61 wished that policy more or less conciliatory, more or less assertive. One conclusion, however, the polls do substantiate: by the winter/spring of 1961 a large majority of those prepared to express an opinion to pollsters saw Castro as an enemy of the United States.

A private firm of market analysts, Sindlinger & Company, questioned almost four thousand Americans in the week following the Bay of Pigs operation about the invasion and their attitude toward the Castro regime. Though only a minority favored an effort by U.S. armed forces to unseat Castro, better than 90 percent "endorsed the attempt of Cuban refugees to get rid of Castro." The claim that the Americans surveyed represented "a scientific cross-section" of the population may be doubted, but the language of the replies has the conviction of direct quotation. Two themes surfaced repeatedly: Castro had betrayed our expectations; Castro's conduct was that of a crazy man. For every assertion that Castro was "a dirty, lousy, low-down rat," there were a half-dozen comments labeling him "insane," "mentally unbalanced," "half nutty," "psycho," "nuts," "a dope fiend," "cracked-up," "haywire," "off his rocker." Running through the replies is a note of resentment. The United States should not be burdened by a "Communist puppet and dictator" in our part of the world. The unexpected turn of events in Cuba could only be explained by the fact that Castro was evil and irrational.[1] In reaction to the figure of Fidel Castro, the response of official diplomacy and the American public found unity.

Foremost among those who saw in Castro a target for personal and ideological animus were spokesmen of the political Right. Such spokesmen were not representative of either administration policy or the American foreign policy public, but they helped influence both and led the march to the excoriation of Fidel Castro that characterized official and popular response by the winter of 1961.

Biographical examples of political conservatism in the years 1959–61 are plentiful, and in no instance was there a reluctance to denounce the Cuban Revolution and advise the Eisenhower and Kennedy administrations on U.S. Cuban policy. In Washington such politicos as Senators Styles Bridges and Roman Hruska and Congressmen Wayne Hays and Keith Thompson called repeatedly for harsher sanctions against Castro and advocated U.S. recognition of an exile Cuban government. In the public at large one could choose among such spokesmen of the Right as George Sokolsky, Robert Welch, General Albert Wedemeyer, Ambassador Spruille Braden, and Paul Bethel, executive director of U.S. Citizens Committee for a Free Cuba.[2] More influential than any of these, however, were Senators James O. Eastland, Barry Goldwater, and George Smathers, and the editor of the *National Review*, William F. Buckley.

James Eastland, as chairman of the Senate Committee on the Judiciary and its Subcommittee to Investigate the Administration of the Internal Security Act and Other Internal Security Laws, was in a position to embarrass the Eisenhower and Kennedy administrations and he was pleased to do so.[3] Eastland was prepared to use his subcommittee as a rival foreign office to the State Department, which he considered rife with leftist sympathizers and homosexuals. He took advantage of the authority of congressional subpoena to turn his committee into a court of inquiry determined to indict U.S. Cuban policy. As with Alice's Queen of Hearts, the sentence would precede the trial: the Department of State, the *New York Times*, and a pro-Castro cell in the U.S. Havana embassy were responsible for undermining Batista and bringing Fidel Castro to power. Muddle-headed left-wingers were responsible for the fact that we "lost Cuba" as earlier we "lost China."

Cuban refugees were warmly welcomed to testify before the subcommittee and encouraged to confirm Eastland's belief that Castro's communist affiliations were well known while he was still in the Sierra Maestra. The first of several carefully staged and televised committee dramas featured Major Pedro L. Díaz Lanz, Castro's air chief who fled Cuba in June 1959. Under the prodding guidance of J. G. Sourwine, the committee's counsel, Díaz offered a rambling account of the expanding authority of the Cuban communists and the persecution suffered by those who resisted their influence. Díaz confirmed that "the word God" had been struck from the new Cuban constitution; that in order to obtain a job it was necessary to file an application for membership in the Communist party; that Cuban students were subjected to Marxist teaching and anti-American propaganda; and that many officers in the Cuban army were beginning to compare the Cuban Revolution to a watermelon: "green outside but red inside."[4]

Equally rambling but somewhat less satisfactory was another witness, General Charles Cabell, deputy director of the CIA. Cabell was called early in November 1959, and Counsel Sourwine had no difficulty in obtaining his agreement that "the Communist movement has made very great progress in Cuba since Castro took over the Cuban Government." Cabell disappointed Chairman Eastland on several counts, however. He denied that "750 North Korean and Communist Chinese" fought with the Castro forces in 1958; he did not believe that the secret Pawley mission in 1958 had been responsible for the "lost confidence" of Batista's army; and he insisted on emphasizing the corruption of the Batista regime and the failure of nerve of Batista's army. Most disappointing of all was his denial that Castro had been a communist while a guerrilla chieftain or was even now a member of the Cuban Communist party. Eastland felt obliged before dismissing Cabell to reiterate that the committee was concerned with results rather than definitions, and the results of Castro's accession to power were clearly visible to all patriotic Americans.[5]

By 1961, Eastland had singled out William Wieland as the prime culprit in the State Department conspiracy to foist Castro upon an unsuspecting U.S. public. In his vendetta against Wieland, one-time director of Caribbean Affairs, Eastland received unstinting assistance from Robert C. Hill, former ambassador to Mexico City. Hill was an embittered man, convinced that his advice had been ignored by his State Department superiors and that his dispatches informing Washington of a secret Mexican intelligence dossier on the young Castro had been kept from "the upper echelon." Hill had quarreled with Wieland during a visit by Milton Eisenhower and Wieland to Mexico City in 1959 and was convinced that Wieland was either a fool or communist. Eastland was prepared to omit the conjunction and, in one of the sorrier episodes of senatorial inquisition, sought by innuendo to attribute Wieland's professional progress to his friendship with former Under Secretary of State Sumner Welles and a State Department circle of alleged homosexuals. The primary thrust of Eastland's attack, however, was Wieland's recommendation for an embargo on U.S. arms to Batista in March 1958. Wieland must have known that this embargo would mean the destruction of the Batista regime and the victory of the communist enemy.[6] Wieland was called before the committee to be grilled and traduced on several occasions. In the process his promised ambassadorial promotion was pigeonholed and his career ruined.

The charge that the Marxist Fidel gained power not through military victory but by means of the knowing assistance of "fellow travelers" in the U.S. government and press provided the central theme of two books that earned the praise of Senator Eastland and his subcommittee colleagues: Nathaniel Weyl's *Red Star over Cuba* and Daniel James's *Cuba: The First Soviet Satellite in the Americas.* Both sought to explain how Cuba had fallen into the hands of the communist enemy. Weyl's book was the earlier and more sensational with its suggestions of conspiracy and treason, and it received the higher praise from Thomas Dodd, subcommittee vice-chairman. Dodd inserted in the *Congressional Record* a brief literary appreciation: "A solid, carefully documented yet dramatic work that tells the story of Castro's rise to power and of the manner in which he was abetted by naive American sentimentalists, deluded liberals and open philo-Communists."[7]

Senator Barry Goldwater also had praise for Weyl and for those who would awake America to the fact that the establishment of a Cuban Soviet Socialist Republic was but the first step in the Kremlin's plan to establish a Latin American Union of Soviet Socialist Republics. Goldwater agreed with Eastland and Weyl that the State Department had sufficient reason to suspect the Red taint of Castro and his movement in the early stages of the Cuban civil war and was culpable for not warning the American people. If our diplomatic officials had done their duty, the public could not have been deceived by such pro-Castro publicists as Herbert Matthews of the *New York Times* editorial board, and would not have swallowed the line that Castro was a democratic reformer. Castro's success in Cuba was a major victory for the USSR in the Cold War.[8]

Goldwater was the leader of a small group in Congress who favored military action to bring down the Castro regime, on one occasion suggesting that Cuba be starved into submission with a naval blockade. He felt a sense of personal betrayal at what he considered the clumsy timidity of the Bay of Pigs operation. As an Air Reserve officer and member of the Military Affairs Committee, Goldwater had his own Pentagon sources, and was quick to disseminate the view that White House interference had mangled a military operation that had a high percentage of success. Goldwater believed that

Adlai Stevenson and other Kennedy advisers—the "Fearful Four-some"—had persuaded Kennedy not to provide promised "air sup-port and sea backup." In a letter to the *Saturday Evening Post,* he criticized the efforts of those who sought to conceal the president's errors and demanded the public exposure of his guilty advisers.[9]

In Goldwater's view, both the Eisenhower and Kennedy adminis-trations had responded to the Cuban crisis with "astounding timid-ity and indecision." Our diplomats appeared mesmerized by "the intellectual theory of nonintervention," when they should have taken a lesson from President William McKinley's successful Cu-ban intervention in 1898—a time before we had "apologists for for-eign ideologies and Red-tinted dictators wielding influence in our newspapers and our Department of State." Seeking to identify the Republican party with a bold alternative to "defensive" contain-ment, Goldwater expressed dissatisfaction with many features of U.S. foreign policy. But in the "theft" of Cuba by our communist enemy he found special cause for rhetorical despair: "The dark night of totalitarianism had descended, obliterating human dignity, cheapening human life, destroying all semblance of human rights. It has set a reign of terror over our neighbors to the south. . . . It has replaced reason with the firing squad. It has ridiculed and perse-cuted religion. It has abandoned property rights and substituted government confiscation."[10]

There were some editorials in the right-wing hate sheet *Ameri-can Opinion* that denounced Castro earlier and more violently,[11] but in the U.S. Senate, Goldwater was in the front rank of Castro-haters as were the most conservative members of both parties. There was indeed a correlation of sorts between the suspicion of a senator for "creeping socialism" at home and his enrollment in the ranks of the Castro-haters. The more suspicious he was of the ex-panding operations of the federal government, the sooner came his decision that Castro was a communist in disguise and a threat to U.S. national security. George Smathers offers but a limited excep-tion to that correlation.

George Smathers was a personal friend of John and Jacqueline Kennedy and as a senator from Florida had a constituency that ex-pected various forms of assistance and subsidy from the federal gov-ernment. He was as much the opportunist as the conservative, and his rating by Americans for Democratic Action was not as low as that of Eastland and Goldwater. He was, however, one of the earlier senatorial opponents of Fidel Castro and as the Cuban emigré population grew in the Miami area, so did his demands that the United States take a tougher stand toward Castro's Cuba.

Smathers meant to carve for himself a position as the senatorial expert on Latin America. In particular, he posed as an expert on U.S.–Cuban relations, and if his proposals lacked consistency, they were at all times a step ahead of the evolving anti-Castro policy of the State Department. He was among the first to denounce the summary trials of the Batistianos, suggesting a national day of prayer for Cuba. In November 1959, he was informing the television audience of "Face the Nation" that Castro's conduct put at risk Cuba's favorable sugar quota; by January 1960, Smathers demanded an end to Cuba's sugar quota and suggested that "the quota money" be used to compensate Americans whose property in Cuba had been confiscated. U.S. citizens should be dissuaded from traveling to Cuba and encouraged to visit instead such friendly Caribbean nations as Haiti. The OAS should organize a naval and air patrol of the Caribbean to prevent Castro's efforts at subversion in Nicaragua, the Dominican Republic, and Panama. With the first months of 1961, Smathers was urging U.S. support for an invasion of Cuba by exile patriots and advising President Kennedy to support "the Varona group," and not the left-leaning Manuel Ray. When Senator Wayne Morse counseled calm after the failure at the Bay of Pigs, Smathers scornfully replied that the solution was "not patience and more debate" but renewed effort to assure the final victory of the Cuban patriots. The United States must demand that the OAS impose severe sanctions on Castro's Cuba and reorganize that body along NATO lines to assure effective joint action. The government should in addition launch a great propaganda offensive against Castro on July 26th, upstaging the anniversary celebrations in Havana and informing the Cuban people that we refused to accept their enslavement.[12]

John F. Kennedy had lost patience with the mounting demands and self-assertion of Smathers by the summer of 1961 and instructed him not to discuss Cuba when visiting the White House. But for the Washington press, Smathers was always good copy. There was no senator more often quoted on the Cuba story in 1959–61 than George Smathers, self-appointed leading challenger of Fidel Castro and the Cuban Revolution. The editor of the *National Review*, though critical of Smathers's vacillating conservatism and White House entrée, quoted Smathers on two occasions. For William F. Buckley, however, the U.S. Senate was on the whole a disappointment, as were other branches and bureaus of the government.

Buckley was among the first journalists to believe that the Cuban Revolution was deserving of suspicion. Fidel was initially characterized as a dangerous left-wing adventurer; by the summer of 1959 Buckley was warning his readers of the expanding influence of Castro's communist advisers and reporting that "many young daughters of army and police personnel had been turned over to Castro units to be used as military whores."[13] Buckley reserved his more abusive adjectives not for the Cuban communists but for Castro apologists and for persons and institutions he identified with the liberal establishment: the *New York Times*, Eisenhower Republicans more concerned for political consensus than national security, Arthur M. Schlesinger, Jr. and New Frontier advocates of socialistic economic planning, C. Wright Mills and proto-Marxist academics.

There was a certain bipartisan evenhandedness in Buckley's denunciations. He had no more use for Eisenhower's "saccharine homilies" than for Kennedy's Cuba White Paper with its "leftist, non-Communist Castroism without Castro line." Proclaiming that "patience that serves only to paralyze decision is . . . a mortal vice," Buckley urged U.S. intervention in Cuba as early as the spring of 1960. A year later he blamed the Bay of Pigs debacle on "a failure of will," and suggested that Harvard University should add to its graduate curriculum "a course or two on Invasions, Amphibious" for the necessary education of "future Harvard Administrations."[14]

It was not, however, the effete academics of Harvard nor the timid bureaucrats of the State Department who provided Buckley with his primary object of scorn. It was a fellow journalist, Herbert L. Matthews.

Herbert Matthews had scored a journalistic coup in February 1957 by making his way past a series of Batista police checkpoints and obtaining a long interview with Fidel Castro in his Sierra Maestra hideout. Matthews had subsequently assumed the role of Castro's champion and sympathetic interpreter of the Cuban Revolution for readers of the *New York Times*. In the years 1959–61,

Buckley remorselessly attacked Matthews and his corrupting influ-ence on public opinion and State Department policy before and after Castro's assumption of power. Buckley was infuriated by Mat-thews's refusal to admit that Castro was a communist and Cuba a Soviet satellite.[15] The *National Review* would periodically reprint an excerpt from Matthews's *Times* article of 16 July 1959 wherein Matthews had assured his readers: "Premier Castro is not only not a Communist but decidedly anti-Communist," and Buckley de-voted a column in January 1961 to chastising his alma mater for inviting Matthews to spend a week as a Chubb Fellow in Timothy Dwight College. Yale was for God and Man but not for a stubborn propagandist whose rhapsodic account of the democratic idealism of Fidel Castro had bowled over the American intelligence service and been responsible for the failure of the State Department to lis-ten to the wise warnings of Ambassador Earl Smith.[16]

Buckley's most detailed indictment of Matthews appeared in an article he wrote for the *American Legion Magazine*. Presumably directed to the danger Castro posed to American security, the title indicated Buckley's chief target: "I Got My Job Through The New York Times." Buckley opened his article with the declaration that the policy question most in need of an answer was "Who betrayed Cuba?" and thereby the security interests of the United States. He then provided the answer:

> The leader of the pro-Castro opinion in the United States is Herbert L. Matthews, a member of the editorial staff of *The New York Times*. He did more than any other single man to bring Fidel Castro to power. It could be said—with little li-cense—that Matthews was to Castro what Owen Lattimore was to Red China, and that *The New York Times* was Mat-thews' Institute of Pacific Relations. . . . It is bad enough that Herbert Matthews was hypnotized by Fidel Castro, but it was a calamity that Matthews succeeded in hypnotizing so many other people, in crucial positions of power, on the subject of Castro.

The star reporter of the *Times* was not a journalist but a propagan-dist, whose "supercolossal mistakes in judgment" made him "an easy mark for ideologues-on-the-make." Belatedly the *Times* had come to the conclusion that the line pedaled by Matthews was "unfit to print," but the damage to the Cuban people and hemispheric security had already been done.[17]

It is not easy to measure the influence of such figures as Goldwater, Eastland, Smathers, and Buckley with any precision. Eisenhower's shift to a get-tough-with-Castro policy in March 1960 was inspired primarily by events in Cuba and Kennedy's decision to authorize and then limit the military operation at Bay of Pigs was inspired by the advice of Bissell and the warnings of Rusk and Stevenson, not by insults in the *National Review*. Both presidents, however, were mindful of the growing hostility in the press and Congress against Castro's Cuba. Attacks on Fidel from the political Right served to stimulate public anger and apprehension. By helping to condition the public context within which American policy was fashioned, the Right exerted a measure of indirect influence on both administrations. The rising anti-Castro State Department rhetoric of 1960–61 was directed not only toward Latin American governments but toward U.S. public opinion, in an effort to convince the voters that Washington was not deceived by the social welfare trappings of the Cuban Revolution but was aware of its Soviet alignment and subversive intent.

The influence of the Right in inciting popular fears of "a Red satellite ninety miles off our shores" was assisted by the comparative uncertainty and ineffectiveness of the leading liberals in Washington. In House and Senate, there were those who initially held high hopes for the Cuban Revolution and who subsequently found distasteful the witch-hunt tactics of Eastland and Dodd. Surprised and worried by the leftward drift of the Cuban Revolution, they failed to offer an alternative to the evolving U.S. Cuban policy of economic sanctions, political isolation, and military threat.

Senator Wayne Morse of Oregon was a recognized liberal and a self-acknowledged maverick, but his response wavered between a fluctuating suspicion that the State Department was unduly influenced by the anxieties of U.S. investors and sporadic anger with Castro for disappointing his American friends by suppressing civil liberties and persecuting Cuban middle-class professionals. Morse warned against the possible boomerang effect of economic sanctions and reminded his constituents that the Cuban Revolution had been inspired by a desire for social justice and national independence that was universal throughout Latin America, but he admitted that once in power the revolutionaries had committed inadmissible acts of brutality. As chairman of the Subcommittee on American Republics Affairs of the Senate Committee on Foreign Relations, Morse approved a report in February 1960 that referred to the danger of communist penetration of the Cuban government and judged the possibility of future domination by the Cuban Communist party "a touch-and-go matter."[18]

A similar uncertainty and unhappiness characterized the response of Rhode Island Senator Claiborne Pell and his older colleague, Paul H. Douglas of Illinois. Douglas in a televised interview of November 1959 urged patience with Castro and advised against any "wholesale condemnation" of the Castro government. Douglas, however, was deeply suspicious of the expansionist designs of the Soviet Union. By the end of 1960, Douglas was convinced that Castro was moving into the Soviet orbit and he offered no objection to Eisenhower's decision to break diplomatic relations with the Cuban government. Claiborne Pell advised patience for a longer period of time and in December 1960 paid a private visit to Cuba in an effort to measure the degree of Castro's hostility for the United States. Pell remained a firm opponent of U.S. "overt or covert action" in Cuba, but by the spring of 1961 favored its political isolation. Cuba was lost to the Free World. The United States should concentrate on the Alliance for Progress, and by encouraging social reform and economic development in Latin America make the region invulnerable to the siren appeal of Castroism.[19]

If Senate liberals offered an option to administration policy, it lay in their greater emphasis on cooperation with the OAS and increased U.S. support for Latin American economic development. Such emphases were advocated by J. William Fulbright, the senator most consistent in his cautionary warnings against military intervention in Cuba. Though Fulbright's liberal credentials were open to challenge on civil rights issues, in his role as chairman of the Senate Foreign Relations Committee he urged cooperation with the UN and OAS, greater concern for world opinion, and an unqualified respect for treaty obligations. Fulbright saw Castro as "a thorn in the flesh . . . not a dagger in the heart." He was increasingly convinced, however, that it was necessary to isolate Castro's Cuba in the Western Hemisphere. Immunization must accompany a policy of diplomatic isolation, and immunization was best accomplished by strengthening the social-economic fabric of Latin America with a speedy and generous implementation of the Alliance for Progress. Castro posed a challenge to Latin America as well as to U.S. Latin American policy, and the challenge should be met by the demonstrable success of economic development in a political framework respectful of democratic values.[20]

The most liberal members of House and Senate appeared to agree by the fall of 1960 that Castro was a danger to American security but were uncertain how best to meet that danger. Their ambivalence was in part the result of a desire not to appear as left-wing pacifists unconcerned with the demands of national security. Moreover, liberals and conservatives alike were conditioned by the Cold War and its Manichaean distinctions.[21] Indeed, some liberal internationalists considered they had more cause to wage battle against the expansionist designs of communism than did right-wing reactionaries. They had envisioned a postwar world in which collective security commitments would be linked with the expanding freedom of international trade and in which New Deal liberalism and reform capitalism would achieve global dimensions. They saw the rival world system of the USSR as the enemy of those expectations. In their convictions that Soviet aggression was responsible for the Cold War and that international communism had conspired to establish a beachhead in the Caribbean, they were at one with their domestic enemies of the Right. Unlike Eastland and Buckley, they did not charge Wieland and Matthews with responsibility for Castro's assumption of power nor did they support the use of military force, but if Douglas and Goldwater differed over the instruments most suitable to the leader of the Free World, they held common fears and antipathies. Indeed, some of the most dedicated anticommunists in Washington were Cold War liberals such as Adolf A. Berle. Berle had been a member of Franklin Roosevelt's Brain Trust, served for many years as chairman of the Liberal party in New York State, and was a personal friend of many left-of-center politicians in Latin America. He was also the man who urged Kennedy to establish a center for Cold War intelligence and propaganda in Latin America.[22]

Granted their conditioning and convictions, liberal politicians could not escape a mounting sense of frustration with the "betrayal" of the Cuban Revolution. That frustration helps explain the ambivalence of their advice on U.S. Cuban policy and the weakness of their influence. They had little impact on administration policy in the years 1959–61 and provided little leadership in the public debate over U.S. Cuban policy.

That debate achieved at points substance and significance, but this was due not to centrists in Washington but to spokesmen of the Left in the urban areas of New York, Chicago, and San Francisco. Spokesmen of the Left were of many hues and spent a large amount of their energy in intramural debate. But if in the final analysis they offer a story of division and failure, they provide as well the most interesting element in the public debate over the U.S. response to the Cuban Revolution.

Chapter Seven

Response of the Left

Division and Defeat

The Left in American history is usually more of an amalgam of views than an institutional reality. Certainly this was the case in the years 1959–61. Its individual spokesmen ranged from I. F. Stone to the officers of the Communist party of the United States; its ideological variety encompassed Catholic socialists, radical pacifists, and Beat poets. It embraced disillusioned members of the old anti-Stalinist Left and rebellious graduate students determined to form a "New Left." Attempts to define the composition of the Left are always more revealing of the describer than the described, and its composition varies according to issue as well as time. Particularly is this true when the issue is one of foreign policy.

When seeking to analyze the response of the Left to Castro's revolution and U.S. Cuban policy, problems of categorization are compounded by the shifting of opinions in the early years of the revolution: the falling off of certain sympathizers and the increasing identification of others, as that revolution came to assume a socialist character. One of the earliest analysts of the response of the Left to the Cuban Revolution was Dennis Wrong, who in an article in *Commentary* sought to distinguish between the responses of the "Old Left," the "New Left," and the "Ethical Radicals."[1] These divisions are adopted in this chapter, but an attempt will be made to subdivide these three groups because each embraces individuals with significant differences in Marxist identification, political goals, and rhetorical fervor. Such efforts at subdivision are liable to the charge of hairsplitting, but liability is not always an excuse for abstention.

Representatives of Wrong's Old Left shared former defeats and current suspicions—for Cold War warriors, witch-hunting senators, and exploiters of the oppressed—but there were important contrasts in diagnosis and prescription. These divisions were largely determined by the measure of acceptance of a Marxist-Leninist frame of historical reference and analysis. The Old Left included a spectrum of anticommunists, neo-Marxists, Marxist-Leninists, and dues-paying members of the U.S. Communist party. Few of its spokesmen—whatever the measure of their socialist faith—had expressed in earlier periods much interest in Cuba or in Latin America, an area often dismissed as unprogressive, corrupt, and medieval in its susceptibility to clerical influence. Attention had been directed to class struggle at home, not the struggle of developing nations to achieve economic and cultural independence. Even fewer had predicted the success of Castro's revolution, but most were quick to proclaim its importance. Less than a year after his assumption of power Fidel Castro was being portrayed as a symbol of Third World rebellion and the antithesis of the establishment values of Eisenhower Republicanism. A trip to Havana, once a staple for thrill-seeking tourists, was now a requirement for American dissenters and radicals.

I. F. Stone, editor-owner of the Washington journal *I. F. Stone's Weekly*, offers an illustration of the response of the segment of the Old Left that sought to combine old-fashioned progressivism with opposition to U.S. Cold War diplomacy. Stone's initial enthusiasm for Castro was shared by many Americans, but what distinguished Stone from Americans for Democratic Action liberals was his early conviction that a powerful anti-Castro sentiment would develop in the United States inspired by anticommunist paranoia and the selfish concerns of certain economic interests. Although Stone was neither a Marxist nor a communitarian socialist, his analysis of public behavior placed emphasis on the influence of greed as well as on the power of fear.

When Fidel came to Washington in April 1959, Stone not only drubbed the Eisenhower administration for "Castro's queasy welcome," but criticized the commentators on the television program "Meet the Press" for their "shrill questions about Communism." The nation appeared anxious only to receive assurance that "his brother is not a Communist, and that he will keep hands off the sugar plantations." If America still held true to its ideals, we would embrace Castro as an authentic hero, a true liberator.[2] Later, when Eisenhower lectured Chilean students on the need to combine social reform with democratic practice, Stone wondered aloud why the U.S. government found no offense in Latin American dictators "sympathetic to American property rights" but was quick to "unleash thunderbolts" when regimes appeared—as in Guatemala and Cuba—"which threaten U.S. interests and move in a socialist direction."[3] Stone's judgments of Castro's intentions evolved as the Cuban Revolution evolved, but three themes were constant: the United States had failed from the beginning to show proper sympathy for the Cuban Revolution; U.S. sanctions and aggressive rhetoric were largely responsible for the radicalization of the revolution and Castro's increasing reliance on Soviet aid; U.S. intervention in Cuba would be criminal folly. A policy of sanctions and belligerence was self-defeating and destructive of our influence in Latin America. We must show imagination and magnanimity and seek to restore friendly relations by means of empathy and concessions.[4]

Stone made a journey to Havana in April 1960, and informed his readers of the new housing developments, the improved social services, and the success of Cuban land reform. A second trip in February 1961 brought a measure of disillusionment. Stone could not but admit his disappointment at the suppression of civil liberties and political dissent and the preferential treatment accorded the Cuban communists:

> Your wistful liberal pilgrim found himself face to face in Havana with a full-fledged revolution, in all its creative folly and self-deceptive enthusiasm. . . . For the first time, in talking with Fidelista intellectuals, I felt that Cuba was on its way to becoming a Soviet-style Popular Democracy. Again for this, the U.S. shares responsibility. . . . The familiar chain reaction of counter revolution is at work, stirring suspicion, strengthening the secret police and arbitrary legal methods.[5]

For a brief moment Stone had hopes for "a fresh start" in U.S. Cuban policy with the inauguration of John F. Kennedy. Possibly the new administration would have the imagination to see the justice of Latin American resentment against U.S. domination and the exploitative effects of U.S. investment. He found Kennedy's Alliance for Progress proposal vague and inadequate, however; it was cast in a banker mentality and such a mentality would never provide Latin America "a peaceful but revolutionary substitute for

Castroism."[6] As for Arthur Schlesinger's Cuba White Paper, it was a "smooth sales talk" to soften up the American people for U.S. intervention in Cuba. It was a personal insult as well.

Stone was understandably upset that Schlesinger had quoted, selectively, from his 27 February editorial with its admission of apprehension that Cuba "was on its way to becoming a Soviet-style Popular Democracy." He was quick to point out that the White Paper neglected to quote his censure of past U.S. policies and his repeated warnings against intervention.[7] When the White Paper was followed by proxy invasion at the Bay of Pigs, Stone renounced all faith in the promise of the New Frontier. The invasion was criminal folly, and it had given Khrushchev "a cheap and easy chance to win a victory of prestige." The only consolation to be derived from this dangerous fiasco was that it might lead to a salutary "cleanup" of Allen Dulles and the CIA. Stone was convinced that the Cuban exile army had been dominated by ex-Batistianos and other right-wingers and bankrolled by "the big sugar and oil . . . companies." It had sought not "a new revolution"—social reform without *caudillo* authoritarianism—but rather a return to the old ways of economic exploitation.[8] Association with reactionaries was the path of defeat for U.S. influence in Latin America, and covert, illegal military operations were as much a danger to Washington as to Havana. They demonstrated "a rapid deterioration in our leadership and in our moral standards." Stone wrote, "We cannot set up government agencies empowered to act lawlessly without infecting the life of our own Republic. To fall back on the conspiracy theory of history, to assume that human convulsion and aspiration are but puppet movements on strings from Moscow, to place our own hopes in counter-conspiracy, is to misread man and history to our own ultimate undoing."[9]

Though admitting his disapproval of Cuba's increasing dependence on the Eastern bloc nations and Castro's short-sightedness in encouraging Soviet–U.S. hostility, Stone never retreated from a conviction that Castro had made life better for the average Cuban. The totalitarian shadow that clouded the Cuban Revolution was more the result of American stupidity than of *fidelista* design, and Fidel Castro was "the first leader of a generation to give Latin Americans genuine social and economic reform."[10]

Stone stood alone among non-Marxist spokesmen of the Democratic Left as a prose stylist, but some contributors to the *Progres-sive*, the *New Republic*, the *Nation*, *Dissent*, and *Commentary* of-fered a similar response. There were differences of emphasis. Some were more or less suspicious of the influence of American inves-tors, slower or quicker to express discouragement with Castro's suppression of civil liberties, more or less convinced that Castro had been driven into an alliance with the Soviets by U.S. sanctions and intransigence. Maurice Zeitlin and Robert Scheer insisted that "the tragic course of Cuba-United States relations" had been deter-mined by the foreign policy of the U.S. government; Morris Rubin believed that though American policy was exclusively at fault during the first phase of the Cuban Revolution, "its democratic, anti-dictatorial, anti-Communist phase," the United States was not alone to blame for Castro's decision to seek aid from the Soviet camp. Rather, "we greased the wheels that carried him there."[11]

Some members of the Democratic Left, veterans of battles of the 1930s and 1940s against Stalinist sympathizers, were more quick to suspect totalitarian tendencies within the Cuban Revolu-tion. When Castro mounted an offensive against certain anticom-munist members of the 26th of July Movement, they gave warning against the corrosive effects of totalitarian methods. At differing points such warnings were offered by Sam Bottone and Michael Walzer and by Daniel Friedenberg, a New York businessman and long-time student of Latin American politics. Friedenberg ex-pressed disenchantment in a brief essay in the *New Republic*. He had visited Castro's Cuba on two earlier occasions and had de-fended the Cuban Revolution against its critics from the Right. Now after a third visit he confessed a loss of faith:

> Castro's was a good fight, perhaps the only clean and unequivo-cal fight since the Spanish Civil War. At least I though so—and still do with that part of my heart my mind tells me is unreli-able. . . . I believed with the best part of me that in the Cuban mixture of good and bad, the good was the higher truth. . . . I [still] sympathize with Fidel Castro and feel the tragedy of his position, but I no longer think history will absolve him. . . . There comes a time when the weight of the facts becomes too heavy, the contradiction between our dream and reality so gross, we must throw off our delusions, or cease being honest

men. And that time has come. . . . I am not saying that Fidel Castro is a Communist, but that in every way he supports Soviet imperialism. . . . The entire machinery of state is directed toward holding the allegiance of these miserable peons of an outworn oligarchy, and the US is used by the Cuban Government much as Hitler used the Jews.[12]

Corliss Lamont claimed to personify the humanist wing of the Democratic Left, and Lamont sustained faith in Castro's Cuba for a longer period and directed his attention primarily against the aggressive acts of the CIA. Max Lerner, however, found in the doctrines of humanism reason to draw up an unfavorable balance sheet against Castro. By a Marxist analysis, Castro was "a liberating leader who defied American imperialism and freed Cuba's masses for a leap forward into economic growth and a socialist way of life," but a humanist analysis would include "social and psychic costs." For Lerner, those costs included "the ignoring of any rule of law, the stifling of press and speech, the ousting of independent professors and their replacement by regime spokesmen, the atmosphere of suspicion . . . [and] hate." Dedicated to the rule of reason and increasingly fearful of the designs of world communism, Lerner was essentially antagonistic to radical revolution. The economic colonialism under which Cuba had long suffered was not to be defended, but the replacement of old elites by new did not prove revolutionary virtue. Revolutionaries must be judged by their impact on the minds and liberties of the people.[13]

C. Wright Mills would probably have classified himself as a member of the Democratic Left, but his exact position is difficult to define. More influenced by Marxist theory than was I. F. Stone, less doctrinaire than the editors of the *Monthly Review*, Mills offers an individualized example of a pro-Castro response, noncommunist and neo-Marxist. If difficult to categorize, Mills's response to the Cuban Revolution was better known and more frequently debated than that of any other member of the American Left. Mills's book *"Listen, Yankee"* was one of the first studies of the nature and objectives of the Cuban Revolution and it enjoyed a sale of 400,000 copies. It became a bible for some and anathema for others.

Mills was a Texas-born professor of sociology who had a deep suspicion of the self-imposed constraints of most academics. As a social scientist he was a student of power, status, and patterns of control and subordination, and was prepared to resist his own conclusion that "knowledge seldom lends social power to the man of knowledge." In Mills's view, the intellectual had obligations that reached beyond the library and professional association; he or she had the obligation to be a committed activist in a world where power and its corruptions imposed conditions of inequality within and among nations. Mills wrote as well as he spoke, and with such books as *White Collar, The Power Elite,* and *The Sociological Imagination,* he gained a general audience and a national reputation. He also gained critical reviews from consensus scholars suspicious of the popularizer and radical Marxists suspicious of the "reformist."

In his writings, Mills paid tribute to both Karl Marx and Max Weber, but in the last years of his tragically short career, it was the influence of Marx that appeared to predominate. Always the independent radical, Mills could not be satisfied with any single explanation of human conflict, but a selective version of Marxian theory, emphasizing the importance of the individual as agent of social change, had increasing appeal.[14] Deeply discouraged by the continuing arms race, the Cold War fixations of American policy makers, and the failure of the United States to respond sympathetically to the problems of underdeveloped nations, Mills saw in the Cuban Revolution the most important development to occur in the Western Hemisphere in the twentieth century and in Fidel Castro a new kind of charismatic hero. Mills went to Cuba in August 1960, spent three days with a hospitable and loquacious Fidel, and then over a three-week period toured the island with his tape recorder, interviewing most of the principal government officials and scores of ordinary citizens. The result was *"Listen, Yankee": The Revolution in Cuba.*[15]

"Listen, Yankee" is more propagandistic than analytical and it suffers from the haste with which it was composed and published. It remains, however, one of the most interesting and personal of all of the pro-*fidelista* books of the American Left. Mills probably rephrased the words of his *campesino* interviewees for greater effect, but he captured the revolutionary élan that many Cubans still felt in the summer of 1960. The book is a study in empathy, and Mills was the willing recorder of revolutionary dedication and pro-

paganda. He went to Cuba convinced that the revolution was capable of furnishing the world with a new example of democratic socialism; convinced that the greatest obstacle to the success of the revolution was the hostility of Washington policy makers concerned with protecting American property interests and promulgating the gospel of anticommunism. His visit affirmed those convictions, and he became a willing proselytizer for the revolution and its indictment of U.S. policy. Mills informed his readers: "I am for the Cuban Revolution. I do not worry about it, I worry for it and with it." He invited their concurrence and their participation in a righteous cause.

For Mills, the cause was not that of Cuba alone, for the voice of the *campesinos* was "the voice of the hungry-nation bloc." To this voice Americans must listen; if we did not we would continue to pursue a policy that could be disastrous for ourselves and for other nations. Press and government had denied citizens of the United States the opportunity to hear the voice of the Cuban revolutionaries; so "Listen, Yankee." Listen as they speak of the past brutalities of American imperialism and of their present determination never to be exploited again; listen as they speak of their pride in the revolution, its successful agrarian reform, its concern for the poor and oppressed, its ability to promote the welfare of the peasants and urban workers alike.

In the final section of his book, Mills cast aside the role of reporter and assumed the role of instructor. This "Note to the Reader" offered a series of unqualified judgments on the nature and future prospects of the Cuban Revolution. The revolution was a "new phenomenon," far more total and successful than the earlier Mexican revolution; U.S. hostility had forced Castro's government to align itself politically with the Soviet bloc contrary to its initial "genuinely neutralist and hence peaceful world orientation"; the Cuban government was a revolutionary dictatorship of the peasants and workers and its authoritarian features were justified by the requirements of socialist reconstruction and "legitimized by the enthusiastic support of an overwhelming majority of the people of Cuba."[16]

With the publication of *"Listen, Yankee"* Mills became a cult figure for certain young radicals and the object of scorn for such Cold War warriors as his Columbia University colleague, Adolf A.

Berle.[17] A man of great personal charm, energy, and versatility—
skillful at carpentry, auto mechanics, and farming—Mills found in
radical politics an avenue of social contribution and a means of
escape from the confines of academia. He became the most sought-
after speaker at rallies of the Fair Play for Cuba Committee and
godfather of the Wisconsin graduate students who would proclaim
the formation of a New Left. He was considered suspect, however,
by those members of the Old Left who found his neo-Marxism too
individualistic and dilute. Mills's heart was in the right place but
his understanding of the inevitabilities of class struggle and the
economics of underdevelopment was painfully insufficient. The
true response of the Left to the Cuban Revolution was to be found
not in the writings of an angry sociologist but in the pages of
Monthly Review.

For its editors and subscribers, the *Monthly Review* not only provided a means of disseminating the radical Marxist response, it was
the radical Marxist response, and never was this more true than in
its articles and editorials on the Cuban Revolution. Those articles
and editorials display a remarkable uniformity of ideological perspective and policy suggestion. Perspective and policy were initially
outlined by its editors, Leo Huberman and Paul Sweezy, in their
1960 book *Cuba: Anatomy of a Revolution,* and no deviationism
was to be observed in the pages of the journal over the next two
years.[18]

For the editors of the *Monthly Review,* the Cuban Revolution
was not a bourgeois national revolution, liable to cooption and
compromise, but a true socialist revolution. It stood as example not
only for Latin America but for all Third World nations that suffered
underdevelopment as a result of the operations of monopoly capitalism. Although U.S. hostility had hastened the radicalization of
the revolution, its socialist direction was primarily determined by
the leadership's recognition of the applicability of Marxism to the
revolutionary situation in Cuba. Only collectivization of the means
of production could effect the political and social changes that
promote modernization and meaningful economic and cultural independence. Only a radical social revolution could assure Cuba
control over its economic surplus and provide the preconditions
necessary to economic growth and social development.

The Cuban Revolution was prophetic and exemplary; it was also unique. It was the first genuine socialist revolution made and led by noncommunists. Castro had wisely not fallen into the trap of the counterrevolutionaries with their diversionary tactic of anticommunism; he had wisely accepted the help of the Cuban communists, as later he had accepted the assistance of the Soviet Union and its allies. But the revolution was a true national social revolution, untainted by alien control. Liberals who made a fetish of political forms might express shock at limitations on the civil liberties of the counterrevolutionaries in Cuba. They would do better to recognize that for the revolutionaries—and this embraced the great mass of the Cuban people—freedom was absolute. The masses had been given new hope and purpose as they joined the revolutionary leadership to blaze a new trail for humanity on its march to a brighter socialist future. For its part, the Cuban leadership understood that social equality and economic development required centralized planning and control.

The Cold War was to be seen as a struggle between world capitalism and world socialism for the political-economic destiny of the Third World nations. In that struggle, North American capitalists were firmly committed to maintaining a status quo that plundered the poor nations for the benefit of the governing classes of the industrialized nations. American capitalists recognized the Cuban Revolution as the first phase of a revolutionary movement in Latin America that could undermine the entire structure of U.S. imperialism not only in the Western Hemisphere but in the rest of the world as well. There was, consequently, nothing accidental or inadvertent in the aggressive hostility of the U.S. government for the Cuban Revolution. Expressions of sympathy for a Cuban people "betrayed" by Castro were hypocritical, and Schlesinger's White Paper a tissue of lies. The Kennedy administration demonstrated its captivity to the corporate elite with its illegal invasion at Playa Girón. It was the duty of every thinking citizen to repudiate such acts of counterrevolutionary aggression and demand of the U.S. government a Cuban policy that recognized the right of self-determination for nations that elected to throw off the fetters of foreign domination and take the path of revolutionary socialism.[19]

As the editors of the *Monthly Review* criticized Mills as theoretically unsound, so were they criticized by the hard-core Marxist-Leninists writing in *Mainstream* and *Political Affairs*. This small band, survivors of the pro-Stalinist Left of the 1940s, held views on the economics of underdevelopment and the imperialist nature of U.S. Cuban policy similar to those of Huberman and Sweezy but on four counts they differed: they were more ready to identify the USSR as leader-guardian of international socialism; they credited the Cuban Communist party with a significant role in the origins and direction of the Cuban Revolution; they denied that Cuba had achieved the status of a socialist society;[20] they saw the alignment of Cuba with the Eastern bloc nations not as a latter-day decision made necessary by American hostility but as a central requirement for the proper orientation of the revolution and its protection from the dangers of *fidelista* deviationism.

Joseph North and Herbert Aptheker both subscribed to these four theorems but with differences of tone befitting a reporter for the *Daily Worker* and a scholar of history. North published a short book in 1961, *Cuba: Hope of a Hemisphere*, which sought both to praise Castro and to prove that it was the members of the Cuban Communist party who were the true heroes of the Cuban Revolution. That revolution "moved along the broad lines" the communists had been advocating for a generation. The PSP had sent volunteers into the Sierra Maestra, many of whom became outstanding figures in the rebel army; the PSP had played an invaluable role in maintaining liaison between the rebels in the field and the revolutionary movement in the cities; the PSP had directed the change from guerrilla tactics to those of positional warfare. It was Blas Roca, the PSP leader, who had instructed Castro to place greater emphasis on the urban working class as a source of revolutionary strength. The PSP had made itself felt in "all corners and areas of the political and economic life of Cuba," and it was the Cuban communists who by uniting the working classes and the intellectuals were directing the revolution's progress *toward* socialism. The Cuban Revolution was a patriotic colonial revolution that was on its way "to being as well a socialist revolution."[21]

The historian Herbert Aptheker agreed that though Cuba had successfully completed a bourgeois national revolution, it was only at midpoint in achieving a radical socialist revolution. An editor of *Mainstream*, Aptheker was instrumental in arranging in the spring of 1961 a "Special Cuba Issue" of the journal, but his most detailed analysis of the Cuban Revolution was a two-part piece for *Politi-*

cal Affairs. For Aptheker, the Cuban Revolution incorporated elements of the three great revolutionary currents of the twentieth century: the Latin American revolution against hacienda feudalism, the post–World War II rebellion of colonial and semicolonial peoples against imperial domination, the socialist revolution initiated by Lenin and the Bolsheviks in October 1917. "As the result of an anti-imperialist, national-liberating, agrarian, anti-feudal, democratic revolution," Cuba was classifiable as "a national-democratic country" that had "the full support of Communists." In the natural course of events, it soon would move into the ranks of the socialist nations.

All supporters of "the heroic Cuban masses" must unite to assure that the revolution could pursue its natural course, and should make every effort to expose and defeat the "malevolence of U.S. monopoly capital exerting itself through the instrumentality of the U.S. government." Aptheker appealed especially to "the working class and the Negro masses." They must not be misled by the propaganda of anticommunism, "the fatal hoax of our century"; rather they must recognize the accomplishments of the revolution in mounting "an all-out assault upon racism and discrimination" and fighting for "the interests and aspirations of the poor and the oppressed."[22]

Aptheker and other Marxist-Leninists made a conscious effort to enlist black Americans in the fight, and so did the U.S. Communist party, which adopted a resolution at its seventeenth convention praising the Cuban Revolution for placing "the elimination of racism as one of its major objectives."[23] The enlistment effort was largely a failure.

There were individual black Americans who offered steady praise for Castro's revolution, and among them were a few supporters of the Communist party such as Richard Gibson and neo-Marxists such as William W. Worthy, Jr. More typical of the black response, however, were Congressman Adam Clayton Powell and the former heavyweight boxing champion Joe Louis. Powell visited Castro's Cuba in the winter of 1959. He returned with glowing reports of the reforms effected by Fidel and called for U.S. economic assistance for the new regime. But when he discovered that the Cuban leaders were not anxious to accept the advice and direction of U.S.

citizens, whatever their color, and when the American press began
to express fears of communist infiltration, Powell's support of the
fidelistas quickly flagged. Sadder was the brief affiliation of Joe
Louis with the Cuban Revolution. Louis was invited to Havana to
publicize a contract signed by the new Cuban state tourist bureau
and a New York public relations firm that included Louis as a
poorly paid honorary member. The State Department suggested to
Louis that he was being misused and that Castro sought to encourage black tourism as part of his anti-American designs. Louis, in
trouble with the Internal Revenue Service, held a press conference
in which he publicly repudiated the contract.[24]

Another example of disillusionment and repudiation was provided by certain citizens of Harlem when Castro visited New York
in September 1960 to address the United Nations. Castro's decision
to leave his midtown hotel for the Hotel Theresa in Harlem was at
first praised by the New York *Amsterdam News* as an illustration
of Castro's democratic convictions. But when his bodyguards made
life difficult for the other hotel residents and when Castro insisted
on being photographed embracing Nikita Khrushchev in the hotel
lobby, middle-class opinion in Harlem took a dramatic turn. A majority of black politicians, disturbed by violent altercations between
Castro's entourage and anti-Castro exiles, decided not to attend a
reception for Castro sponsored by the Fair Play for Cuba Committee, a decision independently reached by the poet Langston Hughes
and the NAACP branch president, Joseph Overton. The Baptist
Ministers' Conference of Greater New York sent Governor Nelson
Rockefeller a telegram deploring "any attempt by Fidel Castro to
make the Harlem community a battleground for his ideologies and
a cesspool of his doctrine of hate and greed."[25]

Black Americans had traditionally shown little interest in joining
left-wing organizations dominated by white Marxists, and the success of the American government and press in identifying Castro
with communism and Soviet influence does much to explain the
failure of the pro-Castro Left to convince black Americans that
Castro was their champion. In the spring of 1959, Castro's speech
proclaiming "The Rights of the Black Man in Cuba" had received
favorable notice in the black press in the Northeast,[26] but the
much-publicized denunciations of America by Castro over the next
year produced the conviction that the Eisenhower administration

was correct: Castro was a self-declared enemy of the United States and of U.S. citizens of all races. Once the issue was made to appear as Cuba versus the United States, the force of nationalism predominated for most black Americans.

Among the minority who remained firm in their support of Castro's Cuba, the most dedicated were several hundred black members of the Fair Play for Cuba Committee. Their most articulate spokesmen were Richard Gibson and William Worthy. Gibson was one of eight black charter members of the committee, and by September 1960, he was its acting executive secretary.[27] Gibson was a Marxist and a man convinced that the hostility of the U.S. government to the Cuban Revolution was largely determined by white racists who feared the example of a society in which black people had equal rights and full access to political power. Racists had interests similar to those of billionaire monopolists; they wanted to keep the exploited in their place at home and abroad. Gibson visited Cuba in August 1960 with the black historian John Henrik Clarke and the poet LeRoi Jones; he returned to report that Castro had eliminated racial discrimination and segregation in Cuba. With his friend William Worthy, a correspondent for Afro-American newspapers in the Baltimore–Washington area, he warned that the sporadic bombing attacks on Havana by Cuban exiles were but a preliminary to a U.S.-sponsored invasion. Following the invasion at the Bay of Pigs, they inserted in several newspapers full-page advertisements with the title, "A Declaration of Conscience by Afro-Americans." American blacks were instructed not to be fooled; their enemies were not in Cuba but in Washington. The Cubans were "our brothers," and black Americans must do everything in their power to stop "criminal aggression against a peaceful and progressive people."[28]

Castro's hard-core supporters within the black community were a small minority and still fewer were those under thirty years of age. Castro generated considerable support among white students but there is no evidence that in the years 1960–61 he was judged a hero by student leaders in black colleges. The New Left, insofar as it found its origins on university campuses at Wisconsin, Michigan, Chicago, and Columbia, was in its early years not only idealistic, impatient, and dedicated but also white.

The movement self-christened the New Left did not exist when the *barbudos* entered Havana, but very soon after its birth it developed a strong emotional identification with the Cuban Revolution. The American New Left may be said to have begun with the last months of 1959 and the publication by a group of graduate students at the University of Wisconsin of the first issues of *Studies on the Left*. Through the year 1961, it retained the character of a radical dissident student movement and its primary heroes were C. Wright Mills and Fidel Castro. Its goal was the establishment of a more humane society marked by the elimination of all instruments of political and economic coercion, and its model was Castro's Cuba. It would have little or no influence on the evolution of the Cuban Revolution or upon U.S. Cuban policy, but in its early years the movement was strongly influenced by its perception of the Cuban Revolution. Indeed, that revolution furnished the prism through which the New Left saw its separation from both the Old Left and the liberal establishment.[29]

The members of the New Left expressed impatience with the doctrinal rigidity of the spokesmen of the Old Left and contempt for Cold War liberals and the leaders of the major political parties. Aptheker was an anachronism; Stevenson a proven disappointment. Neither Marxism-Leninism nor the New Frontier offered the prospect for meaningful change. Seeking a hero model, they looked to the young rebels of Havana; in Cuba they found not only inspiration but a cause, an externalized good. They identified with the youthful spirit of the revolution and particularly with Fidel. Later, when the New Left movement became more ideological and confrontational, posters of Ché Guevara would adorn the dormitory walls of student radicals, but initially Fidel with his rumpled fatigues, unkempt beard, and endless energy appeared the epitome of the rebel with a cause, the enemy of tyranny, materialism, and conformity.[30] In Castro they found revolutionary inspiration and in the Cuban policy of the U.S. government confirmation of the evils of the American political system.

Unlike certain members of the Old Left, representatives of the New Left saw Cuba not as a case study in the economics of Third World underdevelopment but as a happening of unprecedented significance. By proclaiming the virtues of a foreign revolution they would remind their own country of its lost values and present moral crisis. The Cuban Revolution offered the opportunity to attack Cold War ideology and stereotypes and to express a superior if paradoxical patriotism.

The New Left surrounded the Cuban Revolution with a mystique of youthful promise and applauded its invention of a new form of political and economic society. Of particular significance was its bonding of the worker and the intellectual. This union marked its distinction from communist and capitalist societies alike. Castro's Cuba wished not the forced industrialization of Stalin's Five Year Plans but a new humanist socialism linked to moral incentives and egalitarian voluntarism. Castro was neither a communist nor a timid liberal reformer; he was an existential radical, whose actions were rooted in the needs of personal and national salvation. This was the source of his mystical union with the Cuban masses. He was the interpreter of their desires, a modern-day representation of Rousseau's General Will.

The ideas and sentiments of the New Left did not coalesce into a systematic philosophy; most of its members were suspicious of doctrinal rigidity. Its intellectual godfathers were not Marx and Lenin but C. Wright Mills and Jean-Paul Sartre. An early issue of *Studies on the Left* reprinted a portion of Sartre's report on his visit to Havana in the spring of 1959,[31] and Sartre's emphasis on the non-ideological nature of the 26th of July Movement was echoed by the editors. It was Mills, however, whom they saw as their chief advocate. Mills's "Letter to the New Left" was inspiration and justification; his belief that America's best hope lay in its young intellectuals was satisfying to the ego and eminently correct.[32] Mills instructed them in the disutility of the frayed shibboleths of the Old Left, the corruptive capacity of bureaucratic institutions, and the self-contradictions of corporate liberalism. Cloistered scholarship was to be scorned; knowledge must be validated in action and salvation lay in personal participation. Mills's political activism was to be imitated and so too his wholehearted support for the Cuban Revolution. Criticism of specific developments in Cuba could only divide the fraternity of young radicals. Castro was engaged in a pioneering effort to build a new and humane society. His failure would encourage the forces of reaction everywhere; his victory must forecast the success of the New Left in America.[33]

Although Students for a Democratic Society (SDS) did not

achieve formal organization until the latter months of 1961 and the publication of the Port Huron Statement, 15 June 1962, the records of its early meetings demonstrate the close similarity of the graduate students of Michigan with those of Wisconsin in their response to Castro and the Cuban Revolution. In subsequent years, the SDS would adopt a more ideological stance and give birth to the Weathermen and variants of populist totalitarianism, but in its formative period the SDS demonstrated an admiration of Sartre, Mills, and Fidel equal to that of Saul Landau and *Studies on the Left* or Norman Fruchter, editor of the *New Left Review*. The meeting agenda for an SDS meeting in Ann Arbor on the last day of December 1961 had as its headnote a quotation from Mills proclaiming "Knowledge does not now have democratic relevance in America," and the Port Huron Statement warned that Washington's treatment of Castro suggested that the United States had retreated to its "old imperialist ways." Tom Hayden and other SDS organizers maintained that any abuses of democracy in Cuba were the result alone of threats from the United States. Campus radicals must give unstinting support to the young revolutionaries of Cuba.[34]

By the late 1960s the New Left would be characterized more by division and anger than by identification with some externalized good. But in its early years it found hope in the Cuban Revolution and its response to that revolution helped fashion its own self-image.

The portion of the Left that has been referred to as the "Ethical Radicals" did not take a position toward the Cuban Revolution as distinct or uniform as that of doctrinaire Marxists writing for *Monthly Review* or campus dissidents determined to form a New Left. What distinguishes the Ethical Radicals is a note of anguished uncertainty. Many were exponents of nonviolence and they could deplore the Bay of Pigs invasion with a fervor equal to that of the Students' League for Industrial Democracy, but most were strong civil libertarians as well and saw troubling signs of repression in the new Cuba. Embracing a wide range of dissenters—philosophical anarchists, pacifists, Catholic socialists—they displayed a common tone and mood in their response to the Cuban Revolution. The tone was one of reluctant anxiety; the mood was that of wavering hope. Three examples may suffice: the American Friends Service

Committee, the *Catholic Worker*, and the quarreling editors of *Liberation*.

The American Friends Service Committee was quick to express support for the social goals of the Cuban Revolution, and through its publications and the labors of the affiliated Friends Committee on National Legislation, the group waged a modest education campaign to free Cuban–American relations from the ideological rigidities of the Cold War. By fall 1960, however, its publications began to express a note of concern about the distortion of the early goals of the revolution. Hiram Hilty, a professor at Guilford College and a member of the Society of Friends, visited Cuba in August–September 1960 at the request of the committee and reported that the "Twenty-sixth-of-July Non-Communist Revolutionaries" were in danger of losing their political authority to "dedicated communists." Hilty's report was published by the committee, together with an essay by journalist Herbert L. Matthews, in a pamphlet entitled *Understanding Cuba*. In an introduction to this pamphlet, Robert Lyon, a regional officer of the committee, noted that the intransigence of U.S. policy and the anti-Americanism of the Castro regime were mutually reenforcing, with the result that "each side is forced to pattern its behavior according to the other's expressed fears."[35]

The committee called upon the United States to break the circle of mounting hostility and thereby persuade the Cuban leaders to reaffirm their faith in "democratic procedures." Policy makers in Washington did not deserve all blame, but it was the duty of the United States to show magnanimity and take the initiative in reversing "the downward spiral of U.S.–Cuban relations." This conviction was reiterated in a staff study prepared by the Friends Committee on National Legislation in February 1961. Its author, Frances Neeley, admitted the difficulty of negotiating with one "as excitable and as vitriolic as Prime Minister Castro," but urged the U.S. government to seek an alternative to the present "isolation and overthrow policy." Neeley asked, "What would happen if the United States resumed trade with Cuba? Began to purchase Cuban sugar again? Restored diplomatic ties? Offered to negotiate differences? Offered to help finance Cuba's social revolution? Allowed U.S. citizens to travel in Cuba?" There were no certain answers, but the effort was worth the risk. A new and sympathetic U.S.

policy could not only reduce U.S.–Cuban tensions but Cuban dependence on the Soviet bloc. At the least, the United States must terminate policies that had the unintended effect of preventing the restoration of civil liberties in Cuba.[36]

The Bay of Pigs invasion temporarily ended the amicus curiae efforts of the American Friends Service Committee. Appeals for magnanimity were displaced by expressions of anger. Many of the Friends were supporters of the pacifist Fellowship of Reconciliation (FOR) and some of them were signers of the paid advertisement that appeared in the *New York Times* on 23 April 1961. Under the heading "WE CANNOT CONDONE THIS ACT," the FOR charged that irresponsible intervention "could lead to a cruel and desperate civil war that might even be the beginning of World War III."[37] By the end of 1961, the mood of both the American Friends Service Committee and the FOR was one of profound discouragement. Their suggestions, like their pacifist principles, found no audience in the Kennedy administration.

The *Catholic Worker*, the official organ of the Catholic Worker Movement, sought to promote the Christian socialist principles of its founder Peter Maurin. The monthly's editor-publisher Dorothy Day, one of America's more authentic saints, was a proponent of nonviolence, Christian love, and "distributionism." Opposed to the Marxist concept of class warfare and to the domestic and foreign policies of the USSR, the *Catholic Worker* denounced with equal fervor the evils of capitalism, militarism, and economic imperialism. Its primary concerns were the promotion of social justice and nuclear disarmament, and it made no mention of the Cuban Revolution until 1960. The support it then expressed was tempered by reluctant suspicion. Prepared to denounce vigorously the Cuban policy of the U.S. government, it found little to applaud in Castro's foreign policy or the centralization of power in the Cuban state.

An analysis of the response of the *Catholic Worker* is made difficult by the fact that it offered but five articles on Cuba in the years 1960–61, and the longest of these was an excerpt from David Dellinger's *Liberation* essay, "America's Lost Plantation."[38] The editors accepted Dellinger's thesis that U.S. capitalist exploitation provided the primary impetus for Castro's revolution and accepted as well the judgment of William Worthy that American citizens must "mobilize 'Hands Off Cuba' sentiment" against "irresponsible elements in the Pentagon [and] dehumanized cold-war fanatics in the CIA and FBI."[39] In two articles by associate editors of the magazine, however, strictures against the dangerous influence of U.S. investors were unaccompanied by praise for Fidel Castro.

Ed Turner attributed the opposition of the U.S. government to Castro's revolution to "a billion dollars of U.S. investment" and criticized Washington for its readiness to label as communist any move in Latin America that sought an end to exploitation by foreign capitalists, but he was silent on Fidel and the evolving power structure of Castro's Cuba.[40] His fellow editor, Stuart Sandberg, frankly admitted the mixed reaction of a Christian socialist to the political orientation of revolutionary Cuba. There were grounds for concern in recent Cuban developments: "Castro's use of force, his violent suppression of organized resistance, his co-operation with Russia, his naive permissiveness towards communist ideology, his attacks on the Church, and most of all, from a Christian point of view, his virtual deification of the state as that which gives meaning to man's existence." Yet of all nations, the United States had least right to make "blanket accusations" or engage in foolhardy military intervention. Our unjust policies of the past had brought about the revolution; consequently, we had no right to damage or destroy it. Our best policy was one of abnegation and self-examination. We should cease our self-righteous condemnation of the evils committed by others and recognize our own guilt. National redemption must begin with individual penance.[41]

In the final analysis, the *Catholic Worker* called not for new negotiations between Washington and Havana, but for a withdrawal from international politics while the American nation recovered its soul and thereby regained its identification with all humanity.

More political in orientation were the editors of *Liberation*, a journal committed to nonviolent, libertarian radicalism and long identified with opposition to totalitarian dictatorship of the Right or the Left. Its editors in 1959 were David Dellinger, A. J. Muste, Sidney Lens, and Roy Finch, and initially they were united in their praise for the Cuban Revolution. In its tradition of independent radicalism, the magazine offered space to articles by Robert Alexander and Kenneth Boulding that questioned Castro's allegiance to social democracy, but until the winter of 1961, *Liberation* editorials consistently focused on the errors of U.S. policy and the hope that

Castro offered to developing nations seeking to throw off the shackles of economic colonialism. Editorial unity was broken, however, with an article by Roy Finch in which he voiced the opinion that the Cuban Revolution had lost its way and was "pretty well being taken over by totalitarian-minded people." The other editors offered public rebuttal and Finch in turn wrote an "Interview with Cuban Libertarians," expressing his disappointment with the failure of *Liberation* to remain true to its Gandhian principles and to recognize that it was Castro's domestic opponents who deserved the sympathy of Americans committed to individual liberty and freedom of expression. In May 1961, Finch resigned from the editorial board. His "Interview" and resignation precipitated a series of letters, pro and con, as well as further statements by David Dellinger and Sidney Lens.[42]

Dellinger and Lens saw Finch's dichotomy between democracy and dictatorship as too simplistic and of limited relevance for a country such as Cuba, seeking to overcome the political and economic effects of two generations of internal oppression and external dictation. There was no pure libertarian alternative to Castro; one could side only with the Castro regime or the American-sponsored counterrevolutionaries. They too deplored the signs of expanding Soviet influence, but a call to the Cuban people "to overthrow the Castro regime nonviolently" only served to encourage Batistianos in Florida and the CIA in Washington.[43]

Dellinger had early sensed the historical importance of the Cuban Revolution. He had made a trip to Havana in 1960 and had written a historical survey entitled "America's Lost Plantation," which was offered to the readers of *Liberation* as part of its "Cuba Packet." Although Dellinger denied Finch's charge that he was "an uncritical supporter of Fidelismo," he offered a firm defense of the revolution as "a humanist and organically democratic Revolution" in an article in the April 1961 issue of *Liberation*. Dellinger insisted that Castro's Cuba gave the lie to doctrinaire Marxists "who say that economic justice is impossible without overweening state control" and to U.S. liberals and their pretense that "the kind of economic oligarchy we have in the United States is in essence a democratic society." Castro's government was successfully resisting both the murderous sabotage directed by Washington and efforts to gain control of the revolution by "the totalitarian and semi-totalitarian left." Cuba was not "Communist-controlled," but was forging "a genuinely third way." Pacifists must see fundamental economic change as essential to progress and peace; pacifists in a world characterized by the economic exploitation of the poor nations by the rich nations must be revolutionaries.[44]

With the end of 1961 and Castro's declaration of Marxist-Leninist allegiance, the editors of *Liberation* were less certain that Castro could maintain "a genuinely third way." As a result of U.S. harassment and the Bay of Pigs invasion, Cuba was in danger of succumbing to political repression and bureaucratic elitism. There was still a strong possibility, however, that Cuba would fashion "its own form of radicalism, quite different from that of either the Soviet or the neutralist world."[45]

The Left in all of its various divisions and subdivisions provided some of the most intelligent as well as some of the more propagandistic literature on the Cuban Revolution and U.S. Cuban policy. Its impact on the policy makers in Washington was, however, minimal. In part this was the result of its fragmentation and internal sectarian disputes. Too much of the energies of the members of the Left was consumed in internal feuds over issues not unimportant in substance but distracting in effect. Had all segments of the Left spoken with a single voice it is unlikely that it would have significantly influenced the official response of the United States to the Cuban Revolution in either the Eisenhower or Kennedy administrations. It is probable, however, that the splintered quality of the Left and the self-contradictions of its evolving response to the Cuban Revolution diminished the impact of its opposition to official policy and made it easier for both Washington and Middle America to ignore its warnings and dismiss its advice.

Chapter Eight

The Response of Campus and Coffeehouse

t is with no sense of surprise that one finds more support for the Cuban Revolution on the Left of the ideological spectrum than its Right or Center. Similarly, one would expect to find more sympathy for Fidel Castro in the academic and literary communities than in the trade union hall or the investment firms of Wall Street. No segment of the American public demonstrated unanimous support or opposition to the Cuban Revolution, and for all groups attitudes must be correlated to the revolution's chronology, but students, academics, and members of the literary avant-garde were more attracted to Fidel and his revolution than were other subsections of the American public.

The degree of identification exhibited by the graduate students of Wisconsin and Michigan was not typical of the American student population; nor were the free-verse tributes of Lawrence Ferlinghetti representative of the literary community at large, but campus and coffeehouse provided the locale for some of the more articulate interest in the Cuban Revolution. Writers and academics participated in the Fair Play for Cuba Committee and at several points the university campus and literary bohemia generated angry protest against U.S. Cuban policy. The sympathy of student and professorial activists, young novelists, and Beat poets for the Cuban Revolution was neither uniform nor consistent but from Castro's visit to the United States in April 1959 through the summer of 1961, *fidelismo* elicited admiration as well as controversy in academic and literary circles.

Student opinion is always difficult to measure and impossible to quantify with any precision. Only two conclusions appear certain: many American undergraduates were attracted by the youthful spirit and seeming novelty of the Cuban revolutionaries, and one should not project the activism and resentments of American students of the late 1960s back into the years 1959–61. Some students in those earlier years saw in Castro a hero and a cause, and in support of the Cuban revolutionaries found a means of individual assertion and self-definition. But it was only in the years of Lyndon Johnson that posters of Ché Guevara became a major sales item in college bookstores and student activists thought of taking a sabbatical to help *guajiro* cane-cutters.[1]

When Fidel Castro made his visit to Washington in April 1959, he took the opportunity to accept invitations from Harvard and Princeton universities. Princeton would cautiously restrict his appearance to 150 invited members of the Woodrow Wilson School of Public Affairs, but earlier at Harvard Castro had addressed an enthusiastic audience of almost 6,000 at the Dillon Field House. John Leonard, then a Harvard junior, wrote scornfully of the event for the conservative *National Review*—accusing the Harvard undergraduates of failing "to exercise the intellectual and ethical discrimination they went to Harvard to acquire"—but the *Harvard Crimson* found reason to wish Castro success and praise "his personal magnetism and idealism."[2]

The Fair Play for Cuba Committee (FPCC) made a serious effort to establish branch chapters on university campuses and claimed to have more than forty student councils, but that figure was inflated. Only at Harvard, Michigan, Wisconsin, Cornell, Antioch, Oberlin, and several institutions in the San Francisco Bay area was there an effort to give organizational form to student support for the Cuban Revolution. Even on those campuses, support was often erratic and usually took the form of criticism of U.S. government policy rather than serious examination of the goals and programs of the revolutionary regime in Havana. Most student political organizations in these years were of ad hoc variety and, in company with other student groups, were limited by the dictates of the college calendar as well as the annual turnover of student leaders. Survival of Castro's revolution was only one of their concerns and after the Cuban Missile Crisis of October 1962, its priority suffered a sharp decline. Subsequently, campus debates between members of the SDS and Young Americans for Freedom would occasionally focus on the promise and danger of Fidel,[3] but revolutionary Cuba only reemerged as a major student concern when the New Left was radicalized in the late 1960s and Ché Guevara received posthumous beatification.

Professors make their living by talking; consequently it is somewhat easier to analyze faculty response to the Cuban Revolution. Divisions within the academy were in part a reflection of the ambiguous impact of the Cold War on American liberal opinion ever since the days of the Truman Doctrine. Many faculty members categorized themselves as liberal internationalists, and by that classification acknowledged the threat of communist expansion and accepted the theory and practices of containment. As conscious beneficiaries of the Enlightenment, however, they believed in progress, pledged allegiance to social justice and human betterment, and opposed military dictatorships and landed oligarchies. Few had difficulty in applauding the departure of Batista and initially most welcomed the accession of Fidel Castro. By the fall of 1959, however, they had begun to exhibit division and uncertainty. Some continued to see in Castro a fellow liberal anxious to raise the living standards of the oppressed with a Caribbean version of the New Deal; others became convinced that he was an enemy of political democracy and a potential ally of the communists.[4] Among the outspoken, supporters outnumbered opponents, but an increasing number expressed uncertainty and took a stance of watchful waiting.

The fact that the American professoriat could boast of few experts in Latin American politics and still fewer in the history and politics of twentieth-century Cuba increased the likelihood of division and confusion. Such respected Latin American historians as Frank Tannenbaum of Columbia and Hubert Herring of Minnesota had done little field research in Cuba, and only the Hispanic American Institute at Stanford offered specialized study in Cuban/Caribbean history.[5] As a consequence, the earliest books on Castro's revolution were written by a sociologist and two Marxian economists and the first efforts to place the revolution in historical context were those of a member of the *New York Times* editorial board, Herbert L. Matthews, and a free-lance journalist, Theodore Draper.

As noted earlier, C. Wright Mills's book, *"Listen, Yankee,"* had perceptible influence on the representatives of the New Left and Huberman and Sweezy's account became a sacred text for the *Monthly Review,* but in academic circles the disparate judgments of Matthews and Draper received more attention. For patrons of the faculty dining room, Mills was too popular to be trusted and editors of the *Monthly Review* were held in suspicion as ideologues. For academics who would maintain their liberal credentials while criticizing the course of the Cuban Revolution, the betrayal thesis of Theodore Draper gained wide allegiance.[6] For those academics who would sustain support for the *fidelistas* while avoiding association with Marxist analysis, Herbert Matthews's depiction of Castro as a Cuban patriot driven to an unwanted alliance with Russia by the errors of U.S. policy provided a source of quotation.

After a youthful flirtation with Trotskyism, Theodore Draper became disillusioned with the reform potential of Marxism and by World War II was a strong opponent of Stalinist Russia and communist imperialism. A contributing editor for the *Reporter* and the *New Leader*, Draper received a measure of scholarly recognition for his detailed study of the American Communist party. He gained a broader audience with his articles and books on the Cuban Revolution. Initially sympathetic to the 26th of July Movement, Draper soon became convinced that Castro had purposively decided to undermine its authority, ally himself with the Cuban communists, and betray the revolution. He was a middle-class revolutionary who turned his revolution against the middle class; he "promised one kind of revolution and made another." Fidel Castro had not been pushed into the arms of the communists and the Soviet Union; rather he had walked into their embrace with eyes open. Though not a communist when first he seized power, Fidel had decided by fall 1959 that the continued power of his revolutionary elite required a communist-style police state and alliance with the PSP and the Soviet bloc nations. American policy—if occasionally guilty of overreaction—had little responsibility for this transformation. Castro had spurned tentative U.S. aid proposals in spring 1959, and he cultivated the enmity of the U.S. government in an effort to unify the urban proletariat and peasantry while destroying the Cuban middle class. Though there were positive accomplishments to be ascribed to Castro's revolution, the net balance—in terms of human liberty and economic welfare—was clearly and increasingly negative.[7]

Herbert L. Matthews had gained national attention and the George K. Polk Award for journalistic enterprise with his interview with Fidel Castro in the Sierra Maestra in February 1957. Both Castro and Matthews exaggerated the importance of that interview for the success of the 26th of July Movement, but it gave the lie to Batista's claims that Castro was dead and the insurrection ended and indirectly assisted the guerrillas of the Sierra Maestra to gain arms, money, and recruits. Matthews thereafter considered himself a personal friend of Fidel and would assume the role of defender of the Cuban Revolution. The demands of editorial consensus and the increasing anti-Castro suspicions of James Reston and other members of the Washington bureau placed restrictions on Matthews in his Cuba editorials for the *New York Times*, but in late August 1960 he published a long essay in the *Report* of the Hispanic American Institute of Stanford University that received considerable attention in liberal academic circles. Here his criticisms of U.S. policy, anticommunist politicians, and the press coverage of the Cuban Revolution were more blunt and specific.[8]

In Matthews's view the revolution was from the beginning a social revolution and a revolution that enjoyed widespread popular support. Castro was its primary architect and Castro continued to sustain an empathetic identification with the wishes and needs of the Cuban masses. Castro's regime was not controlled or significantly influenced by the Cuban communists, and his growing dependence on Soviet aid was the result primarily of the obdurate refusal of the U.S. government to offer understanding or financial assistance to the revolutionary government. The obstructionist tactics of Castro's domestic enemies and threats by the U.S. government had radicalized the revolution and introduced certain totalitarian features that were no part of Fidel's initial intention. But if the revolution had been radicalized, it had not been betrayed. The *fidelista* program had evolved as a result of an internal revolutionary dynamic and the regime's perception of U.S. enmity. In the process, Castro had reluctantly concluded that it was impossible to achieve national economic independence or a fundamental reorganization of Cuban society within a democratic political system.

American newspapers, radio, and television had reported the Cuban Revolution prejudicially and irresponsibly. They had failed to place the revolution in the context of either the history of Cuba or that of U.S.–Latin American relations. Consequently, they had failed to identify its patriotic and anticolonial components and had erroneously associated Fidel's anti-Yanqui rhetoric with the editorial columns of *Pravda*. The anticommunist phobias of American editors and Washington politicians were largely responsible for Castro's conviction that the United States intended to destroy his regime, and subsequent measures by the Eisenhower administration had confirmed his belief that American policy was dedicated to reestablishing the domination of the Cuban economy by U.S. private capital. It was Castro's perception of U.S. enmity that had driven him to entangle his noble revolution with the retrogressive communists. Matthews acknowledged his disappointment that Castro had not developed the 26th of July Movement into a political force that would have made unnecessary any measure of reliance on the Cuban Communist party, but he insisted that Castro was in a position to suppress the communists in Cuba whenever he chose. Fidel's American friends had reason to regret his increasing reliance on the Soviet bloc for arms and trade, but the revolution had already effected a remarkable improvement in the living standards of the rural and urban poor and its future remained hopeful.[9]

Some academics sympathetic to the Cuban Revolution found Matthews's account too personal and believed he placed too much emphasis on the idiosyncratic features of the revolution. The revisionist historian William Appleman Williams and the young neo-Marxist scholars Samuel Shapiro and James O'Connor put less emphasis on the role of Fidel and more emphasis upon the manner in which the Cuban Revolution demonstrated the inevitable conflict between neocolonialism and national self-determination.

Williams did not profess to be a Latin Americanist or a student of Cuban history. Rather he was an American historian primarily concerned with the relationship between the political economy of the United States and its diplomatic tradition of commercial and territorial expansion. Williams would later be recognized as the godfather of a revisionist school of young diplomatic historians, but in the years 1959–61 his influence was confined to his graduate student disciples at the University of Wisconsin and to the readers of a book-length essay he had published in 1959, *The Tragedy of American Diplomacy*. *Tragedy* was one of that small handful of historical works deserving of the overused adjective "seminal." It initially received mixed reviews and a small sale, but in the Vietnam era it would be among the most quoted works of U.S. history. It offered an overview of American diplomatic history since the 1890s; its thesis was that the foreign policy of the United States was that of an imperial power and the engine force for U.S. expansionism was provided by the needs and political influence of the export sectors of its capitalist economy. Only at times had U.S. expansionism taken the form of territorial acquisition; more usually it had pursued a policy of open-door imperialism. Convinced of the superiority of American political values and industrial products, American officials had aggressively sought to eliminate barriers to the export of American goods and capital in an ever-widening portion of the globe.[10]

Williams's judgments on the Cuban Revolution and U.S. Cuban policy were of a piece with his thesis respecting the causes and consequences of U.S. economic expansion. Initially offered in the form of observations to the graduate student forum at Wisconsin, Williams summarized those judgments in a book published by the Monthly Review Press in 1962, *The United States, Cuba, and Castro: An Essay on the Dynamics of Revolution and the Dissolution of Empire.* Though personally sympathetic to Castro, Williams was less concerned with praising the *barbudos* than with describing the revolution as an example of the conflict between nationalism and neocolonialism and an illustration of the self-defeating nature of an American foreign policy devoted to the preservation of the status quo. Williams saw U.S. policy before and after Castro's assumption of power as the primary cause of Fidel's anti-Americanism and as an important determinant in the "crucial" first six months of the revolutionary regime. Castro had inherited an immediate financial crisis, but "a series of threats from American leaders in and out of Congress" had convinced him that to beg U.S. aid during his Washington visit would "risk slowing the basic drive to transform Cuban society." Draper's "betrayal thesis" was false to the history of the 26th of July Movement as well as to the history of twentieth-century revolutions. From its beginnings, the movement had sought radical social-economic reforms as the only means to break the thralldom of the Cuban economy to U.S. capital. Castro had never promised a middle-class revolution, but his alliance with the PSP and his ties with the Soviet Union were the result of U.S. policy and Cuban counterrevolutionaries.

In the final chapter, "Lessons Waiting to Be Learned," Williams instructed his readers that the United States must revise its attitude toward radical social revolutions abroad and urged the resumption of direct discussion between Washington and Havana. Williams was not a Marxist but rather a modern populist and an advocate of communitarian democracy. He believed that an educated and politically active public could redirect American foreign policy and bring an end to imperial ambitions and global interventionism. The deserved failure of U.S. Cuban policy to date could serve as object lesson that other nations did not wish to be Americanized.[11]

Samuel Shapiro, an assistant professor at Michigan State University, was among the first students of Latin America to visit Castro's Cuba, making personally funded tours of several weeks duration in August 1960 and January 1961, and then again in August 1962. In articles for the *New Republic* and *New Politics*,[12] Shapiro criticized the U.S. policy of attempted economic strangulation and praised the constructive achievements of the revolution, but his advocacy of the *fidelista* regime was not unqualified. Castro's legitimate fears of counterrevolutionaries and their American allies did not justify his imprisonment of some of his early supporters. Shapiro's primary target, however, was the ignorance of the U.S. government and public about the nature and causes of the Cuban Revolution. "Democrats and Republicans, Presidents and Congressmen, universities and newsgathering services" had all failed to understand its nationalist inspirations and its appeal for Latin American peoples desirous of liberation from the economic hegemony of the United States. The Alliance for Progress was a step in the right direction, but Shapiro prophesied that it would prove too modest and too tardy to stem the spread of Castroism. Castro and Castroism would be around for a long time to come, and U.S. policy makers must come to terms with this fact.[13]

James O'Connor's book-length analysis of the revolution was not published until 1969, but in the years 1960–61 he wrote several articles on Cuba for the *Progressive* which were cited in academic circles sympathetic to the problems of the developing nations. An assistant professor of economics at Cornell, O'Connor agreed with Williams and Shapiro that the "unceasing diplomatic warfare" waged by the United States was responsible for Castro's informal alliance with the Soviet Union, but O'Connor believed that Castro's domestic policies "evolved from the elementary needs of the Cuban people." Only the collectivization of the Cuban economy could produce the radical revision of Cuba's social and political structure necessary for economic growth and independence. Though the U.S. policy of sanctions and reprisals was blameworthy, it was also—given the allocation of economic and political power in the United States—inevitable. Determined to protect its economic and political dominance in the Caribbean, the United States could not "passively acquiesce to Cuba's struggle for independence, support a thorough-going agrarian reform, or help finance the nationalization of the monopolies."[14]

Most academics who took a strong and favorable interest in the Cuban Revolution were young social scientists whose audience and reputation was limited to the local campus. There were exceptions, however, and one of the more interesting was the Committee of Correspondence. This ad hoc group was composed of a small band of established scholars who were unhappy with what they saw as the stultifying impact of the Cold War on intellectual debate and government policy. The committee was never a formal organization but rather a discussion network that issued occasional newsletters and position papers.[15] Among its members were the sociologist David Riesman, the psychiatrist Erich Fromm, the political economist Kenneth Boulding, and the economic historian Robert Heilbroner.

The committee's primary concerns were "the sibling rivalry" of the U.S. and the USSR, the evolution of "garrison statism" in America, and the dangerous consequences of the U.S. strategy of nuclear deterrence. Periodically, however, it spoke out against U.S. Cuban policy. Washington's concern for the protection of vested U.S. property interests in Cuba gave the United States a counterrevolutionary image in Latin America; Schlesinger's White Paper on Cuba was guilty of distortions and rhetorical self-intoxication; the Bay of Pigs invasion demonstrated that the "realists" in the Pentagon and CIA were "romantic rattlebrains." Cuban–American relations offered a microcosm of the Cold War and the United States should restore diplomatic and economic relations with Cuba and negotiate a settlement of Cuban–American disagreements. Only then would we be able to concentrate on an effort to promote social reform in Latin America and demonstrate the superiority of democratic institutions to those of communist totalitarianism.[16]

Two issues of the Committee of Correspondence *Newsletter* were devoted exclusively to U.S. Cuban policy. That of 12 May 1961 followed the Bay of Pigs invasion and voiced the disillusionment of liberals such as Riesman with the Kennedy administration. Letters from Erich Fromm and Michael Maccoby and essays by the political scientist Nadar Safran and the social critic Lewis Mumford denounced the dangerous "cult of will-power" that dominated the new administration. For Mumford, Kennedy was "still living in a pre-nuclear world, guided by the stale shibboleths of nineteenth century politics."[17] The *Newsletter* of January 1962 was a symposium entitled "Revolution and Liberal Conscience." The focus of the symposium was a letter to Riesman by his fellow sociologist Nathan Glazer, wherein Glazer had extolled the analysis of Theodore Draper and attacked those liberals who were blind to the tyranny of the Castro regime.[18] With Glazer's permission, copies of this letter were sent to a number of readers and contributors, requesting their response and noting that revolutionary Cuba had become "a serious confrontation, by a new generation of liberals, socialists, and pacifists, with the problem of power, the ethics of revolutionary social change, and the question of American responsibility." Expectedly, most of the contributors attacked Glazer, though several, such as Stephen Thernstrom, a self-proclaimed "young radical" and research fellow at the MIT–Harvard Joint Center for Urban Studies, deplored Castro's "destruction of the opposition and of the right to opposition." Staughton Lynd, then a history teacher at Spelman College in Atlanta, found the analyses of Draper and Glazer flawed by a failure to understand the comparative history of earlier revolutions, and Robert Paul Wolff, a philosophy instructor at Harvard, criticized the readiness of Americans to accept economic repression when it was accompanied "by the forms of political democracy." Roy Finch, former editor of *Liberation*, and Michael Walzer, managing editor of *Dissent*, agreed with Glazer in designating civil liberties and freedom of expression as the prime criteria for evaluating the democratic nature of a political society, but most of the symposium contributors from Christopher Jencks, editor of the *New Republic*, to Al Haber, field secretary of SDS, saw Glazer's letter as an example of the corrupting effects of Cold War ideology on liberal opinion and an attempt to whitewash the past and present sins of U.S. Cuban policy.[19]

Among American scholars who entertained early distrust of the Castro Revolution and apprehension about its consequences for human liberty, probably the most important was Reinhold Niebuhr. It is interesting to compare his views with those of David Riesman and the Committee of Correspondence. Niebuhr was the theologian who provided much of the intellectual rationale for liberal internationalists in the Cold War years of the Eisenhower and Kennedy administrations. Suspicious of the dogmas and the certitudes of radical politics, antagonistic to totalitarian creeds of the Right and the Left, Niebuhr had a strong sense of the fallibility of man and the durability of evil. Enlightenment and Marxist convictions of the inevitability of human progress found little validation in history, and efforts by ideologues to implement their visions usually added to the sum total of human misery. Some of Niebuhr's followers would make a virtual ideology of his intellectual skepticism and in the process celebrate the centrist tradition of American politics and advocate a diplomatic policy of "Realism."

In his attitude toward the Cuban Revolution, Niebuhr's opinions were similar to those of such policy advisers as Arthur Schlesinger and Robert Alexander. These men felt a repugnance to the simplistic analyses of Castro-baiters in press and Congress; they were not unmindful of the political influence of vested interests or the destabilizing effects of economic maldistribution and mass poverty, but they saw the expansion of communism as a defeat for human liberty and the open society. The world system ambitions of Marxism-Leninism in combination with the coercive instrumentalities of the modern state made tyrants of revolutionary ideologues. For Niebuhr, Fidel Castro provided a prime example. He was "an impressive actor in the drama perennially re-enacted . . . the tragic and ironic drama of dreams of justice turning into a nightmare of tyranny."

Niebuhr was prepared, however, to criticize certain features of U.S. Cuban policy. Washington's strategy of economic warfare and diplomatic quarantine was "generating sympathy" for Castro and preventing Latin Americans "from clearly seeing that history, far from absolving him, has convicted him." Strong-arm tactics aroused anti-Yankee resentment throughout the hemisphere, threatened such institutions of mutual security as the UN and the OAS, and enabled Castro to confuse the moral issue posed by his betrayal of the initial goals of the revolution. We must keep our hands off Cuba so that the people of Cuba and all other nations in the hemisphere would have an unobstructed view of a closed society where the promises of freedom had been perverted into the instruments of tyranny.[20]

There were many scholars, of course, who entertained little interest in the Cuban Revolution and many more who publicly expressed neither advocacy nor opposition. And then there were some, such as Henry F. May, who appreciated the historical importance of the revolution, tried to evaluate its consequences and impact, and then took a position of unhappy neutrality. May could not subscribe to the militant certainties of the Luce magazines nor to the pacifist convictions of the Society of Friends; no more, as an academic liberal, could he express sympathy for the lost profits of American investors in Cuban sugar plantations or endorse the economic determinism of the Marxists. He half-envied some of his young students and their emotional investment in Castro's revolution—likening it to the identification of John Reed with the Villistas—but he suspected they were extrapolating their own hopes and ideals. Their approval of certain accomplishments of the new Cuban government was justified; their refusal to place the Cuban leaders in the Marxist camp was not. May found himself advocating renewed negotiations between Washington and Havana, while observing that negotiations alone offered no panacea; advocating a policy of collective action with member nations of the OAS, while noting that no country could be expected to transfer direction of its foreign policy to its neighbors; urging greater efforts in behalf of the Alianza para el Progreso, while admitting that history offered few examples in which one nation had successfully directed the rate of social change for other peoples. For the self-analytical faculty liberal, the answer to the question of "pro" or "con" was often "both."[21]

On only one occasion in the years 1959–61 did a significant number of American academics seek national attention for their views on the Cuban Revolution. This was, of course, in the aftermath of the abortive invasion at the Bay of Pigs, when various professors who had earlier confined their opinions to the faculty club felt driven to seek a public forum.

At Harvard the European intellectual historian H. Stuart Hughes addressed a meeting sponsored by the American Friends Service Committee, denounced the invasion, and informed Kennedy that he had lost the confidence of all persons who had believed the New Frontier would effect needed reforms in foreign and domestic policy. Having taken a measure of pride in the election of an alumnus and in the selection of several members of its faculty as presidential counselors, Harvard University felt it had particular claims on the virtue of the new administration and a responsibility to censure its shortcomings. Forty-one members of the Harvard faculty, spearheaded by Hughes and joined by more than two dozen academicians in neighboring institutions, published an open letter to the president on 10 May demanding that the government "reverse the present drift towards American military intervention in Cuba." Accepting the thesis that U.S. policy had forced Castro into the arms of the Soviet Union, the seventy signatories charged that the government as early as the spring of 1960 had determined to overthrow the Castro regime. Kennedy to his shame had adopted this unjustified and self-defeating policy. Covert military action could only enhance "tendencies toward dictatorship and anti-Americanism latent in any Latin-American social upheaval." Kennedy must reverse course and reopen negotiations with Havana.[22]

This public letter elicited the disapproval of *New York Times* political columnist Arthur Krock and a sharp rebuttal by the Cuban Revolutionary Council in New York. Krock dismissed the signers as humanities professors whose experience "supplies no qualification for passing judgment on foreign and military policy," and the Cuban Revolutionary Council issued a challenge to debate "the entire issue of United States-Cuban relations" with representatives of the Harvard faculty.[23]

The tenth of May also saw the publication of a letter to Kennedy from 181 historians, members of some forty-one universities and colleges. Though less abrasive in tone, the historians' letter criticized Kennedy not only for authorizing the invasion effort of the anti-Castro exiles but also for advocating self-censorship by the press on matters relevant to national security. "Truthful reporting did not create the fiasco in Cuba," and efforts to "fabricate national unity in support of a Cuban policy whose future outlines remain obscure" were misguided and improper. Were the Kennedy administration again to attempt "an ill-starred intervention" in Cuba, it would risk the danger of a general war and, at the very least, "weaken the position of the United States in countries determined to pursue their own development, free of great-power control."[24]

Obviously not all historians, nor all academics, felt a requirement to speak out against the proxy invasion of Cuban territory. Roger Fisher of the Harvard Law School and Arthur Larson, who would later head the Center for the Study of World Law at Duke University, offered detailed analysis of the illegality of the Bay of Pigs operation, but at Princeton University forty-three members of the faculty expressed their opposition to efforts to project the academy into the maelstrom of political debate. They were anxious lest public letters by professors critical of Kennedy's Cuban policy be considered "representative" of opinion in academic circles. For the Princeton professors, aid to Cuban refugees should be seen as "a positive affirmation of the role of the United States in supporting the cause of freedom."[25]

Disunity characterized the American professoriat and so, too, a lack of influence. With a single exception, one cannot point to a speech, article, book, or open letter by an American academic and say with confidence that it influenced either public opinion or government policy.[26] The exception was C. Wright Mills and his book, "Listen, Yankee." As noted earlier, Mills's influence was not noticeable within academia but it was significant for the origins and credo of the New Left. Mills's influence was also evident in the early days of the FPCC, an organization that sought to combine members of the academic and literary communities with activists of the Left in a propaganda exercise that would trumpet the virtues of fidelismo and assure the safety of radical social revolution in Cuba.

The Fair Play for Cuba Committee was fashioned in the spring of 1960 under the leadership of Robert Taber, a CBS newsman who had conducted the first radio/television interview with Fidel; Waldo Frank, a globe-trotting popular historian; and Carleton Beals, a part-time academic and student of U.S.–Latin American relations. Its formation was announced in a full-page paid advertisement in the New York Times and other major city dailies. Its declared aim was to give the American public the opportunity to hear the truth about developments in Cuba and the democratic, reformist goals of the Castro regime. The FPCC promised to issue a newsletter offering information to independent-minded Americans and asked that all inquiries and contributions be sent to its headquarters at 60 East 42nd Street, New York City. Among the sponsors of the committee and its advertisement were James Baldwin, Sidney Lens, Truman Capote, James Purdy, and Norman Mailer.[27]

The most detailed explanation of the committee's purpose and assumptions was published by the Cleveland chapter. By its account, the FPCC stood forth as the only organization prepared to fight the misconceptions entertained by the American public as a result of slanted press coverage and Washington's policy of information control and deliberate deceit. Communists did not control the Cuban government and the Cuban government and people sincerely wished to reestablish friendly relations with the United States if only Washington would cease its policy of economic aggression and covert subversion. American officials had used the smokescreen of communism to stifle rational discussion of the efforts of the revolutionary government to achieve true independence and a decent life for all its citizens. By refusing to assist Castro in his battle against starvation, unemployment, illiteracy, and disease, the United States had given him no choice but to accept economic aid from the Soviet bloc; by threatening to overthrow the revolution by military force, the United States had given Castro no option but to seek military aid from those countries. Despite continual external harassment, the revolutionary government had already made great improvement in the lot of the average Cuban, but how much more could be accomplished if only the American public demanded the immediate restoration of diplomatic and trade relations. The ban on the right of Americans to travel in Cuba must be lifted; the government must offer Cuba economic and financial assistance; the United States must "recognize the sovereignty of the Cuban government and its right to regulate its own affairs under the principle of self-determination." A reversal of current U.S. Cuban policy was essential not only for the sake of the Cuban Revolution but for the preservation of individual freedom in the United States. A nation that embarked on a policy of counterrevolutionary colonialism abroad usually ended by suppressing civil liberties at home. Americans should be forewarned by the example of the effect of the Algerian War on democratic institutions in France. The

FPCC was as concerned for freedom in the United States as for the protection of social revolution in Cuba. On both counts it was essential that the American people refuse to be suborned by the tax-supported propagandists of the State Department and demand of their government a just settlement of all differences with Cuba "in a spirit of understanding and on a level of equality."[28]

By the FPCC's own count, the Cleveland chapter was but one of twenty-one chapters in the United States that collectively had a membership of more than 5,000 persons. In addition, there were four chapters in Canada with a declared membership of almost 1,000. Whether the fluctuating membership of forty campus "student councils" was included in these totals was never made clear. What seems certain, however, is that the chapters in New York, Cleveland, and San Francisco were the most active and the number of dedicated workers never exceeded 2,000.

Many Americans who wished fair treatment of the Cuban Revolution gave wide berth to the Fair Play for Cuba Committee. Some saw it as an organization identifiable with the Left; others suspected that its ranks were infiltrated by members of the Communist party of the United States; a greater number believed the charge that the FPCC was serving as the paid stooge of the Cuban government. These suspicions were influential in limiting the committee's membership, but their validity is open to question.

From the beginning, the committee included members of the Left, but its early advertisements and press releases disparaged the role of the PSP in a manner offensive to the radical Left. By the spring of 1961, the leadership of the FPCC had become more Marxist in orientation, and subsequently there was some infiltration of the organization by Communist party members and sympathizers. Despite the best efforts of several congressional investigators, however, the FPCC was never proven to be a communist front organization. There is evidence, however, that committee officials did accept monetary favors from the Castro government. This was not done with the goal of personal gain, nor did it affect the committee's beliefs and intentions, but on at least two occasions the FPCC was liable to the charge of "accepting Castro's gold." The first of these occasions concerned a committee advertisement paid for in circuitous fashion by the Cuban embassy at the UN; the second involved a subvention by the Cuban government for 340 Americans on a "Fair Play Tour" and their housing and entertainment at the Hotel Riviera.[29]

The committee denied any financial connection with the Cuban regime, and after a time all of its advertisements and public letters proclaimed that its sole source of income was "the contributions of fair-minded Americans." One can doubt that claim and still endorse the FPCC's belief that it was the target of unwarranted persecution. Not only were committee officers subpoenaed by the Eastland Committee and subsequently grilled in public session, but the committee was the subject of FBI investigation and vigilante violence. Supporters of anti-Castro Cuban exiles tried to break up a FPCC meeting in New York, and in Los Angeles, juvenile thugs under the banner identification of "Young Conservatives" engaged in pitched battle with members of the audience at a FPCC-sponsored rally.

April/May 1961 saw further demonstrations against the FPCC by anti-Castro Cubans and "Hungarian freedom fighters"; those months also saw what appeared to be the committee's period of greatest influence. Among the first to react to news of the invasion at the Bay of Pigs, the FPCC sought to direct the response of all citizens worried or angered by the resort to military intervention. Briefly they appeared to succeed, but in the last analysis committee leadership was confined to its own members. The rash of demonstrations that erupted in the fortnight following news of the abortive invasion often included FPCC participation but decreasing FPCC guidance. The goal of the committee was to use the Bay of Pigs debacle to create support for the radicalized, socialist Cuban Revolution, and make Castro's Cuba the kind of ideological touchstone that the Spanish Civil War had been for many Americans in the 1930s. Most of the demonstrations and protests of April/May, however, featured not the virtues of the Cuban Revolution but the sins of the CIA and the danger of a foreign policy that relied on military force.

Initially, the FPCC did appear to be taking charge. It was the Fair Play for Cuba Committee that organized a demonstration outside the UN on 17 April—the first day of the invasion. Daily demonstrations lasted for a week, with the goal of alerting the citizens of New York as well as the diplomats at the UN to U.S. complicity. On one occasion more than 1,000 persons picketed the U.S. mission—with signs rechristening the CIA as the Cuban Invasion Agency. The week's climax came with a Fair Play for Cuba rally at Union Square on 21 April that drew an estimated 3,000 persons. The main speaker was Richard Gibson, recently appointed as acting executive secretary of the FPCC, who informed the audience of the success of Fidel Castro in eliminating racial discrimination and the attraction of the FPCC for all enemies of racial prejudice. The same day the FPCC published a seven-column paid advertisement in the *New York Times*. Titled "An Appeal to Americans," it declared that no nation had the right to conspire to overthrow another government whose domestic and foreign policies did not meet its approval. "If our government's activities are, as we believe, illegal and immoral, then we as a nation stand condemned."[30]

In New York the FPCC was the initial generator of protest against the Bay of Pigs invasion, but this was less true in other major cities or on university campuses. A protest on the Boston Common on 20 April was applauded but not organized by the Boston/Cambridge branch of the FPCC, and the same could be said for a larger rally in San Francisco, where 2,000 people marched from Union Square to the Federal Building. C. Wright Mills had been invited to address the protest meeting in San Francisco but he was hospitalized and could only telegraph his support for the demonstrators and Fidel:

KENNEDY AND COMPANY HAVE RETURNED US TO
BARBARISM. . . . I FEEL DESPERATE SHAME FOR MY COUNTRY.
SORRY I CANNOT BE WITH YOU. WERE I PHYSICALLY ABLE
TO DO SO, I WOULD AT THIS MOMENT BE FIGHTING
ALONGSIDE FIDEL CASTRO.[31]

There were demonstrations of varied enthusiasm and numbers in Detroit, Cleveland, Seattle, New Haven, Baltimore, and Minneapolis, as well as on more than a dozen campuses, but in every case their organization was local and spontaneous. The FPCC could take pleasure in the sum total of speeches and placards that denounced military intervention, but its self-image as director of a national synchronized effort was without basis in fact. Pickets from Antioch College at the capitol in Columbus, Ohio, organizers of a "Bay Students Committee" in San Francisco, and speakers at a protest rally of 500 Cornell students in Ithaca were operating quite independently of the FPCC. So, too, were demonstrators at Independence

Mall in Philadelphia and the 100 representatives of the Non-Violent Committee for Cuban Independence who staged a week-long fast and vigil outside the headquarters of the CIA in Langley, Virginia. The FPCC had kind words for the activities of such pacifist groups as the Committee for Non-Violent Action, the Peacemakers, and the War Resisters League; it praised the courage of student activists and spokesmen for the New Left, but its alliance with such groups was rhetorical and post hoc. The call by the FPCC to organize local picket lines around all federal buildings on two successive Saturdays, 6 and 13 May, met with little cooperation from other groups opposed to the foreign policy of the Kennedy administration.

The FPCC was not without influence in eliciting support for the Cuban Revolution, but by 1962 it spoke for only a segment of the shrinking minority of Castro sympathizers. In the eyes of the New Left it was associated with the ideological "hang-ups" of the grayheads of the Old Left. In the eyes of many liberals it was rendered suspect by charges that it had surrendered its objectivity and independence to Marxist-Leninists at home and Cuban officials abroad. Moreover, many of the literary figures who had once lent a cultural gloss to its list of sponsors had drifted away. Their detachment from the committee was less the result of a fear of contamination than of a congenital distaste for organizational conformity. Beat poets did not make good committee members, nor would Norman Mailer and other politically activist authors let others write their lines.

The appeal of Fidel Castro to many members of the literary avant-garde was partly the result of misperception. They saw Castro as a radical romantic and symbol of rebellion against conformity, bureaucracy, and Establishment authority. In fact, Castro had required of the *barbudos* a standard of conduct that many residents of Greenwich Village would have rejected as puritanical. Beards alone do not make soul brothers, and the hard-working, goal-oriented Fidel probably would not have enjoyed the writings of Jack Kerouac nor approved the lifestyle of Norman Mailer. But if the identification of certain young writers in America with the *fidelistas* was more the result of psychological transference than of careful investigation, more emotional than substantive, it was for a time a badge of distinction and produced several literary tributes.

The poet-playwright LeRoi Jones (before his adoption of Black Muslim separatism) was an active member of the FPCC and, following a trip to Cuba and participation in an anniversary rally outside Santiago, wrote a long piece for the *Evergreen Review*, extolling the Cuban revolutionaries.[32] Lawrence Ferlinghetti, a poet-guru for the literary avant-garde in San Francisco, also visited Castro's Cuba. He offered a sympathetic warning to the new Liberator:

> It's going to be
> a big evil tragedy.
> They're going to fix you, Fidel
> with your big Cuban cigar
> which you stole from us
> and your army surplus hat
> which you probably also stole
> and your Beat beard
>
> History may absolve you, Fidel
> but we'll dissolve you first, Fidel
> You'll be dissolved in history
> We've got the solvent
> We've got the chaser
> and we'll have a little party
> somewhere down your way, Fidel
> It's going to be a Gas
> As they say in Guatemala.[33]

The young novelists Warren Miller and Marc Schleifer were supporters of Castro before their Cuban visits and unqualified admirers thereafter. Miller and his wife arrived in Havana in December 1960 and over the next two months discussed the revolution with left-wing Cuban intellectuals and representatives of the victorious radical wing of the 26th of July Movement. In his account published some months later, Miller found no flaw with the revolutionaries and dismissed Castro's Cuban opponents as a compound of cynicism, corruption, and wishful thinking. Their numbers were in any case dwindling; Castro had the support of the overwhelming majority of the Cuban people. The old Cuba would never return and U.S. foreign policy must free itself of monopoly control and align itself with the new Cuba.[34] Marc Schleifer, a member of the FPCC and editor of the literary quarterly *Kulchur*, was equally convinced that Castro had effected a beneficent transformation of Cuban society. The new Cuba had no similarity with that "Fantasy Cuba of terror and imminent collapse" created by the dishonest press and "filthy officialdom" of the United States. When at the Hotel Riviera the band had swung into a new cha-cha tune, Schleifer was proud to join the audience in chanting, "Cu-ba Si Yan-kee No, Cu-ba Si Yan-kee No."[35]

Norman Mailer never visited Havana, frequented few coffeehouse poetry readings, and was suspicious of Russian motives in assisting the Cuban revolutionary government. He was, however, an admirer of the Maximum Leader and acknowledged his admiration in an open letter to Fidel published in the *Village Voice*: "You were the first and greatest hero to appear in the world since the Second War. . . . There has been a new spirit abroad . . . since you entered Havana. I think you must be given credit for some part of a new and better mood which has been coming to America." In another letter, addressed to President Kennedy, Mailer characterized Castro as "revolutionary, tyrannical, hysterical, violent, passionate, brave as the best of animals." He was perhaps doomed to end in tragedy, but he was one of the "great figures of the 20th century" and "at the present moment a far greater figure than yourself."[36]

It is difficult to determine the extent of support and sympathy for Fidel and his revolution within the community of professional writers. Manifestos in support of the *fidelista* cause and declarations against U.S. policy were seldom endorsed by more than a few dozen mainstream literary figures. Again, it was the Bay of Pigs invasion that elicited the largest response. An open letter to President Kennedy of 15 May 1961 demanding a promise from the administration that it would "not launch or direct any military attack on Cuba" was signed by such respected authors and editors as Edmund Wilson, Philip Rahv, Norman Podhoretz, Mark Van Doren, John LaFarge, and Van Wyck Brooks, as well as those more usually identified with political dissidence such as James Baldwin, Nat Hentoff, and Seymour Martin Lipset.[37]

The major effort by the literary community to give voice to its opposition to U.S. policy came in September 1961 when 111 artists and writers published "A Declaration of Conscience." Proclaiming that "the people of Revolutionary Cuba have the right to determine their own destiny," the signatories declared that "the continuing aggressive attitude of our government" endangers world peace and threatens "our own freedom as Americans" as well as the right of self-determination of the Cuban people. It was not a coincidence that acts of hostility against revolutionary Cuba had been greeted with enthusiasm "by militarists, big business and its press, Southern racists and McCarthyites." The contest was a struggle against the forces of reaction, and creative artists must not shirk the duty of active participation. This declaration was signed not only by such early battle participants as Warren Miller, Marc Schleifer, LeRoi Jones, Lawrence Ferlinghetti, and Norman Mailer, but by Kay Boyle, Allen Ginsberg, Paul Goodman, and several score of lesser luminaries.[38]

It is both easy and cheap to mock the efforts of scholars and writers to influence U.S. Cuban policy and to disparage their motives. Undoubtedly some found release in political activism from the boredom of service on the curriculum committee or the anxieties of writer's block. They were for the most part, however, transparently sincere. That they were also ineffective tells as much of the prestige hierarchy of American society in the years 1959–61 as it does of their limited organizational abilities or internecine divisions. Where scholars and writers can perhaps be faulted is in their measure of persistence and consistency of effort. Few of their attempts at collective action survived the enthusiasm of the moment or the anger generated by a particular event.

Chapter Nine

The Press

Analysis of the influence of the press on the conduct of American foreign policy has become if not a separate academic discipline, at least a thriving cottage industry. Recent studies tend to suggest that the press is more often the reflector than maker of public opinion on foreign policy issues, but the expanding role of press officers in the Oval Office and Department of State over the last few decades indicates that policy makers in Washington have seen the press as a source of influence as well as a subject for manipulation.[1] Few students of American public opinion would deny that the press often serves as a prism for the moods and half-formed judgments encompassed within a pluralistic society, and thereby magnifies as it reflects existing fears and prejudices.

At no time in the years 1959–61 did press opinion determine official U.S. response to the Cuban Revolution, but there were several instances when officials of the Eisenhower and Kennedy administrations identified press opinion with the public mood and consequently altered the tempo if not the objectives of their Cuban policy. The timing of Eisenhower's decision to cancel the balance of the Cuban sugar quota was probably influenced by editorial demands as well as congressional pressure, and Kennedy's decision to give the green light to the Bay of Pigs invasion was in part the result of a fear of press reaction were word to leak that he had denied the "freedom fighters" the opportunity to liberate their homeland.

Any analysis of the response of the press to the Cuban Revolution must obviously begin with an acknowledgment that "press opinion" is more a term of convenience for White House counselors and historians than a quantifiable reality. For the years 1959–61, the term embraced television and radio commentators as well as the print press, newspapers as diverse as the Chicago *Tribune* and the *New York Post*, and weekly periodicals as contrary-minded as

Time and the *Nation*. At no time was there unanimity of journalistic opinion. Yet there was, at every stage, an identifiable majority opinion and most dailies and magazines moved along a similar course. Some journals expressed antipathy to Fidel Castro more virulently and earlier than others; some called for a more militant U.S. policy while others continued to counsel caution and cooperation with the member nations of the OAS. In the evolving position of newspapers and magazines regarding events in Cuba differences of chronology and vocabulary coexisted with a remarkable similarity of direction and emphasis. The direction was toward a conviction that the Cuban Revolution was deserving of censure; emphasis was on the identification of that revolution with communism and the Cold War enemy.

Certain historians of the Cuban Revolution have implied that from the beginning the American press displayed an anti-Castro prejudice. This is an erroneous judgment. In January 1959 the most typical response of American newspapers, magazines, and television commentators to Castro's assumption of power was one of surprise and cautious approval. Incorporated in this initial response was a belated distaste for the cruelties and corruption of the Batista dictatorship, an appreciation that the bearded Fidel was newsworthy as a novelty among Latin American political figures, and a readiness to accept reports from Havana that the program of the *fidelistas* called for American-style political democracy as well as justice for the poor and oppressed. Castro was young and inexperienced and should watch out for radical troublemakers, but the new regime in Havana was a great improvement over the old and deserved the swift recognition that it had received from Washington.[2]

There were a few dissenting voices—such as the New York *Herald-Tribune* and the *National Review*—but the American press generally viewed Castro's triumph with avuncular approval. Newspapers identified with the Republican right wing as well as dailies of more liberal disposition offered good wishes to the revolutionary government of Fidel Castro. Whatever their later emphasis on the danger of communist influence, only a small minority expressed an initial worry that the *fidelista* revolution might prove vulnerable to subversion.[3]

The initial lack of apprehension about communist infiltration and the generally favorable attitude toward the bearded heroes of the Sierra Maestra was not simply the result of Herbert Matthews's favorable assessment in the *New York Times* nor of sympathetic interviews published in *Coronet* and *Look*.[4] The attitude reflected the unspoken assumption that Cuba was irrevocably a part of the geographic sphere of influence of the United States. Even were the new regime to restrict the profit taking of American investors in Cuba, it could not be so foolish as to deny Cuba's special historic relationship with the United States or its dependence on the "American System" for its military security and economic improvement.

The Luce magazines, *Time* and *Life*, which would later engage in a crusade to alert America against the danger Castro posed to the security of the Western Hemisphere, were prepared in winter 1959 to welcome "a new and noteworthy neighboring political leader, the bearded soldier-scholar Fidel Castro."[5] His appointment of Manuel Urrutia as president augured well, and *Life* predicted that "well-groomed people" would now share the functions of power with the *barbudos*.[6] Other magazine favorites of middle-class Americans, such as *Reader's Digest*, agreed that the "daring and determination" of Fidel Castro strengthened "the hope of democracy" in Cuba.[7]

One would expect that if Henry Luce and DeWitt Wallace approved Batista's departure, the new regime in Havana would be the source of still greater optimism for the editors of the *Christian Science Monitor*, the *New Republic*, and the *Nation*. They were, respectively, hopeful, congratulatory, and enthusiastic. Edwin Canham of the *Monitor* expressed the hope that "Cuba will make important strides toward education, economic democracy, and political freedom"; the *New Republic* scouted all suggestions of "Communist penetration in the Castro movement"; the *Nation* declared that the Castro revolution presaged a "new era" for Cuba and offered lengthy reports from Havana by Carleton Beals, a self-proclaimed advocate of social revolution.[8]

During February/March 1959 a few newspapers that had initially portrayed Castro as the champion of Cuban democracy began to adopt a more pessimistic tone. This was usually the result not of premonitions of growing influence by Cuban communists but rather of distaste for the summary execution of certain Batistianos and for Castro's fulminations against the United States. The Eisenhower administration was pursuing a policy of patient noninterference and the excitable Fidel should not seek scapegoats for his domestic problems.

When Castro came to the United States in mid-April, he was besieged by invitations from a wide variety of private groups and organizations and was the recipient as well of generally favorable press coverage. Statements by Castro implying a desire for improved Cuban–American relations and support for the OAS were cited in many editorial columns and there was a distinct revival of optimism for the future course of the revolutionary hero. Fidel had much to learn about the Anglo-Saxon practice of accommodating dissent and he could profit by a course in international economics, but he was not the wild-eyed fanatic portrayed by followers of the discredited Batista.[9]

It was not until the summer of 1959 that any sizable portion of the American press began to take a distinctly anti-Castro position and it was not until the summer of 1960 that the American press—by a large majority—saw the Cuban Revolution as a danger to the national security of the United States. Between June 1959 and July 1960, there was a clear shift of opinion in newspapers across the country, a shift marked by a growing editorial consensus that Castro was a tool of the communists and so an instrument for Soviet penetration in the Caribbean. Some, such as the San Francisco *Examiner*, came to this conclusion early; others, such as the *New York Post*, did not surrender hope for the Cuban Revolution until midsummer 1960, but by the latter date there was no mass-circulation newspaper or magazine in the United States that could not accurately be labeled "anti-Castro."[10]

The theme of communist influence and subversion characteristic of the print press by the summer of 1960 had been the focus much earlier of a television "documentary" aired by CBS and narrated by Stuart Novins. It is difficult to characterize the television and radio press in general terms, but two judgments can be made with confidence: the earliest television programs on Castro and the Cuban Revolution were highly favorable; treatment of both was increasingly critical after the Novins report of 3 May 1959.[11]

Novins had previously served as moderator of a "special edition from Havana" of the CBS news program "Face the Nation," where Castro had done a masterful job of answering the questions of the

panel of interrogators with long rambling replies that assured total obfuscation.[12] Irritated by this Alice-in-Wonderland experience, Novins subsequently obtained permission to report and nar-
rate a thirty-minute "documentary" on the first four months of the
Castro regime. It was aired under the title "IS CUBA GOING RED?"
Novins made clear his belief that the answer should be in the affir-
mative: "The island of Cuba—90 miles off our shores, site of the
American naval base that guards our southern defenses, anchor for
our defense of the Panama Canal, and key to the political future of
Latin America—this Cuban island is today a totalitarian dictatorship and is rapidly becoming a Communist beachhead in the Caribbean." Novins made great point of the difficulties of Castro's Cuban
opponents and the lack of civil liberties and elections. Castro's
refusal to allow a two-party system was indeed seen as indication
of communist sympathies as well as totalitarian vices. Novins
concluded, "But without free constitutional elections . . . it really
doesn't matter whether Castro is a Communist or a willing dupe of
Communists. The result in Cuba is the same."[13]

Novins's telecast received wide publicity, and from such magazines as the *National Review*, high praise. Novins sought to capitalize upon his new-found role as an anti-Castro Jeremiah in a
"Face the Nation" interview on 31 January 1960 with Jorge Zayas, a
Cuban emigré journalist. Mr. Zayas was encouraged to suggest that
the anti-Castro opposition would soon begin a counterrevolution
and that Castro was a communist, though "smart enough not to
carry a card."[14]

Of the three broadcasting systems, CBS showed the greatest interest in Cuban affairs, and was the quickest to portray Castro as a
danger to American security,[15] but the concern of the television
press with the evolution of the Cuban Revolution and Cuban–
American relations was at best sporadic. Whether because of a reluctance to engage in political controversy or because of the increasing inaccessibility of Havana to its cameras, the television
press offered little extended coverage of the Cuban Revolution until
the Bay of Pigs invasion. Scattered evidence indicates that the television press preceded the print press in its distaste for Fidel and its
suspicions of communist subversion, but the evidence is limited
and radio and television archives disappointingly incomplete for
the years 1959–61.

The print press is the more available for research and analysis. The dominant direction, as noted, was toward a position strongly antagonistic to Fidel and the Cuban Revolution. For a few dailies, identified with Cold War belligerence, the accusations of the emigré air commander Major Díaz Lanz before the Senate Internal Security Committee provided sufficient impetus to proclaim Castro's betrayal of the democratic hopes of his countrymen, but it was only with the last months of 1959 that most conservative journals, such as the Chicago *Tribune*, labeled Castro a communist sympathizer and a declared enemy of the United States. With the spring and summer of 1960 this theme was echoed by a growing number of editors and commentators and supplemented by other charges: Castro was plotting revolution in other Caribbean and Central American nations; Castro was waging a personal vendetta against American capital and property in Cuba; Castro was inciting class warfare; Castro was the willing dupe of the Soviet Union, begging military and economic assistance of the Eastern bloc nations. The editorial opinion of big city dailies was divided on whether Castro should be damned primarily as a communist conspirator or as a megalomaniacal dictator, but there was agreement that he was an enemy to democracy in Cuba and to the security of the Caribbean region. Editors of liberal persuasion usually continued to call for restraint by Washington, lest Castro be cast in the role of martyr and thereby "restore" his popularity, but none offered a defense for Castro's diplomatic alignment with the Soviet Union.[16] By the fall of 1960, there was little mention in American newspapers of the social reforms of the Castro regime and increasing coverage of the visits of Cuban officials to Eastern Europe and China. Editorial cartoons portrayed Castro as a dirty slob, a wild-eyed radical, or both.

For the periodical press, one can trace a similar evolution. To review the increasingly anti-Castro tone of magazines as disparate as the *New Republic* and *Reader's Digest* is to describe chronological variations of a single journey.

Among magazines that emphasized public affairs and foreign policy, the *New Leader* and the *Reporter* were among the first to adopt the betrayal thesis. It was the *New Leader* that printed Theodore Draper's essays offering a detailed exposition of that thesis, and subsequently distributed them to a wider readership in the form of special supplements. In its editorials, the *New Leader* stressed the totalitarian features of the Cuban government and reached the conclusion that the United States could no longer pursue a policy of nonintervention, allowing the Soviet bloc to arm the Castro regime "unilaterally." The United States should give arms as well as moral support to the Cuban refugees, because the only alternative to "communist totalitarianism, represented by the Castro regime" was "an emergent democracy represented by the Revolutionary Council."[17] The *Reporter* and its editor, Max Ascoli, were a bit earlier in highlighting "the penetration of Communists" and gave greater attention to Cuban encouragement of "piratical expeditions" against neighboring countries, but they were comparatively less sanguine about the ability of the refugees to provide a solution to the Cuban problem.[18]

The *New Republic* did not assume an anti-Castro stance until December 1960, and even then continued to offer hospitality to contributors of contrary opinion, while the *Nation* surrendered its sympathy for the Cuban Revolution even more reluctantly. As late as the summer of 1960, the *New Republic* sought to distance itself from the anti-Castro scaremongering of those it judged benighted right-wingers. The efforts of demagogic senators to attribute Castro's success against the murderous Batista to second-echelon officials in the State Department was a shameful revival of McCarthyism. The cancellation of Cuba's sugar quota was unwise; for it would be seen as a policy dictated by American oil companies, which recently had suffered property confiscation for their refusal to refine Soviet petroleum. As the year progressed, however, the columns of "TRB," the magazine's Washington correspondent, became increasingly critical of the direction and leadership of the Cuban Revolution. Castro had only gradually, and perhaps quite unintentionally, handed Cuba over to the communists, but the result was nonetheless a Cold War defeat for the United States. The best policy was to eschew either military or covert intervention, observe our obligations under the UN and OAS charters, and hope that given enough rope Castro might arrange his own downfall at the hands of his domestic opponents. One could not, however, ignore the disagreeable fact that Cuba was pursuing a policy antagonistic to the security interests of the United States. The danger lay not in Cuba's Marxist orientation but in its dependence on unfriendly foreign powers:

It is one thing for the U.S. to tolerate, even cooperate with, a militarily neutralist, Marxist-oriented Castroism which has ties to extremist but indigenous Latin American political movements. . . . But it is quite another matter if the strings that lead from Havana are pulled from Moscow and Peking. For that means that Cuban-based revolutionary activities are necessarily antithetical to the United States.[19]

The *Nation* reached a similar conclusion but only after much soul-searching. Through the summer of 1960, its editors and correspondents continued to insist that the Cuban Revolution was not communist but nationalist, and months later it continued to attribute primary blame for the leftward swing of the Castro government to shortsighted policies by the Eisenhower administration. U.S. policy had been guilty of arrogance as well as exaggerated apprehensions; Cuba was victim as well as aggressor. There was no denying, however, that the alliance of Cuba with the Soviet Union was harmful to civil liberty in Cuba and an incentive to Cold War paranoia in America.[20]

Examples of the old tradition of "journals of opinion," such magazines as the *New Leader*, the *Reporter*, the *New Republic*, and the *Nation* had a loyal following including members of what has been labeled the "foreign policy elite"—the minority of Americans who exhibit a sustained interest in foreign relations and international politics. But none of these magazines appealed to a mass audience; none enjoyed the circulation of the Henry Luce inventions, *Time* and *Life*, or the broad middle-class allegiance of the *Saturday Evening Post* and *Reader's Digest*.

One of the more interesting aspects of the editorial evolution of the Luce magazines was the failure of *Life* to keep pace with the anti-Castro virulence of *Time*. After mid-1959, the "World" section of *Time* maintained a steady drumbeat of predictions about the economic ruin facing Cuba under schemes of "central economic planning" projected by the dangerous radicals in Havana. The Agrarian Reform Institute was awarded the adjective "Red-tinged" and Castro was proclaimed "The Reds' best tool in Latin America since Jacob Arbenz fled Guatemala." *Time* wobbled at points in its assessment of the comparative influence of the Soviet Union and "Red China," but it was positive that Cuba was headed for the degrading role of a communist satellite. Havana had exchanged "its prosperous Western look for Iron-Curtain drab" and Castro's lying accusation of a prospective U.S. military intervention was but a "tawdry little melodrama" intended to distract the Cuban populace "from the growing failures of his Marxist revolution."[21]

Life offered no editorial comment that could be accused of advocacy for the Cuban government, but neither did it take the radicalization of that government as a personal affront. It made occasional comments about Cuban communists "coming out of the woodwork" and criticized the "hatchet job" Castro inflicted on the moderate wing of the 26th of July Movement, but *Life* editors appeared less outraged by the sins of Castro than their counterparts at *Time* and less compelled to alert the American public to the imminent danger of a communist beachhead "ninety miles from our shores."[22]

That danger was emphasized by the *Saturday Evening Post* and *Reader's Digest*. Harold Martin, a *Post* editor, warned in August 1959 of the resemblance between the "economic leveling" plans of Fidel and those of the Soviet Union. Four months later, *Post* readers were informed that Castro was "a crackpot surrounded by Communist operators" and instructed that the United States could not accept "a Communist satellite in Cuba."[23] Concurrently, *Reader's Digest* noted that Castro's regime was demonstrating "extreme vulnerability to Communism" and was a likely candidate for "the Kremlin's top-priority work in the Western Hemisphere." In the following year, the *Digest* offered articles describing Ché Guevara as "a hard-core Communist, loyal to Moscow" and proclaiming that an iron curtain had descended on the island of Cuba. Cuba had become a police state and America should listen to the brave Cuban refugees and their tales of persecution, the better to understand the conspiratorial power of international communism. Cuba provided all nations in the Western Hemisphere with "a case history of Communist take-over" and a lesson in the fragility of political liberty and democratic freedom.[24]

Students of the response of the press to the Cuban Revolution have paid particular attention to the months of April and May 1961 and the Bay of Pigs invasion.[25] These analysts differ in their attribution of censure, but they agree that the press was as surprised by the invasion as was the general public and that its inaccurate coverage was the product of bewilderment as well as the deceptive press releases of the public relations hirelings of the Frente Revolucionario Democratico and the CIA.

Nor was this surprise feigned under order of the Kennedy White House. The Kennedy administration had suppressed an article in the *New Republic* associating the CIA with a prospective invasion by Cuban emigrés, and persuaded the *New York Times* to alter a "report from Miami" by Tad Szulc,[26] but lethargy more than coercion or patriotism explains the confusion of the press when it received word of the landing at Playa Girón. That confusion helped assure its vulnerability to protestations of American noninvolvement by government press officers.

Surprise usually was accompanied by expressions of hope for a quick victory by the freedom fighters and prophecies of a "mass uprising" by the Cuban people.[27] There was, however, little demand for the dispatch of U.S. military forces in support of the presumably independent Cuban invaders, even when the initial false reports of insurgent success were succeeded by Associated Press bulletins indicating the possibility of humiliating defeat. Two of the Hearst papers, the San Francisco *Examiner* and the New York *Mirror*, were the only big city papers to call for U.S. armed intervention.[28] Most editors agreed with *Time* that "the U.S. position is that of coach and well-wisher, cheering from the sidelines but forbidden on the playing field."[29]

When obliged to acknowledge Castro's swift and total victory, the typical press reaction was to denounce Fidel and support John F. Kennedy. By the last week of April, few journalists had any doubt that the U.S. government had orchestrated the invasion, but there was a remarkable readiness to rally around the president, and this at a time when Kennedy's mastery of the press was unremarked and when a majority of the big city papers were Republican in political sympathy. Some historians have explained this paradox by emphasizing the contagion of Cold War jingoism. The press could not condemn covert aggression for it shared Kennedy's conviction that any means were justified that might eliminate the threat of Castro's Cuba.[30] Such an explanation fails to satisfy, however. If it helps explain the lack of a "great debate" on the morality and legality of the role of the CIA, it does not explain why there was not a greater readiness to blame the Kennedy administration for the failure of the operation. Editorial restraint was probably the result of a continuing faith in the rightness of U.S. intentions and an instinctive belief that America must show unity in the face of the criticism of the world press and the self-congratulatory declamations of Fidel and Nikita Khrushchev. Some papers were sorry that the operation was attempted; more grieved that it was unsuccessful, but none demanded congressional censure or investigation. The "perfect failure" at the Bay of Pigs had the surprising effect of stimulating sympathy for the new president.

After a time, of course, there were second appraisals and renewed division within the press. Some editors became more belligerent in their calls for Castro's removal, others advocated patience, and a few demanded a major reassessment of U.S. Cuban policy.

The Luce magazines praised Kennedy for his readiness to take full responsibility and for his crusader address to the American Society of Newspaper Editors, but suggested that future operations against Castro should exhibit fewer inhibitions. Now marching in step, *Time* and *Life* deplored the lack of U.S. air cover and the unnecessary secrecy that had limited the operation's chance of success.[31] Latin American governments had made "the fetish of noninterference a formula for collective suicide." As leader of the Free World, the United States should not define its responsibilities by the timidity of its alleged allies nor should it fear the false accusation of imperialism.

Time and *Life* no longer referred to Castro as a "crackpot"; he was now portrayed as a Latin Stalin. The Castro on the *Life* cover of 2 June 1961 was a cold-eyed fanatic, "hungry for power," who represented "a new and nightmarish danger for . . . freedom and order in our hemisphere." *Time* followed suit with a cover story on the relevance of President James Monroe and his doctrine to the Latin American crisis. A military invasion of Cuba, for the express purpose of restoring the island to its freedom-loving inhabitants, would represent a reaffirmation of the Monroe Doctrine.[32]

The belligerence of *Time* and *Life* was matched by the New York *Herald-Tribune*, the *Atlanta Constitution*, the Chicago *Tribune*, and such columnists as Stewart Alsop, David Lawrence, George Sokolsky, and Roscoe Drummond. It was the opinion of the editors of the *Saturday Evening Post* that Castro's Cuba represented a Russian invasion of the West. Consequently, U.S. intervention could not fairly be condemned by our friends and should be "acceptable to Americans."[33]

For other journalists, however, the Bay of Pigs failure was more an incentive for policy review than an inspiration for overt aggression. The *New Republic* was cautious in criticizing the Kennedy administration but advocated for the future less reliance on force and more emphasis on seeking "the ideological defeat of Castroism" by means of the Alliance for Progress. The U.S. government should support "social reform and democratic growth in Latin America." Efforts to arrange an OAS arms embargo were justified but military intervention would be self-defeating.[34]

Reluctant to give support to Kennedy's right-wing enemies, the *New Republic* expressed its troubled doubts about Kennedy's Cuban policy obliquely and sporadically. The *Nation* was more outspoken. Having sought to warn the administration earlier of the stupidity of any form of "preventive war in Cuba," the *Nation* felt no compunction in demanding that the Kennedy administration initiate a total review of its Cuban policy. The president was warned that "History Will Not Absolve Him" were he to authorize further illegal military operations in violation of international conventions and domestic statutes. Neutrality laws should be enforced and "cloak-and-dagger 'spooks' at the CIA" padlocked. Castro had committed many "follies," but the U.S. government must cease inflating the danger of the Cuban regime and get on with the business of supporting essential social and economic change in Latin America.[35]

Any study of press response to the Cuban Revolution and U.S. Cuban policy should take notice of what is usually called "the special interest press"—papers and magazines that serve as acknowledged advocates of a particular group and its concerns and values. The following examples of the business press, the Catholic press, and the veterans press may supplement an analysis of urban dailies and general-audience magazines.

The business press deserves perhaps the most attention, because it offers an opportunity to test the conclusions of those writers who insist that U.S. Cuban policy was dictated by "big business" and a determination to maintain Cuba in its accustomed role as a

source of exploitation and capitalist plunder.[36] Both "radical historians" in the United States and patriot historians of Castro's Cuba
have charged that U.S. policy was shaped by the demands of American investors that Castro be replaced by a Cuban government that
would restore their property and their previous position of economic dominance.[37]

The opinion of the congeries of interests lumped under the heading of "business" is difficult to identify and measure. Certainly a
handful of business journals cannot be said to represent *the* attitude
of business toward the Cuban Revolution. An examination of four
of these publications—*Business Week, Journal of Commerce, Nation's Business*, and the *Wall Street Journal*—can, however, offer a
few clues. Although such analysis does not permit a distinct pic-
ture of what business demanded of U.S. Cuban policy, it does indicate what representatives of the business community refrained
from demanding. It suggests, moreover, that the views of self-cho-
sen spokesmen for the business community were neither monolithic nor in advance of the anti-Castro policy of the government.

Business Week was initially the most optimistic about Cuba's
prospects in the wake of Batista's departure. The end of the civil
war would mean an end to the destruction of American property
and improved prospects for a bountiful sugar harvest. The magazine
noted that the stock exchange had seen a rise in the quotation price
for International Nickel and West Indies Sugar, and that spokesmen
for Fidel Castro had disclaimed any plans to nationalize industry in
Cuba. It was true that the 26th of July Movement had condemned
the domination of Cuba by foreign economic interests, but there
was no reason to believe that the new government would be unmindful of the island's need for private investment.

Throughout 1959, *Business Week*, though occasionally worried
by Castro's propaganda against "rapacious and exploiting imperial-
ists," remained hopeful. Castro was fastening "a one-man rule on
Cuba" but Ambassador Bonsal was demonstrating the goodwill of
the United States and several U.S. companies in Cuba were pro-
ceeding with expansion plans, convinced that "the worst is over."[38]
There was no solid evidence that Castro had communist leanings;
rather, his policies exemplified a "violent case of Latin American
nationalism." It was not his "democratic-minded reform goals" but
his dictatorial methods that were deserving of censure. Castro's

government was a major improvement over his predecessor, honest and "without Batista-type bribes and deals."[39]

It was only with the last days of 1959 that the "International Outlook" editorials of *Business Week* became apprehensive about the future course of the Castro regime. The shift was occasioned in part by growing signs that Fidel was planning "the nationalization of many foreign-controlled companies," but more important was the trial of Major Hubert Matos, which seemed to indicate the rising influence of the Cuban communists in the government and army. The editors remained convinced that the Eisenhower administration had been wise to follow a wait-and-see policy—"economic reprisals . . . would have imperiled our whole position in Latin America and reputation as a good neighbor"—but they now worried that Castro might "lead the Cuban people into disaster."[40] Though Mikoyan's visit to the Havana trade fair incited further fears respecting "the leftward slide" of the Cuban government, the editors admitted that U.S. businessmen in Cuba were divided on whether the revolutionary regime was committed to the international communist movement or was "still an independent national socialist reform group." The dilemma of U.S. policy makers was how to show Castro that we meant business while making sure that we did not drive Castro "into Moscow's arms."[41]

By 9 July 1960, *Business Week* had decided that patience was not its own reward. An editorial entitled "Time to Blow a Whistle" concluded that Castro had proven false to the democratic social reforms he had promised and had "taken Cuba into the Communist camp." Cuba had needed land reform and economic diversification; instead it now had an inefficient "State-controlled economy" and a "Communist-line dictator." Eisenhower was fully justified in cutting the Cuban sugar quota, and it was to be hoped that we could "muster support from the other American states for a tougher line against Castro."[42] In the following months, the magazine opposed military intervention by the United States while favoring a total trade embargo and Cuba's diplomatic and economic isolation by the OAS. Its editors doubted whether Castro's domestic opponents were "strong enough now" to overturn the government but expressed a fluctuating hope that their strength was on the rise. Eisenhower's proposed aid program for Latin America was wise if tardy and should persuade our Latin American friends that we were interested in their economic development as well as their recognition of "the Communist threat."[43]

With the advent of the Kennedy presidency, *Business Week* continued to express gloom and counsel caution. The Cuban Revolution was demonstrating "the classic revolutionary pattern." Having passed through the earlier stages of the rule of the moderates and the accession to power of the extremists, it was now well into "a reign of terror." The magazine saw no easy solution. If Castro remained in power, he would give the communists "an open channel into the rest of Latin America"; were he to be overthrown by external intervention, his martyrdom would help spread *fidelismo* throughout Central and South America.[44] The Cuba White Paper, released by the State Department in early April, was judged a "shrewd diplomatic maneuver," but an editorial of 15 April seemed less certain about the desirability of "U.S. support to Cuban insurgents."[45]

The first response of *Business Week* to news of the Bay of Pigs invasion was, at least by implication, critical. The editorial was entitled "What the U.S. Risks in Cuba," and it concentrated on the effects of possible failure for our global alliance system and the international reputation of the new administration. Subsequently, the editors of *Business Week* regretted the impact of the operation's failure on "the standing of the U.S. around the world," while praising politicians in Washington for their bipartisan determination "to close ranks." It was to be hoped that the administration had learned from the failure of this "desperate venture" and would pursue a more hardheaded and less ambitious strategy toward "the forces of change in a revolutionary world." The best policy was to galvanize the members of the OAS "into a political and economic quarantine of Cuba."[46] *Business Week* had discarded its initial hopes for the Cuban Revolution and saw Castro as an instrument of communist penetration and a danger to the United States, but its advocacy of a multilateral and cautious policy remained constant.

The *Journal of Commerce*, *Nation's Business*, and the *Wall Street Journal* can be analyzed more summarily, for their response is interesting primarily for purposes of comparison. None of these publications gave as much space to Cuban developments as did *Business Week*; all were more quick to denounce Castro and his agrarian land reform and sympathize with the economic losses of foreign investors, but their major point of attack was Castro's relations with international communism. They believed there was a connection between Castro's efforts to nationalize the Cuban economy and his alignment with the Warsaw Pact nations, but it was Castro's alleged role as the agent of communist infiltration that was the primary focus of their evolving antipathy to the Cuban Revolution.

The *Journal of Commerce* was the earliest to make reference to Cuba as a potential Soviet satellite but *Nation's Business* offered the more excited rhetoric. Though initially supportive of the "restrained" policy of the Eisenhower administration, its editors by the winter of 1961 were advancing an early version of the domino theory. The Soviet Union was following Lenin's plan of global domination: first Eastern Europe, then Asia, and then a carefully staged invasion of the Western Hemisphere. Cuba was but the first step in the Soviet plan for Latin America; it would be followed by communist coups in Central America and Mexico. Finally, the United States would fall, "like an overripe fruit."[47]

The *Wall Street Journal*, as a daily newspaper that sought an audience beyond the membership of the National Association of Manufacturers and the stockbroking community, attempted for a longer time a posture of evenhanded reportage.

The *Journal*'s initial response to Castro's assumption of power was confined to conflicting statements of its probable impact on sugar prices. A week later it reported that a U.S. businessman in Havana discounted all suggestions of communist leanings on the part of the *barbudos*: "They're just nice kids." For the first six months of 1959, the *Journal* refrained from attacking the economic goals and decrees of the Castro regime.[48] Only with July and the implementation of the Agrarian Reform Law, the charges of Major Díaz Lanz before the Eastland Committee, and the deposition of President Urrutia, did the *Journal* announce its displeasure with Fidel and his revolution. It was by no means certain that he was a communist, but it was obvious that he had a "reckless disregard of property rights and economic sense" and was prepared to deny his opponents the freedom "which was the sole ostensible reason for his revolution."[49] Were Castro to come under the control of the communists, the danger to the United States was "not so much on account of Cuba itself" as its consequences for Latin America: "A

Red Cuba would be, like the one-time Red Guatemala was, a staging area for infiltration elsewhere. It would be a Soviet political base in the Western Hemisphere."[50]

For some months more the *Journal* appeared uncertain whether the Cuban leaders were a susceptible "bevy of beatniks" or agents of communist subversion.[51] It noted a similar confusion within the business community about the proper direction for U.S. Cuban policy. An article of 11 April 1960 cited a State Department official who reported that though a majority of business leaders had recommended to the Department a get-tough policy, others urged caution and the need to reach a modus vivendi with the Cuban government, and a few advocated that Washington offer economic aid to the revolutionary regime the better to reverse its "leftward drift." Some businessmen advised economic sanctions—cutting the Cuban sugar quota and freezing Cuban assets—but sanctions were opposed by manufacturers who still exported to Cuba and by certain American sugar producers who feared the impact of any revision of the current marketing arrangement.[52]

The acceleration of Castro's expropriation program and reports of strengthened ties between Cuba and the nations of Eastern Europe clarified the issue for the *Journal* as well as for Congress. When the latter gave the Eisenhower administration authority to slash the Cuban sugar quota, the *Journal* applauded. Castro's angry response, expropriating telephone and electric utilities and all U.S.-owned sugar mills, was unwarranted and called for retaliatory sanctions. The U.S. government was not to blame for the communization of Cuba —even now it was not clear how we could have prevented Castro's accession except by armed intervention in behalf of the detested Batista regime, which would have been impractical and immoral—but Washington should have no qualms in pressuring the other members of the OAS to quarantine Cuba.[53]

With other business publications, the *Journal* praised Kennedy's White Paper on Cuba. It was a "hard-hitting account" that made clear the nature, direction, and goal of the Castro regime: "the nature is Communism; the direction, a Soviet satellite; the goal, a Red hemisphere." The *Journal* apparently did not suspect that the White Paper was a prelude to military adventure; rather it concluded that the primary task of the United States was to contain *fidelista* communism within Cuba.[54] The first reports of the Bay of

Pigs invasion inspired no elation—it was not clear that the Revolutionary Council would have the popular support to govern Cuba effectively—but the failure of the operation provided the goad for increased militancy. Subsequent weeks saw the *Journal* adopt a more belligerent stance. For the time being the United States could be content to give Castro's domestic enemies supplies and sympathy, but the day might come when military intervention would be judged "the only means" of assuring Castro's destruction.[55]

No sweeping generalizations can be derived from this limited survey of the business press. In comparison with certain "journals of opinion," the business press devoted more attention to the details of Castro's expropriation policy; in comparison with the *New York Times*, it was quicker to label Castro a victim of communist control. It did not, however, advocate a policy of military intervention nor was it at any point in 1959–61 as bellicose as the Chicago *Tribune* or the *National Review*. It was initially hopeful that U.S. business would not suffer serious restraints in Castro's Cuba, and it reflected for many months thereafter the confusion and uncertainty of the Eisenhower administration. It was unwilling to believe that the Maximum Leader would be able to jettison Cuba's longtime economic and diplomatic dependence upon the United States. When the business press did shift to a get-tough posture in summer 1960, it was more the result of its fears of communist expansion than of its anger at the confiscation of American-owned property.

The business press tended to reflect the caution as well as the profit orientation of twentieth-century American capitalism. Containment of "Cuban Communism" was essential and the restoration of a free market economy in Cuba was desirable, but military intervention and involvement in a Cuban civil war could be costly and disruptive.

The scattered evidence available on the response of union labor to the Cuban Revolution reveals a surprising similarity to that of *Business Week* and the *Wall Street Journal*. In 1959–61 the leadership of the AFL-CIO was determinedly anticommunist. George Meany and Walter Reuther welcomed the advent of Castro but after Fidel's successful move to block the expulsion of communists from the Cuban labor federation, and after Mikoyan's visit to Havana, they took an increasingly anti-Castro position. The Cuban revolutionary regime was the subject of suspicion and attack in the publications of the AFL-CIO, and in May 1960 the AFL-CIO Executive Council declared that the Castro government was endangering the peace of the Western Hemisphere. In the same month, the allegedly radical International Longshoreman's Association announced a boycott on the loading and unloading of Cuban ships in U.S. ports.

Neither the AFL-CIO Executive Council nor the Longshoreman's president, Harry Bridges, saw reason to bemoan the investment loss of Gulf Oil, but—with the *Wall Street Journal*—they decided that the Cuban Revolution was, like a watermelon, "green on the outside and red on the inside." Cold War fears of communist conspiracy and expansion determined their attitude toward Fidel and *fidelismo* by spring–summer 1960.

The same could be said of the other two examples of the special interest press, those speaking for American Catholics and U.S. veterans. Examples of the former are the magazines *Commonweal* and *America*; for the latter the obvious choice is the *American Legion Magazine*.

Commonweal was a respected organ of liberal Catholic opinion, and its first response to Fidel Castro was one of congratulatory approval. Not only did Castro promise needed reforms for the Cuban people but he appeared grateful for the quick recognition accorded his government by the Holy See in Rome and the pledge of cooperation by the archbishop in Havana. Later there were some editorial warnings about anti-American propaganda and the summary trials of Batistianos, but *Commonweal* was reassured by Castro's speeches during his visit to the United States in April 1959. All who met him were "much taken by Premier Castro's obvious sincerity and dedication to his people." The Agrarian Reform Law was long overdue and there appeared little likelihood that Castro would allow the Cuban communists to pervert the *fidelista* revolution. By November 1959, the editors noted that "important conservative Cuban Catholics" had broken with Castro, but assured their readers that "other influential Catholics continue to support him." There was reason to deplore Castro's disrespect for the civil liberties of his domestic critics, but no cause to lose hope that the inexperienced leadership in Havana would learn from its mistakes.

Only in the early months of 1960 did *Commonweal* give credence to charges that Castro was falling under the influence of "Communist advisors," and only in August 1960 did it denounce the regime in Havana. *Commonweal's* evolution paralleled that of the church hierarchy in Cuba. After the Cuban bishops issued a pastoral letter condemning "the growing advance of Communism in our country," the editors of *Commonweal* portrayed Castro as "betrayer" of the revolution. Castro's charge that anticommunism was counterrevolution was false to fact and false to the initial ideals of the Cuban Revolution. When Castro denounced the church leaders as "provocateurs" and "scribes and pharisees ... serving Yankee imperialism," *Commonweal* decided that Fidel had become an instrument of oppression. The "communization of the Cuban government ... grew wider and swifter" with each passing day.

Commonweal editors, however, were cool to Eisenhower's economic and diplomatic sanctions against the Cuban government. Sanctions would allow Fidel to play the role of martyr and give advantage to Kremlin propagandists. The United States should be vigilant against the danger of armed subversion by the Castro government in the Caribbean, but the best antidote to the spread of Castroism lay in imaginative projects of hemispheric development and cooperation.[56]

America addressed itself to a working-class Catholic audience and made few pretensions to intellectual depth or liberal sensitivities. And yet for all of its differences with *Commonweal*, its judgments on Fidel Castro were quite similar. *America* was earlier in suspecting the rising influence of Cuban communists in the labor unions; it was more supportive of Eisenhower's trade restrictions, but, with *Commonweal*, it did not declare the Castro government a victim of communist subversion until Castro began his campaign against the Catholic hierarchy in Cuba. Then its editors ceased to advocate negotiation. Unless sanity was soon restored in Havana, it would be necessary "to assume those responsibilities which are the corollaries of power." Castro's enmity toward the church was evidence not only of the influence of Cuban communists but also of his identification with the Soviet bloc. American Catholics must recognize that the Cuban Revolution was now "a political maneuver of international communism rather than a home-grown reform."[57]

Commonweal and *America* were declared opponents of Castro by the fall of 1960; nevertheless, they refrained from calling for U.S.

military intervention then or later. The American Legion saw no need for such restraint nor did its official magazine. At its convention at Miami Beach in October 1960, the Legion called for "a total economic boycott against Cuba and if necessary a military blockade of the island to force overthrow of the Fidel Castro regime."[58] Six months later it deplored the failure of the Bay of Pigs invasion and expressed the hope that this failure would be redeemed by a bolder and more successful effort in the near future. The *American Legion Magazine* was predictably early in associating Fidel with communism and asserting the necessity of stemming "the deadly contagion" of the Moscow-dominated Cuban regime. Printing anti-Castro jeremiads by William F. Buckley and Edward Tomlinson, the *Legion Magazine* declared the Monroe Doctrine in grave danger and gave extensive space to the execution by "a communist firing squad" of Howard F. Anderson, former commander of Havana Post 1, American Legion. Anderson, operator of a chain of auto service stations in Cuba, had been accused of sabotage during the Bay of Pigs invasion and was executed "without trial or defense." Anderson's brutal death demonstrated anew why it was necessary to eliminate "a Soviet bastion 90 miles from the shores of the United States." Washington must do all in its power to establish an anticommunist provisional government in Cuba and then offer immediate recognition and support.[59]

A survey of press attitudes in the years 1959–61, whatever the number of newspapers and periodicals and however conscientious the content analysis, allows few positive conclusions. It cannot settle the long-standing question of whether the press is a subdivision of public opinion or its most important expression; nor can it answer the question of whether the press shapes public opinion or only serves as its reflecting glass. Such a survey does, however, suggest a few hypotheses about the relationship of press opinion and policy makers in Washington.

A large majority of the big city newspapers and mass-circulation magazines began to turn against Castro and his revolution by fall 1959 and were increasingly antagonistic to both by fall 1960. Editors did not need to be beguiled by administration press spokesmen to accept a get-tough-with-Castro policy, for press antagonism *preceded* the escalation of economic and diplomatic sanctions by

Washington. This does not mean, however, that the press inspired the tougher anti-Castro policy in Washington. It would appear, indeed, that the relationship of the policy attitudes of press and State Department was one of concurrence rather than influence. Neither dictated the views of the other, though the prejudices of the one made easier the anti-Castro strategy of the other. Editor and bureaucrat were inspired by similar fears, antipathies, and convictions.

For a majority of American journalists, it was the belief that Castro had succumbed to communists at home and abroad that primarily determined their anti-Castro stance in the last months of 1959 and throughout 1960. This judgment anticipated any significant degree of Cuban military dependence on the Soviet Union, but the power of apprehensions lies not in their measure of present reality. There was a high correlation between the strength of editorial conviction that Fidel was a communist agent and the level of editorial antagonism to the Cuban Revolution.

The attitude of the American press toward the Castro regime and U.S. Cuban policy was primarily shaped within the context of Cold War fears of expanding communist and Soviet influence in the Caribbean and not by the confiscation of the property of U.S. corporations in Cuba. Expropriation of property was criticized as was Castro's treatment of his domestic enemies and his denunciations of the United States. The press blamed Castro for the refugee problem in Florida, for his refusal to hold elections, and for his unwillingness to confine the Cuban Revolution within the limits of a moderate, bourgeois, nationalist reform movement. But the three primary charges directed against the Castro government were its infiltration by Cuban communists, its efforts to export revolutionary sedition to its neighbors, and its dependent relationship with the Soviet bloc nations. Castro had joined the communists, was using Cuba as a base for communist infiltration into the Americas, and was determined to make Cuba a Soviet satellite. Those charges were interrelated and all were inspired by Cold War belief in the expansive and conspiratorial nature of international communism.

The U.S. press—like the government—viewed Castro and the Cuban Revolution almost exclusively in terms of the values and interests of the United States. Only token attention was given to the needs and wishes of the Cuban people. Editors and policy makers alike judged the evolving revolution in terms of its correspondence to American values and its ratio of advantage/disadvantage for U.S. diplomatic influence and national security. A majority of the mass-circulation press and the special interest press decided—a few months earlier than the Washington bureaucracy—that the Cuban Revolution was un-American.

THE MIRROR

Chapter Ten

Response as Illustration

U.S. response to the Cuban Revolution serves in many ways as a mirror of the beliefs and discontents of the American public, its conviction of national righteousness and its periodic sense of national frustration. But perhaps the first point to emphasize is the parallelism between public sentiment and official policy in the U.S. response to Fidel Castro and the radicalization of the Cuban Revolution.

There were differences. The initial reaction of a majority of the press to Batista's departure was comparatively more enthusiastic than that of Christian Herter. Elements of the business community labeled Castro a Marxist before Ambassador Philip Bonsal did, and both the Longshoreman's Union and the American Legion criticized the vacillating policy of the Eisenhower administration in the early months of 1960. Finally, when the CIA laid plans to overthrow the Castro regime in a covert, paramilitary operation, it outdistanced the level of anti-Castro sanctions advocated by a majority of the public, as did John Kennedy at the Bay of Pigs.

These differences are not unimportant, but the path to antagonism toward the Cuban Revolution taken by American public opinion and the Department of State was remarkably similar. If Washington was initially more cautious about Castro and then less rhetorically censorious and still later the more ready to give covert military assistance to Castro's enemies, it is nonetheless true that every economic and diplomatic sanction officially imposed upon the Cuban government was endorsed by a majority of the American public. Except for a small though vocal group of leftist critics and academic/literary dissidents, the public kept step with U.S. Cuban policy in the period between November 1959 and April 1961; at points it was in the lead.

The similarity of response of Washington and majority public opinion was not the result of manipulation or pressure. Each served to reenforce the apprehensions and antipathies of the other. This process of reenforcement was, in turn, the consequence of shared assumptions. Of these, five were of major importance:

1. The assumption that communism was inherently expansionist and innately evil.
2. The assumption that no people ever willingly accepted a Marxist-Leninist government. Communist governments were the result of subversion or conquest, and the communization of Cuba must be the result of the conspiratorial tactics of Cuban communists and the Soviet Union. Castro's Marxist regime was by definition repressive and unpopular.
3. The assumption that it was unnatural as well as dangerous for the Soviet Union and communism to invade the Western Hemisphere, a region distinct and separate from the rest of the world. There was a historic association between the United States and Latin American republics—proclaimed by President Monroe, implemented by the Good Neighbor Policy and guaranteed by the Rio Treaty—and any Latin American state that sought to deny that association was a danger to Latin America as well as to the United States.
4. The assumption that the Caribbean was within the sphere of influence and part of the defense perimeter of the United States.
5. The assumption that Cuba owed its independence to the United States, and was properly dependent on the latter for its diplomatic security and economic prosperity. A Cuban leader who sought to destroy Cuba's historic ties with the United States could not be acting from motives of concern for the Cuban people but must be a power-hungry dictator with regional ambitions.

It was the last assumption in particular that was responsible for the belief of Main Street as well as Pennsylvania Avenue that as a result of Castro's increasing alignment with Marxism and the Soviet Union, we had "lost" Cuba. Unlike the earlier charge levied against the Truman administration about the "loss" of China, this conviction was not confined to right-wingers or partisan enemies of an incumbent administration. Nor was the conviction confined to the investment community or to those Americans who had seen Havana as a playground for winter vacations. Branch members of the Foreign Policy Association along with officials in Washington appeared ignorant of the history of anti-Yanqui resentment in Cuba and unaware of the Cuban conviction that the United States had been an obstacle to political democracy and social-economic reform. The myth of the grateful, smiling Cuban working for the Yankee dollar was not less powerful for its lack of historical validity. Some Americans were prepared to admit that the United States had made errors in its dealings with such dictators as Machado and Batista, but Cuban friendship for the United States was automatically assumed. Who else could help them in their effort to achieve a better life and a closer approximation of the American standard of living? U.S. capital and U.S. markets were essential to Cuban progress. Geography and history had prescribed for Cuba the role of loyal friend and dependent ally, and any bearded charlatan who sought to take Cuba into the communist camp was guilty of theft. For Cuba to turn against the United States represented a perversion of history.

The conviction that Cuba belonged by right on the U.S. side explains much of the bitter reaction of policy makers and the readers of *Time* to the radicalization of the Cuban Revolution. Only a minority blamed left-leaning bureaucrats in the State Department; most saw conspirators in Havana as the responsible agents. Fidel had fooled the American people and in the process taken Cuba behind the Iron Curtain. Behind castigations of Castro's Cuba was a half-conscious sentiment of having been cheated, gulled, tricked. It was a sentiment that helped explain both the oscillating policy of the Eisenhower administration and Eisenhower's approval of the CIA training camp in Guatemala. It was a sentiment that explained the conviction of the New Frontiersmen that Castro was an agent of international communism and a personal enemy. It was a sentiment that linked the evolution of U.S. Cuban policy with the evolution of editorial opinion in *Business Week* and the *Christian Science Monitor*. Finally, it was a sentiment that helps explain why Cuba became an issue of such political volatility that demagogic senators would seek to capitalize upon it and presidential candidates in the election of 1960 would find it both irresistible and dangerous.

European observers frequently commented on the strange fix-ation of the United States, the world's richest nation, with a tiny island whose population was less than that of New York City. Their bemused censure demonstrated a lack of understanding of the dip-lomatic history and psychology of the American people.

The U.S. response to the Cuban Revolution not only serves as a general illustration of the tendency of the American people and government to claim certain nations as natural allies and diplo-matic subordinates; it also provides a mirror for U.S. Cold War cer-titudes, U.S. policies toward Latin America, and U.S. apprehensions about revolutionary movements in "the less developed nations."

Castro's Cuba would not have assumed for many Americans the character of a dangerous evil had it not been for the growing convic-tion that Castro in alliance with the Soviet Union was determined to bring the Cold War to the Caribbean and the Western Hemi-sphere. Americans had grown accustomed to resisting communist expansion in Greece, West Berlin, and Korea—even in the Congo and Laos—but for the Soviet Union to invade our defense perimeter was seen as an affront as well as an act of aggression. Events in Cuba heightened the sense of impatience experienced by many Americans with the apparent inability of the United States to win the Cold War, but the resulting discontent led not to a demand for a review of the basic assumptions of our Cold War policies but to a demand that they be more successful. The assessment of the aggressive, conspiratorial nature of communist ideology and its monolithic character and subservience to Soviet imperialism was not subject to question. Events in Cuba simply offered further proof of its accuracy. What was needed was a more effective implementa-tion of the containment policy. If the United States had been able to contain communist expansion in central and southern Europe, surely it should be able to find ways to deny communism a Soviet satrapy in the Caribbean.

Chester Bowles, hardly the most dogmatic of Cold War warriors in Washington, informed the National Farmers Union in spring 1961 that the Cold War was reaching "a historic watershed which may determine the shape of human society for generations and even centuries to come." The choice was between the "universal enslavement" of Marxism-Leninism and the values of the American Way—"our belief in human dignity, our dedication to personal freedom, to spiritual progress, and to justice under law."[1]

The judgment of U.S. policy makers that national security was synonymous with anticommunism was shared by a majority of the foreign policy public. This view shaped our policy toward the Cuban Revolution and public response to that policy—a response that offered a mirror image of the doctrinal fixations of U.S. Cold War psychology.

U.S. response to the Cuban Revolution also illumines the assumptions and priorities of the nation's Latin American policy. The Cold War did not change U.S. policy in Latin America; rather it reaffirmed its goals while modestly altering its tactics. Traditionally, the United States had sought order and stability for its Latin American neighbors. Order and stability would provide a satisfactory context for U.S. trade and investment and serve as a barrier to foreign ideologies and adventurism. Fear of communist subversion accentuated a determination to maintain the status quo and then to support certain evolutionary social reforms that would encourage economic development. Recognition that economic growth and social welfare programs were a better barrier to communism than were military juntas and right-wing dictators found implementation in Eisenhower's approval of the Inter-American Bank and in Kennedy's Alliance for Progress. These programs reflected a determination to confine the threat of Castroism to the island of Cuba.

Castro was not alone responsible for the increased appropriations for economic assistance to Latin America, but the Cuban Revolution and Castro had an impact unequaled in the twentieth-century history of U.S.–Latin American relations. Perón had been a nuisance to the State Department, but Perónism had little influence beyond the borders of Argentina. Castro was the first Latin American leader capable of gaining wide sympathy among Latin American intellectuals and the Cuban Revolution was the first political event in Latin America in the century to gain the sustained attention of U.S. policy makers.

The Alliance for Progress, despite the claims of the New Frontiersmen, did not represent a new dawn in U.S.–Latin American relations. It embodied an intelligent appraisal of the long-term value of Latin America as a market for U.S. exports and an appreciation that right-wing oligarchies were a natural target for *fidelismo* and its supporters. Alianza para el Progreso was designed to promote social and economic progress within approved boundaries, and it reflected a long-standing American presidential tradition of equating progress in Latin America with U.S. values and example.

As the Cuban Revolution enhanced U.S. fears of violent revolution in Latin America, so it strengthened the identification of revolutionary change with communist gain in underdeveloped Third World nations. If it was difficult for the United States to understand the determination of Castro's Cuba to exist as a separate historic personality divorced from U.S. economic and diplomatic influence, so was it difficult for the nation to empathize with revolutionary movements in Asia and Africa. That difficulty preceded the radicalization of the Cuban Revolution, but the latter was seen as an example of the probability that international communism would take advantage of popular authoritarian movements in the Third World. The Cuban Revolution strengthened the determination of U.S. policy makers to restrict and manage change in the underdeveloped nations.

Americans could not identify easily with peoples with a long history of material insufficiency. By the late 1950s, the Cold War witnessed a struggle for the allegiance of the underdeveloped nations, and American observers and policy makers refused to recognize the dissimilarity between themselves and the recently decolonized. Americans believed that two-party elections, a free press, and other institutions of political democracy were—for all nations—the proper base on which to raise a structure of economic development and social reform. They would not acknowledge that the reverse might be true; that it might be necessary to change a nation's economic structure before attempting to reform its political institutions and practices. Radical revolutions were seen as a forerunner of communist infiltration and influence. Cuba served as an example.

In its suspicion of foreign revolutions, the United States appeared the advocate of the status quo and the enemy not only of revolution but of Third World nationalism.

Castro's revolution in Cuba affected American policies in Latin America and in regions as distant as Iraq and Cambodia. American response to that revolution offered a mirror for U.S. Cold War morality and an illustration of the long-standing belief that U.S. capital investment was a necessary instrument for order and stability. More significantly, however, U.S. Cuban policy reflected the ambivalence of the much-cited "global revolution" in U.S. foreign policy in the generation after World War II—the adoption of diplomatic responsibilities and aspirations in areas beyond the Western Hemisphere.

The response to Castro's revolution demonstrated that the United States clung to the idea of the Americas as the natural sphere of interest of the United States even as it sought to pursue the foreign policy of a global superpower. Regionalism and globalism combined to determine the goals and apprehensions of policy makers in the years 1959–61, and neither the foreign policy public nor the Eisenhower and Kennedy administrations recognized any self-contradiction in the requirements of regional and global ambitions. Nor did they recognize any self-contradiction in U.S. insistence on clinging to the old idea of the American republics as a "separate sphere" while establishing military bases throughout the globe. In the UN, the United States insisted that the problem of Castro's Cuba was a regional issue and should be settled by the OAS. Interference by extrahemispheric powers was unwarranted aggression and so was infiltration by alien doctrines. The doctrine of Marxism-Leninism was foreign to the Western Hemisphere and inherently dangerous to the security and welfare of the United States, the hemisphere's natural leader and guide.

U.S. response to Castro's Revolution provided a case study in the conviction of the American government and people that godless communism was an evil doctrine that sought global domination. Its conspiratorial designs imposed on the United States the requirement of achieving military and diplomatic superiority in order to promote peace, stability, and order. The international community was polarized between the alliance systems of the Soviet Union and the United States, and Soviet–American relations was the prism through which all international relations must be viewed. International politics was a zero sum game; a gain for one side was a loss for the other. The Soviet bloc aimed at the enslavement of the world under totalitarian communism. The Free World alliance, forged by the United States, supported political democracy and nonsocialist economic progress. Any international development that enhanced the strength of the Free World was in the interest of peace and justice. Any development that aided the Soviet bloc was harmful to both. Consequently, for Cuba treasonably to desert the Free World alliance and align itself with the Soviet bloc was a catastrophe of global dimensions. Not only did the defection of Cuba promote the diplomatic prestige of the Soviet Union but it enhanced the psychological momentum of international communism as well. For all the doctrinal quarrels among communist governments, the expansion of communism and Soviet influence were still synonymous. Similarly, communist governments were synonymous with totalitarianism. Castro's Cuba, despite its rhetoric of concern for the poor and oppressed, was an example of the identification of Marxism-Leninism with one-party dictatorship. Cuba by going communist had become a bad country and an enemy of free peoples and democratic governments.

Castro's Cuba not only represented the intrusion of an alien doctrine into the Western Hemisphere; it implied that old beliefs in the inevitable movement of history toward liberal democracy were subject to question. Americans had assumed, perhaps only half-consciously, that history was on the side of the United States and its values of constitutionalism, civil liberties, and reformed capitalism. The evolution and appeal of Castro's revolution cast doubt on the benevolence of history and the goodwill of the masses in Latin America and the Third World. Castro's ability to ignore the censure and wishes of the United States suggested that America power was not unlimited and that her good intentions were not universally acknowledged. By the late 1950s, Americans allowed themselves occasional expressions of defeatism in reaction to the protracted struggle of the Cold War. For some, Cuba represented the most disagreeable and frustrating development in that war.

According to Reinhold Niebuhr, "arrogance is the inevitable consequence of the relation of power to weakness."[2] It is perhaps equally true that when the weak do not bow to the will of the strong, the natural reaction of the latter is one of bewilderment, frustration, and anger. All three sentiments characterized U.S. response to the Cuban Revolution. Nor did that response escape a flavor of ethnic superiority. American policy makers and businessmen had long regarded Latin Americans as lesser people and so too the racially mixed population of Cuba. This is not to say that had the island population been composed exclusively of the descendants of New England Puritans that the course of the Cuban Revolution would not have been seen as a serious threat to U.S. interests and influence. But the presumed cultural inferiority of the Cubans made their successful resistance to U.S. demands a source of additional insult.

The United States proved unable to recognize that Castro, whatever his distortion of the original aims of the Cuban Revolution, represented a broad-based movement for independence from the Cuban past—a past dominated by U.S. economic and diplomatic influence. In the view of Washington and a majority of the articulate public, Castro had not simply changed the aims of the revolution, he had purposely betrayed them to the advantage of the Soviet Union, thereby committing an act of international treason. By 1961, apprehensions about the evil nature of the Castro regime had become certainties.

For some Americans there had been a half-wishful quality to those apprehensions, just as in Havana the radical faction of the 26th of July Movement had both desired and deplored overt antagonism from Washington. The final break in Cuban–American relations was, of course, the result more of ideological differences and conflicting diplomatic ambitions than of psychological conflict and wishful thinking, but by 1961 the stereotypical fears of both nations had found confirmation in the actions of the other. The subsequent course of Cuban–American relations would be characterized by mutual and self-righteous enmity.

Notes

CHAPTER I

1. Two of the better chronologies of the revolution are to be found in Facts on File, Inc., "Cuba, the U.S. and Russia," and "Chronology of Important Events in United States–Cuban Relations, 1957–1962," National Security Files, Country—Cuba, Kennedy Papers, Box 46 (17 May 1963).

2. See Alexander, "Castro's Challenge to America," 7–15; Alexander, *Prophets of Revolution*, 282–84.

3. See Castro speech of 26 October 1959 in Kenner and Petras, *Fidel Castro Speaks*, 55–73.

4. See O'Connor, *The Origins of Socialism in Cuba*, 5–11, 39–54. A scholar sympathetic to Cuban socialism, O'Connor offered in the early 1960s some of the most informed essays on the political economy of Castro's Cuba. See O'Connor, "Cuba's Counter-Revolution," 8–11; O'Connor, "On Cuban Political Economy," 233–47; O'Connor, "Cuba," 97–117; O'Connor, "The Organized Working Class in the Cuban Revolution," 3–30.

5. See Castro speeches of 1 May 1961 and 26 July 1961 in Kenner and Petras, *Fidel Castro Speaks*, 74–98.

6. Bender, *The Politics of Hostility*, 8.

7. See Domínguez, *Cuba*, 130–32.

8. James, *Cuba: The First Soviet Satellite in the Americas*, 42.

9. This interpretation is accepted, in part, by Kevin B. Tierney in his interesting analysis of "American–Cuban Relations, 1957–1963," 225.

10. See summary of Castro speech of 2 December 1961 in Herbert L. Matthews Papers, Box 4.

11. Draper, *Castro's Revolution*, 3–57; Draper, *Castroism*, 34–56.

12. Compare, for example, Halperin, *The Rise and Decline of Fidel Castro*, 2–3 and Benítez, *The U.S., Cuba, and Latin America*, 4–5.

13. Alexander, "Castroism vs. Democracy," 3–5.

14. See rough draft, "Chapter I: The Revolutionary Tradition," Draper Papers, Box 23.

15. Thomas, *Cuba*, 1214; Smith, *What Happened in Cuba?*, 284–310.

16. For examples of later explanations by these "moderates" see Casuso, *Cuba and Castro*; Rivero, *Castro's Cuba*; and López-Fresquet, *My 14 Months with Castro*.

17. Johnson, "Cuba: The Domestic Policies of the Castro Regime," 3–16.

18. Goldenberg, *The Cuban Revolution and Latin America*, 242–44.

19. Domínguez, *Cuba*, 143.

20. Suchlicki, *University Students and Revolution in Cuba*, 112–21.

21. For contrasting views of *fidelista* economics see Scheer and Zeitlin, *Cuba: Tragedy in Our Hemisphere*, 209–21; Bailey, "Latin America since the War," 115–25; and Flores, "Economics of Liberation," 75–82.

22. Lehmann, "The Trajectory of the Cuban Revolution," 203–13.

23. Halperin, *Castro and Latin American Communism*, 1–3. See also Horowitz, *Cuban Communism*, 11–13.

24. O'Connor, "Political Change in Cuba," 312–47; Dewart, *Christianity and Revolution*, 24–34, 71–84.

25. Zeitlin, "Cuba: Revolution without a Blueprint," in Horowitz, *Cuban Communism*, 81–82; Wilkerson, *Fidel Castro's Political Programs from Reformism to Marxism-Leninism*, 92–93; Friedman and Kraus, "The Two Sides of Castro's Cuba," 57–58.

26. Morton, *Castro as Charismatic Hero*, 7–18. See also Valdés, "Revolution and Institutionalization in Cuba," 1–38.

27. Davis, "Revolutionary Cuba," 7–11.

28. Ruiz, *Cuba*, 4–7.

29. Gonzalez, "Castro's Revolution," 39–68. See also Gonzalez, "Relationship with the Soviet Union," in Mesa-Lago, *Revolutionary Change in Cuba*, 81–104; Gonzalez, *Cuba under Castro*, 113–26.

30. For Soviet aid policy, see Walters, "Soviet Economic Aid to Cuba, 1959–1964," 74–86 and Dark D. Burks, "Soviet Policy for Castro's Cuba," in Te Paske and Fisher, *Explosive Forces in Latin America*, 3–26.

31. Robert F. Smith, "Castro's Revolution: Domestic Sources and Consequences," in Plank, *Cuba and the United States*, 45–68.

32. Suárez, *Cuba: Castroism and Communism*, 140–41.

33. Blasier, "The Elimination of United States Influence," 72–75.

34. Suárez, *Cuba: Castroism and Communism*, 100–114.

35. For an example of this thesis, see Karol, *Guerrillas in Power*, 201–7; Scheer and Zeitlin, *Cuba: Tragedy in Our Hemisphere*, 142–54, 207; Williams, *The United States, Cuba, and Castro*, 41–42, 82–86.

36. For an illustration of this countermyth, see U.S. Congress, Senate Committee on the Judiciary, "Castro's Broken Pledges," *Memorandum Prepared for the Subcommittee to Investigate the Administration of the Internal Security Act*, 91st Cong., 2d sess., (Washington, D.C., 1970), vol. 3.

37. Nelson, *Cuba*, 24–27.

38. R. Aron and A. Grosser, "A European Perspective," in Plank, *Cuba and the United States*, 148.

39. See Fagen, Brody, and O'Leary, *Cubans in Exile*, 113–17; Fagen, *The Transformation of Political Culture in Cuba*, 3.

CHAPTER 2

1. Smith, *The Fourth Floor*, 158–63; Langley, *The United States, Cuba, and the Cold War*, viii.

2. Smith, *The Fourth Floor*, 229–30; Smith, *What Happened in Cuba?*, 263–68;

Dorschner and Fabricio, *The Winds of December*, 245–47, 350–51, 449–50. Similar versions of this "conspiracy thesis" were offered by Robert C. Hill, former ambassador to Mexico, in testimony before the subcommittee of the Senate Judiciary Committee, 12 June 1961, and, earlier, by publications of a Batista-sponsored lobby in Washington that offered a periodic "Report on Cuba" under the alleged authorship of "Universal Research & Consultants, Inc." See Senate Committee on the Judiciary, *Hearings to Investigate Internal Security Act*, 87th Cong., 1st sess., "Communist Threat . . . Through the Caribbean" (12 June 1961), 793–96, 802–15; Universal Research & Consultants, Inc., "Communist Activities of the Cuban Rebels" (Washington, D.C., 1958).

   3. See, for example, Department of State *Bulletin* 41 (26 October 1959); 42 (11 July 1960), (26 September 1960).

   4. Department of State, *American Foreign Policy Current Documents*, 15, 28 January 1959, Document no. 75, 76, 328–29. (Hereafter cited as Department of State, *Current Documents*.) Insurgent suspicion of the U.S. military missions had been explicit before Castro's assumption of power. In August 1958 J. Miró Cardona, as self-styled "Coordinator" of the "Cuban Revolutionary Civilian Front," had written President Eisenhower demanding their withdrawal. Cardona to Eisenhower, 26 August 1958, copy, Matthews Papers, Box 1.

   5. Allen Dulles testimony, 23 April 1961, "Memorandum for the Record," first meeting of General Maxwell Taylor's Board of Inquiry on Cuban Operations Conducted by CIA, Declassified Documents (sanitized), 1978/436B; Blasier, *The Hovering Giant*, 26–27; Blasier, "The Elimination of United States Influence," 47–49.

   6. The indecision of the State Department and the Eisenhower administration was the result not only of doubts about the legality and morality of U.S. intervention but of confusing reports from the CIA station chief in Havana and other intelligence sources about the political orientation of Castro's movement and its relationship to the Cuban communists. See Department of State, Bureau of Intelligence and Research, Division of Research and Analysis for American Republics, 42, Report no. 7780, 15 August 1958 (declassified 18 September 1978); Christian A. Herter memorandum to the president, 23 December 1958, Declassified Documents (sanitized), 1977/219E (declassified 19 July 1977). The Herter memorandum was perhaps the most interesting single record of official attitude toward Castro in the month preceding his assumption of power. While declaring that "there is insufficient evidence . . . that the rebels are communist-dominated," Herter admitted that the State Department "does not want to see Castro succeed to the leadership of the Government. . . . Therefore, we have been attempting in every appropriate way, through all means available, without openly violating our non-intervention commitments, to help create a situation in which a third force could move into the vacuum between Batista and Castro. . . . [Our goal is] a government broadly based on popular consent and support." Herter made mention of U.S. economic interests in Cuba, but he laid particular stress on the possibility of "appalling mob violence" and a "blood bath" were the Castro forces to gain unrestrained power after pitched battle with the Batista forces in the streets of Havana. In the memoir of his presidential years, Eisenhower wrote that it was only "in the last days of 1958" that the CIA suggested that a Castro victory "might not be in the best interests of the United States." He re-

called that he was "provoked" that "such a conclusion had not been given earlier." *Waging Peace,* 520–21.

7. See Blasier, "The Elimination of United States Influence," 49.

8. Department of State, *Current Documents,* 28 January 1959, Document no. 76, 329.

9. Bonsal, "Cuba, Castro, and the United States," 267.

10. Matthews, *The Cuban Story,* 248; Meyer and Szulc, *The Cuban Invasion,* 46–47. For a contrary and more erroneous criticism of Bonsal, see Bethel, *The Losers,* 127–28. Bethel denounces Bonsal as an enemy of U.S. business interests in Cuba.

11. Department of State press bulletin, no. 190, 16 March 1959.

12. Eisenhower, *Waging Peace,* 523.

13. See Safford, "The Nixon-Castro Meeting of 19 April 1959," 425–31.

14. General A. J. Goodpaster memorandum of conference with president, 18 April 1959, Declassified Documents, 1978/455C.

15. Christian A. Herter memorandum to the president, 23 April 1959, Declassified Documents, 1976/58F.

16. See the persuasive analysis in Blasier, "The Elimination of United States Influence," 50–53.

17. Blasier, *The Hovering Giant,* 182.

18. Senate Committee on the Judiciary, *Hearings to Investigate Internal Security Act,* Robert C. Hill testimony, 12 June 1961, 802–4.

19. Bonsal, "Cuba, Castro, and the United States," 268–69; Blasier, *The Hovering Giant,* 187.

20. Department of State, *Current Documents,* 11 June 1959, Document no. 86, 342–43. It has been argued that January–June 1959 was the period when the United States had the best opportunity to influence the evolution of the Cuban regime and failed, as it pursued a policy characterized by uncertainty, confusion, and an admixture of optimism and antagonism.

21. John C. Dreier, U.S. representative on the Council of the OAS, had also relayed the concern of the government of Haiti over "the growing tension in the Caribbean area, which it feels constitutes a serious danger to its peace and tranquillity." Ibid., 10 July 1959, Document no. 91, 348–49.

22. Eisenhower, *Public Papers of the Presidents,* 7:522.

23. Department of State, *Current Documents,* 13 August 1959, Document no. 95, 354–58.

24. Ibid., 18 August 1959, Document no. 96, 359–64; Department of State *Bulletin* 41 (31 August 1959): 41 (7 September 1959): 301, 332; Smith, "The United States and Latin American Revolutions," 89–104.

25. Bonsal to Matthews, 14 August 1959, Matthews Papers, Box 1.

26. *Revolucíon,* 14 August 1959 as quoted in Blasier, *The Hovering Giant,* 183.

27. Department of State, *Current Documents,* 27 October 1959, Document no. 100, 377–82; Department of State *Bulletin* 41 (16 November 1959): 715–18.

28. Bonsal was discouraged by the reorganization of Castro's cabinet in November, which seemed to give increased authority to Guevara and others whom he classified as extremists. Bonsal later recalled that this development precluded "any further possibility of rational dialogue between our two governments." Castro's pur-

pose thereafter "was to promote the beleaguered-citadel mentality which he had found so favorable to the extension of his authority." "Cuba, Castro, and the United States," 270.

29. Department of State, *Current Documents*, 28 October 1959, Document no. 101, 382.

30. Ibid., 4 November 1959, Document no. 105, 387.

31. General A. J. Goodpaster memorandum of conference with president, 25 January 1960, Declassified Documents, 1978/209D.

32. Department of State, *Current Documents*, 26 January 1960, Document no. 67, 195–97; Department of State *Bulletin* 42 (15 February 1960): 52; Bonsal, "Cuba, Castro, and the United States," 270–71.

33. Thomas, *Cuba*, 1263.

34. Bonsal, "Cuba, Castro, and the United States," 271.

35. Department of State, *Current Documents*, 18 February 1960, Document no. 70, 198–99.

36. See Stebbins, *The United States in World Affairs*, 297.

37. Bonsal, "Cuba, Castro, and the United States," 267–71.

38. Blasier, "The Elimination of United States Influence," 57–60.

CHAPTER 3

1. Nixon then and later sought to portray his Washington interview with Castro of 19 April 1959 as a dramatic confrontation between a deceitful witness and a perceptive interrogator. Jeffrey Safford has uncovered the complete memorandum of that three-hour conference, and unlike the abbreviated version that appears in Nixon's memoirs, it shows a Nixon uncertain about Castro's political beliefs and intentions. Nixon believed Castro inexperienced and insufficiently conscious of the evil intent of the Cuban communists, but the two men found common ground in their distaste for "unfair reporting" by the American press. Nixon offered the opinion, "Whatever we may think of him he is going to be a great factor in the development of Cuba and very possibly in Latin American affairs generally." "The Nixon-Castro Meeting of 19 April 1959," 425–31.

2. Draper, *Castro's Revolution*, 62; *Miami Herald*, 17 January 1960, cited in "Economic Aggression against Cuba" notes, Draper Papers, Box 24.

3. Taylor Commission Memorandum, 23 April 1961, Declassified Documents, 1978/436B.

4. See Eisenhower, *Waging Peace*, 533.

5. Blasier, *The Hovering Giant*, 207–10.

6. Gordon Gray memorandum of meeting with president, 29 June 1960, Declassified Documents, 1978/119C. At this same meeting Eisenhower observed that he did not think Khrushchev "would enter into a mutual security treaty" with Castro.

7. Blasier, *The Hovering Giant*, 191.

8. Department of State, *Current Documents*, 6 July 1960, Document no. 77, 205–6.

9. In his analysis of the Sugar Act of 3 July Blasier points out that at no time did

the Senate Foreign Relations Committee or the House Foreign Affairs Committee hold hearings on the measure or offer opinions concerning its implications for U.S. diplomacy. No member of Congress publicly voiced the opinion that its probable effect would be the strengthening of Cuban–Soviet economic ties. "The Elimination of United States Influence," 66–67.

10. These expropriation measures were directed exclusively against properties owned by U.S. nationals. Compensation was linked to increased Cuban sugar sales to the United States.

11. Bonsal, *Cuba, Castro, and the United States*, 151–52; Alexander, "Cuba and the Sugar Quota," 3–5; Whitaker, "Our Reaction to Communist Infiltration in Latin America," 111–13. Ramon Hulsey observes that Article XVI of the Charter of the OAS specifically prohibited economic sanctions by one member nation against another. "The Cuban Revolution," 165.

12. Bonsal, *Cuba, Castro, and the United States*, 154.

13. Department of State, *Current Documents*, 9 July 1960, Document no. 78, 207.

14. Ibid., 9 July 1960, Document no. 79, 207–8.

15. Vann, *American Policy and the Cuban Revolution*.

16. Department of State, *Current Documents*, 14 July 1960, Document no. 82, 210–12. The theme of Cuban/Soviet responsibility was elaborated in greatest detail in a State Department memorandum to the OAS Peace Committee, succinctly entitled "Responsibility of Cuban Government for Increased International Tensions in the Hemisphere." It was a lengthy document with many sections and complaints, but it sought to make two major points: Cuba was establishing close relations with the Sino-Soviet bloc, and a clear pattern of dictatorial political control was emerging in Cuba. Department of State *Bulletin* 63 (29 August 1960): 317.

17. Department of State *Bulletin* 63 (21 July 1960): 207.

18. In June 1960 the CIA had encouraged the formation of the Frente Revolucionario Democratico as an umbrella organization for the recruiting of Cuban exiles and in July 1960 the nucleus of the projected military force was dispatched to a jungle area in Guatemala for training. Taylor Commission Memorandum, 23 April 1961.

19. Gordon Gray memorandum of meeting with president, 12 July 1960, Declassified Documents, 1978/310F. Eisenhower, however, explicitly approved an additional $13 million for CIA Caribbean operations on 13 August 1960.

20. August saw Eisenhower sending a message to Congress urging the appropriation of funds for Operation Pan America and the next months saw a U.S. representative signing the Act of Bogotá and endorsing its recommendations for increased economic cooperation among the American States. Department of State, *Current Documents*, 8 August, 13 September 1960, Document no. 121, 288; Document no. 124, 293.

21. See Gordon Gray memorandum of meeting with president, 12 July 1960.

22. See *New York Times*, 11, 25 August 1960.

23. Department of State, *Current Documents*, 24 August 1960, Document no. 86, 219; Fitzgibbon, "The Organization of American States," 81. The ministers unanimously agreed that "the acceptance of a threat of extracontinental intervention by any American state endangers American solidarity and security," but this was

quickly followed by a reaffirmation of "the principle of nonintervention by any American state in the internal or external affairs of the other American states."

24. General A. J. Goodpaster memorandum of conference with president, 30 August 1960, Declassified Documents, 1978/308C.

25. See, for example, Herter's address to the United Press International Conference of Editors and Publishers, 8 September 1960, Department of State *Bulletin* 43 (26 September 1960): 469; speech of U.S. representative James Wadsworth to UN, 12 October 1960, Department of State, *Current Documents*, Document no. 87, 222–37; address of Thomas C. Mann, assistant secretary for Inter-American Affairs, at Baylor University, 11 November 1960, cited in Vann, *American Policy and the Cuban Revolution*, 66–67. Wadsworth's speech was in answer to Castro's lengthy attack on the United States in the UN on 26 September 1960, in which Castro charged the United States with supporting colonialism "all over the world" and making false charges of communist influence in Cuba the better to prepare a pretext for a U.S. invasion of Cuba. Smith, *What Happened in Cuba?*, 284–301.

26. Eisenhower, *Waging Peace*, 612; General A. J. Goodpaster memorandum of conference with president, 13 October 1960, Declassified Documents, 1978/320B; Vann, *American Policy and the Cuban Revolution*, 62; Department of State *Bulletin* 43 (20 November 1960): 789; Aron and Grosser, "A European Perspective," in Plank, *Cuba and the United States*, 152–53.

27. Department of State *Bulletin* 43 (5 December 1960): 852; Rivero, *Castro's Cuba*, 59; Bonsal, *Cuba, Castro, and the United States*, 169–71. Bonsal was recalled for "extended consultations" on 20 October and never returned to Havana.

28. *New York Times*, 3 December 1960; Department of State *Bulletin* 43 (12 December 1960): 888–89.

29. Stebbins, *U.S. in World Affairs*, 328. The Eisenhower administration was receiving in late December a series of reports from the State Department Bureau of Intelligence and Research emphasizing the increasing political role of the Cuban Communist party. According to these reports, "virtually all institutions of Cuban life are being remodeled in the likeness of a typical Communist society." Report no. 8385, 27 December 1960, abstract, Declassified Documents, 1979/71C.

30. Department of State, *Current Documents*, 31 December 1960, 3/4 January 1961, 11 July 1960, Document no. 94, 250; Document no. 95, 251; Document no. 97, 253; Document no. 119, 283; Department of State *Bulletin* 44 (16 January 1961): 104–14.

31. Smith, *What Happened in Cuba?*, 282–83. Two weeks later, Eisenhower would totally ban the travel of U.S. citizens to Cuba.

32. See Blasier, "The Elimination of United States Influence," 76.

33. Bender, *The Politics of Hostility*, 9.

34. Robert J. Alexander makes this point in "Castroism vs. Democracy," 4.

35. Bender, *The Politics of Hostility*, xii–xiii.

36. Fagen, *The Transformation of Political Culture in Cuba*, 30–31.

CHAPTER 4

1. Kennedy, "The Cuban Situation," 79–95; Kennedy, *The Strategy of Peace,* 132–41; Smith, *What Happened in Cuba?,* 304–5.

2. Kennedy, "The Cuban Situation," 90; 93–94. Kent M. Beck in his detailed analysis of the role of Cuba in the 1960 campaign suggests that Kennedy was fairly circumspect on the issue of Cuba until the press release statement of 20 October, and concludes that as there was little fundamental difference in the positions of Kennedy and Nixon, Cuba was not an important factor in the election results. "Necessary Lies, Hidden Truths," 37–59.

3. Berle Diary, 18 December 1960; 6 January 1961, roll 8.

4. Department of State *Bulletin* 44 (27 February 1961): 298.

5. Ibid. (6 February 1961): 175.

6. Department of State, *Current Documents,* 13 March 1961, Document no. 132, 343–47.

7. Ibid. See also Kennedy's message to Congress on Latin American aid, 14 March 1961, in which he warned that unless the United States was willing to commit its resources to the task of social progress and economic development, "desperate peoples will turn to communism or other forms of tyranny," and "Remarks by President Kennedy to the Council of the OAS on Pan-American Day, April 14, 1961," in which he insisted that "only governments which guarantee human freedoms, respect human rights, and vindicate human liberties can advance human progress." Vann, *American Policy and the Cuban Revolution,* 85; Department of State *Bulletin* 44 (1 May 1961): 615–17; Department of State, *Current Documents,* 14 April 1961, Document no. 78, 260–63.

8. Dean Rusk memorandum to the president, 24 February 1961, Kennedy Papers, President's Office Files, Country—Cuba, Box 115; Department of State *Bulletin* 44 (6 February 1961): 178; Smith, *What Happened in Cuba?,* 248.

9. Department of State, *Current Documents,* 3 February 1961, Document no. 86, 284.

10. Kennedy to Ribicoff, 17 March 1961, Department of State *Bulletin* 44 (13 April 1961): 490.

11. In his memoir, Eisenhower made no effort to repudiate his influence on Kennedy's Bay of Pigs decision: "to the incoming administration, we left units of Cuban refugees busily training and preparing hopefully for a return to their native land." *Waging Peace,* 614. When President-elect Kennedy visited the White House on 10 January to receive a briefing on various foreign policy issues, Eisenhower had informed him that "in the long run the United States cannot allow the Castro Government to continue to exist in Cuba." Robert S. McNamara memorandum to Kennedy, 24 January 1961, Declassified Documents, 1978/355A. Kennedy and his advisers presumably accepted the judgment of the Eisenhower administration that its covert intervention in Guatemala in 1954 was a great success. Whitaker, "Yankeephobia," 15–19.

12. See Taylor Commission *Report,* part 1, 13 June 1961.

13. At subsequent meetings Arleigh Burke, chief of Naval Operations, and White House aide Arthur M. Schlesinger, Jr. would join the Cuba Group.

14. McGeorge Bundy memorandum to the president, 8 February 1961, Declassified Documents, 1977/250A.

15. McGeorge Bundy "eyes only" memorandum of discussion on Cuba, 8 February 1961, Declassified Documents, 1977/250B.

16. Sherman Kent memorandum to director [of the CIA], 27 January 1961; 10 March 1961, (declassified 15 June 1976), Kennedy Papers. See also Robert Amory, Jr., oral history transcripts, 9 February 1966, in which Amory declared that Richard Bissell used Kent's estimate "time and again" in his effort to convince Kennedy that "time was running out" and the United States "can't mañana this thing."

17. Central Intelligence Agency, Office of Current Intelligence, Weekly Information Report, Summary no. 026, 7 February 1961 (sanitized copy); Information Report OOK3/182/230, 27 March 1961, Declassified Documents. The CIA was, of course, in the advantageous position of gathering information on the domestic scene in Cuba and then evaluating that information for its policy relevance.

18. Central Intelligence Agency, Weekly Information Report CS-3/463,320, 16 March 1961, CS-3/470,587, 6 April 1961; Summary no. 0274/61, 6 April 1961.

19. See State Department Bureau of Intelligence and Research, Report no. 8390, 30 January 1961, Declassified Documents, 1979/72A.

20. Tracy Barnes of the CIA provided on request examples of "the use of air power . . . by revolutionary forces against governments in power" in Latin America. Barnes to McGeorge Bundy, 15 March 1961, Declassified Documents, 1977/168D.

21. Quoted in Bender, *The Politics of Hostility*, 3.

22. Schlesinger's most detailed analysis of the political and diplomatic dangers of a beachhead operation will be found in his memorandum to the president, 5 April 1961, Kennedy Papers, President's Office Files, Country—Cuba—General, Folder 3. Schlesinger did not take an active role, however, in the discussions of the White House Cuba Group and his objections received written expression too late to have perceptible influence on Kennedy's decision. If the operation "could be swift and surgical," Schlesinger wrote, "I would be for it," but he doubted that an invasion would inspire a general uprising. There was the likelihood of a protracted struggle with subsequent pressure for the involvement of U.S. marines. Overt U.S. intervention could make Cuba "our Hungary" in the eyes of world opinion and admirably serve the purposes of communist propaganda. Schlesinger acknowledged the difficulty of "demobilizing" the "brave men we have gathered in Guatemala," but declared that "on balance, I think the risks of the operation slightly outweigh the risks of abandonment." See also Schlesinger memorandum to the president, 31 March 1961, Kennedy Papers, Subject Files, Box 5, and his memorandum of 15 March 1961, Declassified Documents, 1977/250E; Schlesinger to Rusk, 7 April 1961, Schlesinger Papers, Subject Files, Box 5; Schlesinger to Tracy Barnes, undated, Declassified Documents, 1977/250E.

23. Fulbright memorandum to JFK, 29 March 1961, cited in Meyer, *Fulbright of Arkansas*, 195–97.

24. Chayes to Schlesinger, 5 April 1961, Kennedy Papers, Subject Files, Box 5. Thomas Mann argued for efforts to arrange a total embargo of Western trade with Cuba as a safer "first step." McGeorge Bundy memorandum to president, 18 February 1961, Declassified Documents, 1977/250C.

25. Halle, "Lessons of the Cuban Blunder," 14.

26. Robert Amory, Jr., oral history transcripts, 9 February 1966.

27. National Security Action Memorandum no. 31, Declassified Documents, 298/C.

28. Schlesinger, *A Thousand Days*, 256.

29. See note attached to early draft of the Cuba Paper (undated) sent to Adolf Berle, Thomas Mann, Tracy Barnes, and McGeorge Bundy in Schlesinger Papers, Subject Files, Box 6.

30. Draper, "Castro's Cuba," 6–23.

31. In a memorandum to the president of 25 March 1961, enclosing a "semi-final version" of the Cuba Paper, Schlesinger wrote, "The function of this document, I take it, is to win over those who had some initial sympathy for the Cuban Revolution, to give them reasons for changing their minds and thus provide them a bridge by which they can accept the necessity of hemisphere condemnation of Castro." See "Cuba White Paper 4/61 folder," in Schlesinger Papers, Subject Files, Box 6.

32. Department of State, *Cuba*.

33. For a harsh appraisal of the "echo" response of the press, see Mintz, "The Cuban 'Episode' and the American Press."

34. Tomlinson, "What We Have Lost in Latin America," 12–13; *Mainstream* 14 (May 1961) 3–5. *The Commonweal* expressed some concern that prophecies about the victory of democracy in Cuba might suggest overt U.S. aid to Castro's enemies. 74 (21 April 1961): 92.

35. Some critics have charged that the press consciously elected to cooperate with the Kennedy administration in deceiving the American public. See Light and Marzani, *Cuba versus CIA*, 38–41.

36. Schlesinger memorandum to Kennedy, 6 April 1961, Schlesinger Papers, Subject Files, Box 5; Schlesinger, *A Thousand Days*, 261.

37. Department of State, *Current Documents*, 12 April 1961, Document no. 89, 288–89.

38. *New York Times*, 14 April 1961. See also Reston's column, "United States and Cuba: The Moral Question, I," *New York Times*, 12 April 1961.

39. The brigade owed its name to the serial number of its first casualty, Carlos Rodríguez, killed while training in Guatemala.

40. The most recent and detailed account is Wyden, *Bay of Pigs*. See also Meyer and Szulc, *The Cuban Invasion*, and Johnson et al., *Bay of Pigs*.

41. The airfield had been lent to the CIA by the cooperative Somoza regime and rechristened "Happy Valley." It was 750 miles from the Bay of Pigs and the distance seriously restricted the operational effectiveness of the antiquated bombers. Kent M. Beck suggests that Gallup polls during the campaign of 1960 indicated a lack of support for a U.S. invasion of Cuba, and that this "easily forgotten fact" encouraged Kennedy to "lower the noise level" of the exile assault and maintain efforts to disguise the extent of U.S. direction. "Necessary Lies, Hidden Truths," 57–59; Gallup, *The Gallup Poll*, 3:1680.

42. The airstrip at Girón, though briefly held by San Román's forces, never became operational for lack of essential ammunition and fuel.

43. Bonsal, *Cuba, Castro, and the United States*, 183; Sorensen, *Kennedy*, 309.

44. Wyden, *Bay of Pigs*, 31–32.

45. See Meyer and Szulc, *The Cuban Invasion*, 59.

46. When Raúl Roa on Saturday, 15 April charged the United States with responsibility for the raids on three Cuban airfields, Stevenson checked with Washington and received assurances from Harlan Cleveland and other unwitting members of the State Department that the United States had no foreknowledge of the raids and that they were the work of defectors from Castro's air force. Stevenson accepted the truth of the explanation and that afternoon proclaimed the innocence of the American government to the Political Committee of the UN General Assembly. "United States Categorical Rejection Of Cuban Charges Of United States Participation In Air Attacks On Certain Cuban Installations: Statement Made by the U.S. Representative in Committee I of the U.N. General Assembly, April 15, 1961," Department of State, *Current Documents*, 15 April 1961, Document no. 92, 290. By the following Monday (D-Day), Stevenson had reason to suspect he had been tricked into touting a CIA cover story, but he was still not aware of the extent of U.S. complicity in the exile invasion. He was instructed by the State Department to ignore the specific charges of the Cuban representative and to emphasize that the subversive intent of the Castro government represented a challenge to the OAS. Secretary of State to USUN, 12 April 1961, for Stevenson from Harlan Cleveland re Cuba, copy, Schlesinger Papers, Subject Files, Box 5; "United States Denial Of Cuban Charges Of United States Aggression Against Cuba And Of Invasion From Florida: Statement Made by the U.S. Representative in Committee I of the U.N. General Assembly, April 17, 1961," Department of State, *Current Documents*, 17 April 1961, Document no. 95, 293. On 18 April Stevenson dutifully informed the General Assembly that it was the "hostility of Cubans, not Americans, that Dr. Castro has to fear." *Ibid.*, 18 April 1961, Document no. 99, 298.

47. The Taylor Commission Report is composed of two separate documents: "Narrative of the Anti-Castro Cuban Operation Zapata" (letter with memorandums and report), 13 June 1961, and "Memorandums for Record of Paramilitary Study Group Meetings," 22 April–25 May 1961. A declassified "sanitized" version is available on microfilm (Declassified Documents 1977/35A [National Security Files]), but may be more conveniently read in *Operation Zapata* (Introduction by Luis Aguilar).

48. The CIA had little practice in long-range military planning and apparently considered an optimistic scenario to be a sufficient substitute. That scenario assumed the swift establishment of a beachhead, a wide-scale insurrection by a rebellious population, transport of the Revolutionary Council to Cuba and its self-baptism as the provisional government, recognition of that government by the United States followed by unconcealed deliveries of money and military supplies. In addition there were vague plans to raise troops in Latin America to fight for the provisional government so its core army would grow to 5,000 men at D-Day plus 30, and to distribute in some unspecified way "arm packs" to 30,000 anti-Castro guerrillas wherever they were to be found.

49. Wyden, *Bay of Pigs*, 309–10.

50. Briggs, *The Anatomy of Diplomacy*, 199 n. 7; Bonsal, *Cuba, Castro, and the United States*, 185.

51. Bonsal, *Cuba, Castro, and the United States*, 182.

52. Khrushchev had sent Kennedy a message on 18 April saying that the USSR would extend to the Cuban government "all the necessary aid" for repulsing external armed attack, but this message had little relevance to Castro's military success and no effect on Kennedy's decision not to save the invasion brigade by the introduction of U.S. armed forces. Department of State, *Current Documents*, 18 April 1961, Document no. 96, 295.

53. See Wyden, *Bay of Pigs*, 324.

CHAPTER 5

1. Department of State, *Current Documents*, 20 April 1961, Document no. 102, 299–302; Department of State *Bulletin* 44 (April 1961): 659–61.

2. For a somewhat exaggerated view of the favorable press treatment given Kennedy and his speech, see Mintz, "The Cuban 'Episode' and the American Press."

3. One Gallup poll gave Kennedy a 61 percent approval rating for his handling of the Cuban problem. Another poll, however, found that only a 44 to 41 percent plurality favored giving military supplies to Castro's Cuban enemies. Gallup, *The Gallup Poll*, 3:1712–17; 1721; 1771; 1787.

4. *Today and Tomorrow*, 2 May 1961, File of Walter Lippmann columns. See also Arthur Larson, "The Cuba Incident and the Rule of Law," *Saturday Review* 44 (13 May 1961): 28. The *New York Times*, though disinclined to chastise Kennedy for authorizing the invasion, did criticize his suggestion to the Bureau of Advertising of the American Newspaper Publishers Association that the press impose "the self-discipline of combat conditions" and engage in self-censorship in support of U.S. foreign policy. See lead editorial, "The Right Not to Be Lied To," 10 May 1961; Aronson, *The Press and the Cold War*, 161.

5. William S. White, "The Good Old Summertime," *Harper's Magazine* 223 (August 1961): 83–84; Stuart Alsop, "The Lessons of the Cuban Disaster," *Saturday Evening Post* 234 (24 June 1961): 26–27; 68–70.

6. See President's Office Files, Countries—Cuba, Box 114, Kennedy Papers; Murphy, "Cuba: The Record Set Straight," 92–97; 223–36.

7. Nixon, "Cuba, Castro and John F. Kennedy," 283–300.

8. Kennedy was careful, however, when choosing a successor to Allen Dulles as CIA director to select "a prominent Republican," John McCone. See Robert Amory, Jr., oral history transcripts, 9 February 1966.

9. Statement by the president, 24 May 1961, Department of State, *Current Documents*, 24 May 1961, Document no. 109, 309. See also Statement by President John F. Kennedy, 20 May 1961, copy, President's Office Files, Countries—Cuba, Box 114a, Kennedy Papers.

10. Johnson, *Bay of Pigs*, 231–46; Goldwater, *Why Not Victory?*, 87.

11. At one point, Castro moved from a demand for an admission of U.S. guilt to a demand that the United States arrange the release of an equal number of political

prisoners from jails in Guatemala, Puerto Rico, and Nicaragua. *New York Times,* 8 June 1961.

12. Department of State, *Current Documents,* 21 April 1961, Document no. 103, 303.

13. Department of State *Bulletin* 44 (8 May 1961): 681–82. The Kennedy administration insisted, contrary to fact, that Castro used Russian-built MIG fighters to defeat the assault force at the Bay of Pigs.

14. See CIA Office of National Estimates Staff Memorandum no. 23–61, Declassified Documents 1976/10B. Kennedy expected that Khrushchev would raise the issue of U.S. hostility to Cuba at their June meeting in Vienna and had the State Department prepare a position paper citing the objections of the United States to "an aggressive dictatorship subservient to Soviet foreign policy aims" in the Caribbean and denying any parallel between U.S.–Cuban relations and those of the USSR with Iran. "Cuba," Department of State Position Paper, 25 May 1961, Declassified Documents 1976/124D.

15. See "Strengthening Freedom in the Americas," State Department memorandum, 26 April 1961, Declassified Documents 1977/219F. Kennedy's rejection of any type of direct negotiation with the Castro regime was unwavering. When presidential adviser Richard Goodwin had an unscheduled meeting with Ché Guevara in Montevideo, Uruguay, on 17 August 1961 and subsequently proposed in a memorandum to Kennedy that there might be value in establishing a "below-ground dialogue," the suggestion fell on stony ground. Richard Goodwin memorandum to the president, 22 August 1961, Declassified Documents 1978/303A; Arthur M. Schlesinger, Jr. memorandum to Richard Goodwin, 31 August 1961, Schlesinger Papers, Box 5.

16. Mansfield to Kennedy, 19 April 1961, President's Office Files, Countries—Cuba—General, Box 114a, Kennedy Papers. Two weeks later, Mansfield offered further reasons for such a policy: "the Alianza para Progreso . . . is the key to our relations with all of Latin America in the next decade, and unless it is turned, *Castroism is likely to spread elsewhere in Latin America whether or not Castro remains in power in Cuba.* . . . If it works, there is a good possibility that Castro will either wither on the vine or be eventually overthrown by the Cubans themselves." Mansfield to Kennedy, 1 May 1961.

17. Department of State, *Current Documents,* 19 June 1961, Document no. 140, 372; 29 June 1961, Document no. 141, 380–81; State Department Position Paper (R. A. Hurwitch), Declassified Documents 1978/101D.

18. Report by the President's Special Representative to the Secretary of State, 24 June 1961, Department of State, *Current Documents,* 24 July 1961, Document no. 144, 385–90; Department of State *Newsletter* (August 1961): 10. Stevenson also wrote a classified report for Kennedy which gave greater emphasis to the ignorance of Latin American officials about "actual conditions in Cuba" and urged Kennedy to arrange personal meetings with the presidents of Argentina and Brazil, whose "concurrence to further collective sanctions against Cuba is crucial." Report to the president on South American mission, 27 June 1961, Declassified Documents 1977/236C. See also Comments on Gov. Stevenson's Trip by Ellis Briggs, June 1961, State Department Memorandum, Declassified Documents 1977/236D.

19. Department of State, *Current Documents*, 17 August 1961, Document no. 145, 393; Document no. 146, 395–98. The State Department in November held several regional conferences in Central and South America to provide further explanation of the goals of the Alliance to U.S. and Latin American officials. Department of State *Newsletter* (November 1961): 18.

20. Department of State, *Current Documents*, 17 December 1961, Document no. 155, 433–35.

21. Bender, *The Politics of Hostility*, 23–28; Replies Made by the Secretary of State to Questions Asked on the CBS Television Program "At the Source," 29 June 1961, Department of State, *Current Documents*, 29 June 1961, Document no. 141, 380–81.

22. Declassified Documents 1977/351A. In its Memorandum no. 4, the Cuban Study Group suggested (Recommendation no. 5) that the Kennedy administration review "any treaties or international agreements which restrain the full use of our resources in the Cold War" and urged (Recommendation no. 6) that "new guidance [be] provided for political, military, economic, and propaganda action against Castro."

23. Schlesinger, *Robert F. Kennedy and His Times*, 493–95.

24. See "Review of the Cuban Situation and Policy," undated, President's Office Files, Countries—Cuba, Box 114a, Kennedy Papers. It should be a major objective of U.S. Cuban policy "to continue to tighten the noose around the Cuban economy." Concurrently, the Kennedy administration sought to restrict the activities of the small pro-Castro minority in the United States. On 2 June 1961, the FBI was directed to establish a special counterintelligence program to monitor and harass such groups as the Fair Play for Cuba Committee.

25. This policy of economic denial would gain its most detailed explanation in a 1964 memorandum by George W. Ball; see Department of State, *U.S. Policy toward Cuba*.

26. See Thomas, "The Organization of American States and Subversive Intervention," 19–23.

27. Department of State *Bulletin* 46 (19 February 1962): 270.

28. Statement Made by the U.S. Representative before the Council of the OAS, 4 December 1961, Department of State, *Current Documents*, 4 December 1961, Document no. 117, 320–23. Two days later Morrison submitted to the Inter-American Peace Committee a long memorandum charging the Castro regime with "the training of foreigners in Cuba in sabotage and subversive techniques" and offering evidence for the U.S. position that Cuba served "as a bridgehead of Sino-Soviet imperialism within the inner defenses of the Western Hemisphere." See "The Castro Regime in Cuba: Summary," *Current Documents*, 6 December 1961, Document no. 119, 324–26.

29. Department of State *Bulletin* 46 (19 February 1962): 270–76.

30. *Ibid.*, 277.

31. Lynn Bender convincingly describes the association of the stated policy of containing "the Castro contagion" and the intent of "choking off the Castro regime through political and economic suffocation." *The Politics of Hostility*, 23.

32. An undated draft memorandum of State Department origin listed as "themes

for the audience in Cuba" the following points: "Resistance forces continue the struggle inside and outside of Cuba"; "Cuba is isolated in Latin America"; "Although the Cuban Revolution has been betrayed Reforma con Libertad will triumph in Cuba." Declassified Documents 1977/337A.

33. Schlesinger, *Robert F. Kennedy and His Times*, 511–13; Senate Committee to Study Government Operations, *Interim Report: Alleged Assassination Plots Involving Foreign Leaders*, 139–41. (Hereafter cited as Church Committee, *Interim Report*.) The Special Group Augmented was composed of Lansdale, General Maxwell Taylor, and Robert F. Kennedy.

34. Church Committee, *Interim Report*, 142; Tierney, "American-Cuban Relations," chap. 6.

35. Church Committee, *Interim Report*, 80–83; 91–97; 117–32.

36. Ibid., 123–24.

CHAPTER 6

1. Sindlinger & Company, Inc., "Attitudes and Opinions of the U.S. Public in the Cuban Refugee Invasion: April, 1961," Schlesinger Papers, Subject Files, Box 6.

2. Bethel's judgments will be found in his propagandistic history *The Losers*, especially 7–8, 51–55, 109–24, 144–50, 249–50, 299–301, 322–24.

3. Other members of the subcommittee were Senators Thomas J. Dodd (vice-chairman), Olin D. Johnston, John L. McClellan, Sam J. Ervin, Jr., Roman L. Hruska, Everett M. Dirksen, Kenneth B. Keating, and Norris Cotton. Its aggressive counsel was J. G. Sourwine and its Director of Research, Benjamin Mandel.

4. Senate Committee on the Judiciary, *Hearings to Investigate Internal Security Act*, 86th Cong., 1st sess., 14 July 1959, 1–32.

5. Ibid., 5 November 1959, 141–78.

6. For Hill's testimony, see ibid., 87th Cong., 1st sess., 12 June 1961, 793–823; for Wieland's persecution, see ibid., 87th Cong., 2nd sess., 9 January, 8 February 1961; 2 February 1962. See also "Scapegoat for Castro?," editorial, *Washington Post*, 27 December 1961.

7. *I. F. Stone's Weekly*, 1 (23 January 1961). For a contrary appraisal see James Wallace's review of Weyl's book in *Wall Street Journal*, 4 January 1961.

8. See Goldwater, *Why Not Victory?*, 69–87.

9. *Saturday Evening Post* 234 (29 July 1961): 6.

10. Goldwater, *Why Not Victory?*, 69, 80, 84.

11. See John Matthews, "Some Truths about Castro"; and Robert Welch, "Fidel Castro Communist." Equally vituperative were various refugee publications in Miami. See File of The Truth about Cuba Committee, Inc., Draper Papers.

12. See mimeographed "Summary of Economic Aggression against Cuba," Draper Papers, Box 24; Sherrill, *Gothic Politics in the Deep South*, 168–69; CBS News, *Face the Nation—1959*, 5: 354; *Saturday Evening Post* 232 (4 July 1959): 10; Smathers to John F. Kennedy, 29 March 1961, Kennedy Papers, President's Office Files, Countries—Cuba—General; Tanner, *Counter-Revolutionary Agent*, 145.

13. *National Review* 7 (16 May 1959): 4; (27 June 1959): 7.

14. Ibid. 7 (9 May 1959): 40 (16 May 1959): 4; vol. 8 (2 January 1960): 7 (30 January 1960): 63 (13 February 1960): 95 (27 February 1960): 129 (23 April 1960): 253–55 (2 July 1960): 419; vol. 9 (16 July 1960): 13–14 (23 July 1960): 4 (6 August 1960): 4 (17 December 1960): 369–70; vol. 10 (7 January 1961): 6 (14 January 1961): 6–7 (22 April 1961): 238 (6 May 1961): 269 (20 May 1961): 307; vol. 11 (16 December 1961): 404–5.

15. See ibid. 8 (2 January 1960): 7; vol. 9 (31 December 1960): 404; vol. 11 (16 December 1961): 404. Buckley did not label Matthews a communist; rather he charged him with "cretinism."

16. Ibid., 9 (31 December 1960): 404.

17. *American Legion Magazine* 70 (March 1961): 18–19, 46–48.

18. Meyer and Szulc, *The Cuban Invasion*, 32; *Washington Post*, 22 December 1959; Senate Foreign Relations Committee, "Soviet Bloc Latin American Activities and Their Implications for U.S. Policy." In the House, another Oregonian, Charles O. Porter, was a strong initial champion of Castro and one of the more reluctant to abandon belief in the democratic character of the Cuban Revolution. Porter was defeated for reelection in November 1962, having been attacked in the campaign for his pro-Castro stance.

19. CBS News, *Face the Nation—1959*, 5: 350; Schlesinger memorandum to president, with enclosures, 13 May 1961, Kennedy Papers, President's Office Files, Countries—Cuba, Box 114a.

20. Fulbright memorandum to John F. Kennedy, cited in Meyer, *Fulbright of Arkansas*, 197–205; Smith, *What Happened In Cuba?*, 335–37; *Congressional Record*, 87th Cong., 1st sess., 9 May 1961, 7117–19; *I. F. Stone's Weekly* 9 (10 July 1961): 2.

21. When Eleanor Roosevelt wrote in her column *My Day* that perhaps a socialist economy was most suited to the development needs of Cuba and some other Central and South American countries, she was the object of angry criticism. See *New York Post*, 14 December 1960; Rivero, *Castro's Cuba*, 65.

22. Welch, "Lippmann, Berle, and the Cuban Revolution," 102–20.

CHAPTER 7

1. Wrong, "The American Left and Cuba," 92–103. Wrong's article is based on a careful study of articles and correspondence columns in *Dissent, New Leader, Catholic Worker, Liberation, Monthly Review, Nation, New Politics, New Republic, Studies on the Left,* and *Village Voice.*

2. *I. F. Stone's Weekly* 7 (27 April 1959).

3. Ibid. 8 (18 April 1960).

4. See ibid. 7 (23 November 1959); vol. 8 (8 April 1960) (5 September 1960) (24 October 1960) (31 October 1960) (28 November 1960); vol. 9 (16 January 1961).

5. Ibid. 9 (27 February 1961).

6. Ibid. (20 March 1961).

7. Ibid. (10 April 1961).

8. Ibid. (17, 24 April 1961).

9. Ibid. (1 May 1961).

10. Ibid. (3 July 1961).

11. The views of Scheer and Zeitlin are best summarized in their 1963 book *Cuba: Tragedy in Our Hemisphere*, especially 60, 66–67, 86, 126–27, 138–42, 207. For Rubin's views, see "The Tragedy of Cuba," 9–26.

12. Daniel Friedenberg, "History Will Not Absolve Castro," 11–13. See also Friedenberg's review of James, *Cuba: The First Soviet Satellite in the Americas* in *New Leader* 45 (19 March 1962): 24–26. Sam Bottone, charter editor of *New Politics*, was convinced by fall 1961 that "ideologically, Castroism is now all but indistinguishable from Communist totalitarianism." Bottone did not offer excuses for U.S. policy, which he judged stupidly hostile at a time when it might have influenced the 26th of July Movement to remain true to its initial goals of democratic humanism, but he believed "the counter-democratic course" taken by the movement after fall 1959 "was essentially indigenous in nature." The elitist tendencies within Castro's movement fed upon U.S. hostility, and in the process all dissent was stifled and those "who held to the original spirit of the Revolution" were denied "a political existence." Castro's determination to separate political and economic democracy was a perversion of true socialism. "Cuba: Socialist or Totalitarian," 23–35. Michael Walzer, managing editor of *Dissent*, expressed a similar view in the Committee of Correspondence *Newsletter*, January 1962.

13. See Corliss Lamont's advertisement for his pamphlet "The Crime against Cuba," in *Monthly Review* 13 (July/August 1961). Lerner published a column in the *New York Post*. See especially his columns of 18 October 1960; 19 April 1961.

14. Among the better studies of Mills's work are the following: Introduction by Horowitz to *Power, Politics and People*, 1–20; Fowler, *Believing Skeptics*; and Cleere, "The Intellectual as Change Agent in the Writings of C. Wright Mills."

15. An excerpt from Mills's book was the feature article in the December 1960 issue of *Harper's Magazine* 221: 31–37 (" 'Listen, Yankee': The Cuban Case Against the United States"). His book was published in the same month in hardback (McGraw-Hill) and in paper (Ballantine).

16. Mills, "*Listen, Yankee,*" 177–85.

17. See Berle Diary, 10 December 1960.

18. *Cuba: Anatomy of a Revolution* was first published by the Monthly Review Press in 1960; a second and expanded edition was published in 1961.

19. See Huberman and Sweezy, *Cuba: Anatomy of a Revolution* (2d ed., 1961), 85–94, 116, 133–47, 150–62, 171–73, 175–89; "The Theory of U.S. Foreign Policy," *Monthly Review* 12 (September/October/November 1960): 273–79, 321–33, 353–62; "The Criminal Invasion Plan" and "Notes from the Editors," *Monthly Review* 13 (May 1961): 1–7; "Notes from the Editors" for a special issue on "Cuba and Communism," *Monthly Review* 13 (July/August 1961). See also advertisement for "Cuba Packet," back cover, *Monthly Review* 13 (July/August 1961). Paul A. Baran, professor of economics at Stanford University, was—with Huberman and Sweezy—a leading authority on the revolution for the *Monthly Review*. See his *Reflections on the Cuban Revolution*; and "Cuba Invaded," 84–91. For an extreme version of the correlation of "liberation from underdevelopment" with "liberation from the

United States," see Morray, "Cuba and Communism," 3–55.

20. See B. A. Lesham's review of the Mills and Huberman and Sweezy volumes in *Mainstream* 14 (May 1961): 83–88.

21. North, *Cuba: Hope of a Hemisphere*, 7–9, 13–18, 91–92.

22. Editorial in *Mainstream* 14 (May 1961): 3–5; Aptheker, "The Cuban Revolution," pt. 1, 47–52, pt. 2, 35–45. Similar judgments of the revolution and U.S. Cuban policy were made by James S. Allen, a former foreign editor of the *Daily Worker*. See his pamphlet, *The Lessons of Cuba*.

23. *Political Affairs* 39 (March 1960): 96.

24. For Powell, see Eisenhower, *Waging Peace*, 524; Herbert L. Matthews to W. P. Gray, 23 March 1959, Matthews Papers, Box 1; *New York Times*, 26 September 1960. For Louis, see Senate Committee on the Judiciary, "Cuba and the American Negro," *Hearings to Investigate Internal Security Act*, 87th Cong., 1st sess., pt. 11 (5 June 1961), 789–90; *Time* 75 (18 April 1960): 37.

25. *Amsterdam News*, 1 October 1960; Senate Committee on the Judiciary, "Cuba and the American Negro," *Hearings to Investigate Internal Security Act*, pt. 11, appendix; *New York Times*, 26 September 1960.

26. A good summary of this speech is found in Sutherland, *The Youngest Revolution*, 145–46.

27. *New York Times*, 21 September 1960.

28. This advertisement first appeared in the Baltimore *Afro-American*, 22 April 1961. Its twenty-seven signers included W. E. B. Du Bois, Lonnie Cross, and Julian Mayfield. It was published in the *New York Post*, 25 April 1961. For a prejudiced view of the labors of Gibson and other black members of the Fair Play for Cuba Committee, see Senate Committee on the Judiciary, "Cuba and the American Negro," *Hearings to Investigate Internal Security Act*, pt. 11 (5 June 1961).

29. The following analysis of New Left characteristics and ideas is indebted to three studies: Wrong, "The American Left and Cuba," 98–103; Radosh, "The Cuban Revolution and Western Intellectuals," 37–55; Lyons, "The New Left and the Cuban Revolution," 211–46.

30. Lyons offers an interesting assessment of the evolution of the New Left, dividing its history between 1959 and 1970 into four phases: the "Humanist phase," 1959–63; the "Populist phase," 1963–65; the "Socialist phase," 1965–68; the "Communist-Leninist phase," 1968–70. "The New Left and the Cuban Revolution," 211–14.

31. *Studies on the Left* 1, no. 3 (1960): 7–16.

32. Ibid. 2, no. 1 (1960): 63–72.

33. "The editors consider the Cuban Revolution to be the most important and least understood social development in the recent history of the Western Hemisphere. . . . Further acquiescence to this attempt of cold war ideologues to crush the new humane society in Cuba might seriously thwart the chances of constructing a humane society in the United States." Ibid. 1, no. 3 (1960): 1–3. On the identification of campus radicals with the Cuban revolutionaries, see Johnson, "On the Ideology of the Campus Revolution," 74–75.

34. See SDS Papers, Microfilm Roll no. 1.

35. American Friends Service Committee, *Understanding Cuba.*

36. Neeley, "Controversy over Cuba," copy, Schlesinger Papers, Box 6.

37. *New York Times,* 23 April 1961. Among the signers were A. J. Muste, Erich Fromm, Clarence Picket, William C. Davidon, and Kermit Eby. A month earlier the FOR had protested against the refusal of the State Department to allow a FOR-sponsored "peace team" to visit Cuba. *I. F. Stone's Weekly* 9 (10 April 1961): 2. An ad hoc adjunct of the FOR, The Nonviolent Committee for Cuban Independence, led a two-week vigil outside CIA headquarters April–May 1961.

38. *Catholic Worker* 27 (February 1961): 1, 4–8.

39. Ibid. 26 (July/August 1960): 1.

40. Ed Turner, "Cuba," ibid. 27 (April 1961): 1.

41. Stuart Sandberg, "Cuba and the American Dream," *Catholic Worker* 27 (May 1961): 1.

42. Wrong, "The American Left and Cuba," 100; Lyons, "The New Left and the Cuban Revolution," 219; *Liberation,* February–May 1961 and Summer 1961. See, especially, Letter to Editors from Dick Jones in April 1961 issue; "Comment by A. J. Muste" in May 1961 issue of *Liberation* 6: 15, 51.

43. Dellinger editorial, *Liberation* 6 (Summer 1961).

44. Dellinger, "A Pacifist Revolutionary Looks at the Campaign against Castro," 8–12.

45. See Lens, "Cuba Revisited," 17–19.

CHAPTER 8

1. The years 1959–61 saw a few student sympathizers travel to Cuba. For an example of one who returned to the campus with convictions confirmed, see Margolies, "Report from Cuba," 41–46.

2. *National Review* 7 (9 May 1959): 40; *Harvard Crimson,* 27 April 1959. For preparations for Castro's Harvard visit, see *Harvard Crimson,* 6, 25 April 1959. Castro's visit was sponsored by the Law School Forum.

3. For an early denunciation of Fidel by the Young Americans for Freedom, see the *New Guard,* January 1962, 3–4.

4. Richard R. Fagen of Stanford well expressed the dilemma of the academic liberal when he subsequently wrote that the revolutionary quality of Cuban developments "awakened . . . the ambivalence that well-fed children of the enlightenment so often suffer when confronted with such profound translations. On the one hand, I was attracted by the audacity and creativity with which the revolutionaries were attacking the old order and building the new. On the other hand, I was disturbed by the ruthlessness and the thoroughness with which civil liberties and conventional freedoms were swept aside whenever they were seen by the revolutionary elite as inhibiting the developmental effort." *The Transformation of Political Culture in Cuba,* vi.

5. Tannenbaum would in later years write perceptively of the Cuban Revolution, but in June 1961 he offered the judgment that Castro's efforts to free himself from

U.S. tutelage would be unavailing: "The outflow of American energy is so all embracing that . . . not even Russia can save Cuba from American influence." "The United States and Latin America," 161.

6. Particularly was this true of professorial subscribers to the *New Leader*, the *Reporter*, and *Dissent*, magazines that expressed, as early as summer 1959, strong reservations about Fidel Castro. Among U.S. academics, John P. Roche, Nathan Glazer, Walt Rostow, Russell H. Fitzgibbon, and Robert J. Alexander were, with differing degrees of acknowledgment, proponents of the Draper betrayal thesis. Alexander was a long-time student of Latin American politics and his criticism of the evolution of the Cuban Revolution was the best balanced. See Roche, "Confessions of An Interventionist"; Nathan Glazer to David Riesman, Committee of Correspondence *Newsletter*, 19 June 1961, 24–25; Fitzgibbon, "The Revolution Next Door," 113–32; Alexander, "Cuba and the Sugar Quota," 3–5; Alexander, "Communism in Latin America," 15–19; Alexander, "Castroism vs. Democracy," 3–5; Alexander, *Prophets of the Revolution*, 267–86.

7. Draper, "The Nature of Cuba's Revolution," 3–4; Draper, "Castro's Cuba," 6–23 (reprinted in *New Leader*, 5 June 1961); Draper, "New Stage in Cuba," 7–9; Draper, "Cubans and Americans," 59–77. As noted in chapter 4, Draper's first *Encounter* article gained the endorsement of the Kennedy administration, particularly that of presidential counselor Arthur M. Schlesinger, Jr. For later writings by Draper on the Cuban Revolution, see *Castro's Revolution: Myths and Realities*; "Castro and Communism"; "Five Years of Castro's Cuba"; and *Castroism: Theory and Practice*.

8. Matthews, "The Cuban Revolution," 1–8.

9. Ibid., especially 5–7. See also Matthews, *The Cuban Story*.

10. Williams, *The Tragedy of American Diplomacy*, especially 11–44, 165–83, 204–12.

11. Williams, *The United States, Cuba, and Castro*, especially 31–42, 82–86. See also Williams, "Cuba: Issues and Alternatives," 72–80.

12. Among non-Marxist journals of opinion, the *Nation* offered the Cuban Revolution the most space and sympathy.

13. Shapiro, "Cuba: A Dissenting Report," 8–26; Shapiro, "Castro's Cuba Revisited," 15–16; Shapiro, "Castro's Challenge to America," 16–22. Shapiro's first article in the *New Republic* inspired a number of letters to the editor. The angriest was that of Earl E. T. Smith; the most laudatory, that of Robert Paul Wolff, an instructor at Harvard University. *New Republic* 143 (3 October 1960): 21–23. Shapiro's sympathy for the Castro regime, however qualified, inspired charges by a Lansing, Michigan, television commentator that he was a communist. Shapiro sued for slander, but his contract was not renewed by Michigan State University, a fact that I. F. Stone judged "disgraceful." *I. F. Stone's Weekly* 10 (17 December 1962): 3.

14. O'Connor, "Cuba's Foreign Policy and Ours," pt. 1, 8–11; pt. 2, 20–23. See also O'Connor, "Patria or Patriarchy," 43–46; O'Connor, "On Cuban Political Economy," 233–47; O'Connor, *The Origins of Socialism in Cuba*.

15. The committee had its origins in a March 1960 conference at Bear Mountain, New York, which deplored "the present course of arms competition" as a threat to

life on earth. In its first year, the committee operated from David Riesman's Harvard office but in 1961 its newsletter assumed a more professional format as "The Correspondent: Critical Dialogue and Research on Home and Foreign Affairs" and was published in New York. Among the more active contributors apart from Riesman were William C. Davidon, Michael Maccoby, Jerome Frank, Robert W. Gilmore, Robert Jay Lifton, Clarence Picket, Stewart Meacham, Marcus Raskin, Roger Hagan, Harold Taylor, Eric Larrabee, H. Stuart Hughes, and A. J. Muste. The committee had branches in Urbana, Illinois and Berkeley, California, and in spring 1962 it became the Council for Correspondence. It survived until autumn 1965. For an unfriendly appraisal, see the editorial in *Life* 50 (12 May 1961): 32.

16. Some contributors had expressed doubts about particular Castro policies. Though one compared him sympathetically to Gamal Abdel Nasser, another found a measure of similarity between Castro and Juan Perón. See Committee of Correspondence *Newsletter*, 10, 25 September 1960.

17. "Cuba," Committee of Correspondence *Newsletter*, 12 May 1961.

18. Earlier Glazer and Riesman had participated in an exchange of letters criticizing and defending the "Cuba" *Newsletter* of 12 May. See Committee of Correspondence *Newsletter*, 19 June 1961, 24–30.

19. "Cuba II," Committee of Correspondence *Newsletter*, January 1962.

20. Niebuhr, "Mistaken Venture," 3–4; Niebuhr, "Drama on the Cuban Stage," 11.

21. May, "In a Time of Unmanifest Destiny," 541–53.

22. Schlesinger, *A Thousand Days*, 285–86; Rivero, *Castro's Cuba*, 60.

23. Four faculty members accepted: Eric Bentley, professor of drama; Donald Fleming, professor of history; David Riesman, professor of sociology; and Hughes. *New York Times*, 19 May 1961; Houghton, "The Cuban Invasion of 1961 and the U.S. Press," 431. Bentley and Professor Barrington Moore, Jr. were the Harvard professors most denunciatory of the failure of American liberals to damn the Bay of Pigs invasion on moral grounds. For Moore, liberalism had been exposed as "a shabby fig-leaf for second-rate naked power politics." See "Correspondence" by Bentley and Moore in *New Republic* 144 (15 May 1961): 24; (29 May 1961): 22–23.

24. A copy of the historians' letter is in Schlesinger Papers, Subject Files, Box 5. For many signers, such as Douglas Adair and Gordon Wright, this was their baptism in political activism and few if any were associated with political radicalism. I. F. Stone congratulated the professors on their "courage to try and mold (as well as teach) history." *I. F. Stone's Weekly* 9 (22 May 1961): 4.

25. Bethel, *The Losers*, 296; *New York Times*, 1 June 1961. Among the signers of the Princeton letter were Oskar Morgenstern, Whitney J. Oates, Gardner Patterson, and Eugene P. Wigner.

26. History professor Arthur M. Schlesinger, Jr. had the title of presidential assistant, but his major contribution to Cuban policy was to draft a White Paper that offered justification for a political decision already determined.

27. *New York Times*, 6 April 1960. See also Wrong, "The American Left and Cuba," 95; Thomas, *Cuba*, 1277. Under grilling by the counsel of Senator Eastland's Internal Security Subcommittee, Carleton Beals would later seek to excuse himself

from all responsibility for initiating the FPCC. See Senate Committee of the Judiciary, "Fair Play for Cuba Committee," *Hearings to Investigate Internal Security Act* (29 April 1960, 10 January 1961).

28. Cleveland *Call and Post*, 20 May 1961; Draper Papers, Box 24, FPCC Folder; Richard Gibson, acting executive secretary, to FPCC membership, 7 April 1961, copy, Senate Committee of the Judiciary, "Fair Play for Cuba Committee," *Hearings to Investigate Internal Security Act* (25 April 1961).

29. See Letter to Editor by Dr. Harry Gideonse, *New York Times*, 29 April 1961; Schleifer, "Cuban Notebook," 72–83; Richard Gibson testimony of 25/26 April 1961 in Senate Committee of the Judiciary, "Fair Play for Cuba Committee," *Hearings to Investigate Internal Security Act*; Letter to Editor by Richard Gibson, *New York Times*, 10 May 1961; FPCC *Newsletter*, 10 May 1961 (entitled "Eastland Tries Again").

30. *New York Times*, 21 April 1961; Schlesinger, *A Thousand Days*, 285–86. The same paid advertisement was refused by the St. Louis *Post-Dispatch* and all four Chicago dailies. Light and Marzani, *Cuba versus CIA*, 42. The New York headquarters of the FPCC—now moved to 799 Broadway—claimed to have distributed over 300,000 leaflets including 100,000 "Stop the Attack Leaflets" in the third week of April 1961.

31. *The Militant*, 1 May 1961 as cited in Schlesinger, *A Thousand Days*, 286.

32. LeRoi Jones, "Cuba Libre," *Evergreen Review* 4 (November/December 1960): 139–59.

33. Ferlinghetti, *One Thousand Fearful Words For Fidel Castro*. The poem was first read by Ferlinghetti at a pro-Castro rally in early January 1961. See also *Liberation* 6 (March 1961): 10–14.

34. Miller, *90 Miles from Home*. Miller's book is a strange collage of personal commentary, travel journal, newspaper clippings, and poems and songs of the New Cuba.

35. Schleifer, "Cuban Notebook," 72–83.

36. *Village Voice*, 27 April 1961; Wrong, "The American Left and Cuba," 100. Mailer's letter to Castro was published in late April 1961, but by Mailer's account written several months earlier. The open letter to President Kennedy was composed and published shortly after the invasion at the Bay of Pigs.

37. *I. F. Stone's Weekly* 9 (15 May 1961). Norman Thomas drafted the letter on 4 May and was its first signatory.

38. *Monthly Review* 13 (September 1961): 230–31.

CHAPTER 9

1. See Cohen, *The Press and Foreign Policy*, 133–68 for a persuasive analysis of presidential dependence on the press for gauging public attitudes.

2. See the editorial judgment of the *Washington Post*, 2, 3 January 1959. The *Post* coupled "rejoicing" over Batista's departure with observations that Castro was "untested" and much would depend on his "wisdom and self-restraint." It believed that Castro would favor "moderate progressivism" as did Puerto Rico's Muñoz Marin.

Consequently, the United States should extend "all the aid and comfort it can."

3. Francis, "The U.S. Press and Castro," 257–66. Francis surveyed seventeen U.S. dailies and their coverage of the Cuban Revolution from January 1959 to April 1961. He divides the initial response of these newspapers into three categories: "critical," "skeptical," and "hopeful." Among the first he lists the Los Angeles *Times*, the Chicago *Tribune*, and the New York *Mirror*. He assigns to the second category the New York *Daily News*, the Detroit *News*, and the Dallas *News*.

4. St. George, "A Visit with a Revolutionary," 74–76; Laura Berquist, "Interview with Castro," *Look* 32 (24 February 1958): 24–30.

5. *Life* 46 (12 January 1959): 10; *Time* 72 (14 January 1959): 33.

6. *Life* 46 (12 January 1959): 10; (19 January 1959): 31.

7. Editorial foreword to Chapelle, "Remember the 26th of July!" 50.

8. *Christian Science Monitor*, 3 January 1959; *New Republic* 142 (12 January 1959): 5; *Nation* 188 (17 January 1959): 43. Max Ascoli, editor of *The Reporter*, offered a similar endorsement: "Our sympathies . . . are all with Fidel Castro." *The Reporter* 20 (22 January 1959): 2.

9. During this visit, Castro not only visited the campuses of Princeton and Harvard but met with Henry Luce and the president of United Press International. *Saturday Evening Post* now viewed Fidel with a cold eye and criticized the students of "sophisticated universities, like Harvard and Princeton" for their enthusiastic welcome of the new Cuban dictator. *Saturday Evening Post* 232 (4 July 1959): 10.

10. A Gallup poll in the summer of 1960 declared that 81 percent of Americans surveyed had "an unfavorable opinion" of Fidel Castro. However accurate the figure, the poll suggests that public opinion and press opinion had traveled in tandem, whatever their cause-and-effect relationship. *The Gallup Poll*, 3: 1680–81.

11. The earliest documentary film was that shot by Robert Taber and Wendell Hoffman in the Sierra Maestra in April 1957 and aired by CBS in late May as "The Story of Cuba's Jungle Fighters." It was highly laudatory of the efforts of Castro and the *barbudos*. See Llerena Papers, Box 1. Once in power, Castro cooperated with June Cobb of NBC in an hour-long television program similarly sympathetic to *fidelista* aspirations.

12. CBS News, *Face the Nation—1959*, 5: 8–14. Castro had also successfully parried the questions of Lawrence Spivak during the NBC program "Meet the Press" on 19 April 1959, at the time of Castro's visit to Washington, D.C.

13. Typescript of "Is Cuba Going Red?," CBS Television, 3 May 1959, copy, Matthews Papers, Box 8.

14. CBS News, *Face the Nation—1960*, 6: 32–38.

15. See, for example, the commentary of Bill Downs in his interview with Francis O. Wilcox, assistant secretary of state for International Organization Affairs, 11 September 1960, CBS News, *Face the Nation—1960*, 6: 303.

16. The *Washington Post* had decided by November 1959 that there was a strong pro-Communist faction among Castro's supporters and that Castro's efforts to export *fidelismo* served the purpose of a communist offensive in Latin America. *Washington Post*, 23, 24 November 1959. *Christian Science Monitor* decided only in December 1960 that the Castro revolution had fallen prey to "Communist doctrine and control imposed by conspirators taking advantage of great social need."

Washington, however, should recognize that "the overthrow of the Castro govern-ment [was] . . . the business of Cubans, not Americans." Any attempt by the United States to direct the efforts of "reform-minded Cuban exiles" would play into the hands of Castro. *Christian Science Monitor*, 10 December 1960; 3, 5, 6 January 1961.

17. *New Leader* 43 (14 March 1960): 3–6 (4/11 July 1960): 3–4; vol. 44 (10 April 1961): 7–9 (24 April 1961): 2–4 (5 June 1961): sect. 2.

18. *Reporter* 21 (17 September 1959): 41–42; vol. 22 (7 July 1960): 23–25 (15 September 1960): 16–20.

19. *New Republic* 143 (30 May 1960): 8 (25 July 1960): 8 (31 October 1960): 2 (5 December 1960): 5–6. The editors' evolving judgment respecting the "antithetical" nature of the Cuban regime did not prevent continued publication of the pro-Castro analyses of Samuel Shapiro. See the interesting debate between Shapiro and Daniel Friedenberg in the *New Republic*, 143 (8 August, 12 September, and 10 October 1960): 8, 8–26, 11–13.

20. *Nation* 190 (23 January 1960): 69; vol. 191 (23 July 1960): 41–42, 45–47 (6 August 1960): 64 (1 October 1960): 190. The *Nation* offered the earliest revelation of the CIA training camp in Guatemala. 191 (19 November 1960): 378–79.

21. *Time* 74 (6 July 1959): 5 (27 July 1959): 31 (17 August 1959): 36 (7 December 1959): 34; vol. 76 (8 August 1960): 36 (10 October 1960): 45 (24 October 1960): 44 (5 December 1960): 31; vol. 77 (13 January 1961): 29.

22. *Life* 47 (27 July 1959): 27 (3 August 1959): 14–17 (17 August 1959): 34–36; vol. 48 (28 March 1960): 35.

23. *Saturday Evening Post* 232 (1 August 1959): 13–15, 40–41 (19 December 1959): 10.

24. *Reader's Digest* 76 (January 1960): 67–74; vol. 77 (September 1960): 164–70; vol. 78 (March 1961): 112–15 (May 1961): 112–16; vol. 79 (July 1961): 59–64.

25. Francis, "The U.S. Press and Castro," 260–66; Houghton, "The Cuban Inva-sion of 1961 and the U.S. Press," 422–32; Bernstein and Gordon, "The Press and the Bay of Pigs," 5–13; Cozean, "Profile of U.S. Press Coverage on Cuba," 18–53. Cozean surveyed five publications for the period November 1960 to April 1961, comparing their response to particular developments in Cuban–American relations by means of content analysis.

26. Schlesinger memorandum to Kennedy, 6 April 1961, Schlesinger Papers, Sub-ject Files, Box 5; Mintz, "The Cuban 'Episode' and the American Press." See also James Reston column in *New York Times*, 10 May 1961, belatedly bemoaning the failure of the press to demonstrate more initiative and courage in the weeks before the invasion.

27. See, for example, *Washington Post*, 18, 19 April 1961. The theme of its lead editorial of 18 April was summarized by a Herblock cartoon showing a brave Cuban invader with a handkerchief banner attached to his rifle: "Freedom Si, Castro No!"

28. Francis, "The U.S. Press and Castro," 264–65.

29. *Time* 77 (21 April 1961): 32.

30. See Bernstein and Gordon, "The Press and the Bay of Pigs," 12. Jon Cozean in-dicts the press for leading the public and the policy makers to believe that Castro

had little popular support in Cuba and could be easily overthrown. "Profile of U.S. Press Coverage on Cuba," 33.

31. *Time* erroneously claimed that Castro's success was due to "a dozen jets, some of them MIGs, flown by Czech pilots." 77 (28 April 1961): 21.

32. *Life* 50 (28 April 1961): 28B (2 June 1961): 81–92; *Time* 77 (28 April 1961): 9, 21–22 (5 May 1961): 58–59. See also Swanberg, *Luce and His Empire*, 418. Early in May 1961, Henry Luce had lunch with President Kennedy in the White House and advised him that the solution to Castro was "a strong application of the Monroe Doctrine." Henry Luce Interview, 11 November 1965 (recorded by John L. Steele), oral history transcripts.

33. *Saturday Evening Post* 234 (20 May 1961): 10.

34. *New Republic* 144 (17 April 1961): 3–5 (24 April 1961): 4 (1 May 1961): 4. *Christian Science Monitor* advocated a similar course for fighting Castro, and was even more indirect in its criticisms of Kennedy's Cuban policy. 12, 14, 21 April 1961.

35. *Nation* 192 (6 May 1961): 383 (13 May 1961): 401–2.

36. See Scheer and Zeitlin, *Cuba: Tragedy in Our Hemisphere*, 95.

37. When Castro came to power in January 1959, the total book value of U.S. business enterprises in Cuba was greater than in any other Latin American country except Venezuela. U.S. investment was especially predominant in Cuban sugar production and public utilities. The United States was, moreover, Cuba's major customer and supplier. Johnson, "U.S. Business Interests in Cuba and the Rise of Castro," 440–59.

38. *Business Week*, 25 July 1959: 105–6.

39. Ibid., 1 August, 31 October, 14 November 1959: 70–4, 99–100, 45–6.

40. Ibid., 19 December 1959; 13 February 1960: 102, 107.

41. Ibid., 20 February, 2 July 1960: 47–53, 72.

42. Ibid., 9 July 1960: 34, 148.

43. Ibid., 16, 30 July, 13, 27 August 1960: 34, 148, 103–4.

44. Ibid., 11, 18 February 1961: 74, 98.

45. Ibid., 8, 15 April 1961: 112, 148.

46. Ibid., 22, 29 April 1961: 27–8, 41, 128.

47. See *Nation's Business*, February 1961: 71, and "Management's Washington Letter," July 1961: 9. Only slightly less fervent in tone were certain editorials in *Fortune*, Henry Luce's monthly directed to a business audience. It denounced the Agrarian Reform Law at its inception—a "body blow to big foreign companies like Atlántica del Golfo . . . Cuba–American Sugar, and United Fruit"—and it linked the destruction of "free economic activity" with advantage to Cuban communists and the Soviet Union. "If [Castro] . . . wrecks the Cuban capitalist system, Communism will almost certainly follow." *Fortune* 60 (July 1959): 77–78 (September 1959): 110–13, 264–74.

48. *Wall Street Journal*, 5, 8, 15, 19 January 1959; 20 March 1959.

49. Ibid., 17 July 1959.

50. Ibid., 20 July 1959.

51. Ibid., 29 July 1959.

52. Ibid., 11 April 1960; Smith, *The United States and Cuba*, 180.

53. *Wall Street Journal*, 21 November 1960; 5 January 1961.

54. Ibid., 4, 5 April 1961.

55. Ibid., 18, 20, 21 April 1961.

56. *Commonweal* 70 (1 May 1959): 118 (29 May 1959): 221 (31 July 1959): 383 (4 September 1959): 466; vol. 71 (13 November 1959): 197–98 (1 January 1960): 386; vol. 72 (10 June 1960): 269 (19 August 1960): 413; vol. 73 (21 October 1960): 84 (4 November 1960): 141 (20 January 1961): 423; vol. 74 (5 May 1961): 139–40 (14 July 1961): 387. See also Dewart, *Christianity and Revolution*, 154–65 and Glick, "Castro and the Church," 67–69. The two American prelates most outspoken against Castro were Francis Cardinal Spellman of New York and Richard Cardinal Cushing of Boston.

57. *America* 102 (5 December 1959): 314 (23 January 1960): 491 (6 February 1960): 543 (27 February 1960): 631 (5 March 1960): 668 (26 March 1960): 754; vol. 103 (9 April 1960): 33 (18 June 1960): 366 (2 July 1960): 406 (23 July 1960): 468 (6 August 1960): 506 (20 August 1960): 546 (27 August 1960): 566; vol. 104 (3 December 1960): 331 (7 January 1961): 434. *Catholic World* came to a similar conclusion but rather later. By April 1961 it declared that American Catholics should have little doubt that "there is an open battle against the religion of Christ in Cuba." 193 (April 1961): 38. With other examples of the Catholic press, it became convinced that Castro was a Red when he attacked the church in Cuba. As a communist, he was an enemy of the United States as well as of the church.

58. *New York Times*, 21 October 1960.

59. *American Legion Magazine* 69 (August 1960): 12–13, 39–42; vol. 70 (January 1961): 10–11, 37–40 (March 1961): 18–19, 46–48 (June 1961): 28–29.

CHAPTER 10

1. Department of State *Bulletin* 44 (3 April 1961): 480.

2. Niebuhr, *The Irony of American History*, 112.

Bibliography

LIBRARY COLLECTIONS

Boston, Mass.
  John F. Kennedy Library
    Oral history transcripts of Robert Amory, Jr., Adolf A. Berle, Richard M. Bissell,
      Arleigh Burke, Lyman B. Kirkpatrick, Jr., Walter Lippmann, and Henry Luce
    John F. Kennedy Papers
    Arthur M. Schlesinger Papers
Cambridge, Mass.
  Harvard University Libraries
    Document Library, Microtext
      Students for a Democratic Society (SDS) Papers
Hyde Park, N.Y.
  Franklin D. Roosevelt Library
    Adolf A. Berle Diary
New Haven, Conn.
  Yale University Libraries
    Walter Lippmann Papers
    File of Walter Lippmann's "Today and Tomorrow" columns
New York, N.Y.
  Columbia University Libraries
    Butler Library Archives
      Herbert L. Matthews Papers
  New York Public Library
    File on Fair Play for Cuba Committee, vols. 1 and 2
Stanford, Calif.
  Hoover Institution on War, Revolution and Peace
    Theodore Draper Papers
    Mario Llerena Papers
Washington, D.C.
  Columbus Memorial Library
    Library of the Organization of American States
      File on Cuba
  Department of State Library
    Press Reports on the Situation in Cuba, March 1960–6 January 1961, 10 vols.

NEWSPAPERS

Afro-American (Baltimore)
Amsterdam News (New York)
Christian Science Monitor
Harvard Crimson
New York Post

New York Times
Village Voice
Wall Street Journal
Washington Post

PERIODICALS

America
American Legion Magazine
American Opinion
Business Week
Catholic Worker
Catholic World
Christian Century
Commentary
Commonweal
Dissent
Fortune
Harper's Magazine
Hispanic American Historical Review
Hispanic American Report (Stanford
   University)
I. F. Stone's Weekly
Journal of Commerce
Liberation

Life
Look
Mainstream
Monthly Review
Nation
National Review
Nation's Business
New Leader
New Politics
New Republic
Political Affairs
Progressive
Reader's Digest
Reporter
Saturday Evening Post
Social Research
Studies on the Left
Time

NEWSLETTERS

Committee of Correspondence *Newsletter*
Cuba Resource Center Newsletter
Cuban Studies Newsletter (University of Pittsburgh)
Fair Play for Cuba Committee (FPCC) *Newsletter*
The Truth about Cuba Committee *Bulletin on Cuba*

PUBLIC DOCUMENTS

Central Intelligence Agency. Office of Current Intelligence. Weekly Information Report. Memorandum of Office of National Board of Estimates. *Is Time on Our*

Side in Cuba? By Sherman Kent. Washington, D.C., 27 January 1961; 10 March 1961.

Congressional Record. Washington, D.C., 1959–60.

Declassified Documents Quarterly Catalogue, Washington, D.C., Carrollton Press, 1976–79 (microfiche).

Department of State. *American Foreign Policy Current Documents* for 1959, 1960, 1961, 1962. Washington, D.C., 1963, 1964, 1965, 1966.

———. Bureau of Intelligence and Research. Weekly Intelligence Report. International *Bulletin* for 1958–62, vols. 42–46.

———. *The Castro Regime in Cuba.* Washington, D.C., 1961.

———. *Cuba.* Inter-American Series 66, publication no. 7171. Washington, D.C., 1961.

———. *Events in United States–Cuban Relations: A Chronology, 1957–1963.* Washington, D.C., 1963.

———. *International Communism in Latin America.* Inter-American Series 60, publication no. 7084. Washington, D.C., 1960.

———. *U.S. Policy toward Cuba.* By George Ball. Inter-American Series 88, publication no. 7690. Washington, D.C., 1964.

Organization of American States. Pan American Union. *Meeting of Consultation of the Ministers of Foreign Affairs, Punta del Este, Uruguay, 1962: Actas y. documentos.* Washington, D.C.: Pan American Union, 1963.

Taylor Commission. National Security Files (declassified). *Taylor Commission Report.* Part 1: "Narrative of the Anti-Castro Cuban Operation Zapata." 13 June 1961 (sanitized version declassified, 8 May 1977). Part 2: "Memorandums for Record of Paramilitary Study Group Meetings." 22 April–25 May 1961 (sanitized version declassified, 23 June 1978).

U.S. Congress. House. Committee on Foreign Affairs. "The Communist Threat in Latin America." *Hearings before the Subcommittee on Inter-American Affairs.* 86th Cong., 2d sess. 1960.

———. "Cuba and the Caribbean." *Hearings before the Subcommittee on Inter-American Affairs.* 91st Cong., 1st sess. 1970.

———. Committee on Interstate and Foreign Commerce. "Trade with Cuba." *Hearings before the Committee on Interstate and Foreign Commerce.* 87th Cong., 1st sess. 1961.

———. Senate. Foreign Relations Committee. "Soviet Bloc Latin American Activities and Their Implications for U.S. Policy." Report no. 7 of the Subcommittee on American Republics Affairs. 1960.

———. "United States Policy towards Cuba." *Hearings before the Committee on Foreign Relations.* 91st Cong., 2d sess. 1970.

———. "Castro's Broken Pledges." *Memorandum Prepared for the Subcommittee to Investigate the Administration of the Internal Security Act and Other Internal Security Laws.* 91st Cong., 2d sess. 1970.

———. Judiciary Committee. "The Communist Threat to the United States through the Caribbean." *Hearings before the Subcommittee to Investigate the Administration of the Internal Security Act and Other Internal Security Laws.*

86th Cong., 2d sess. 1960. 87th Cong., 1st sess. 1961. 87th Cong., 2d sess. 1962.
_____. "Cuban Aftermath—Red Seeds Blow South: Implications for the United States of the Latin American Conference for National Sovereignty and Economic Emancipation and Peace." *Hearings before the Subcommittee to Investigate the Administration of the Internal Security Act.* 87th Cong., 1st sess. 1961.
_____. "Cuba." *Hearings before the Subcommittee to Investigate the Administration of the Internal Security Act.* 91st Cong., 2d sess. 1970.
_____. "Fair Play for Cuba Committee" and "Cuba and the American Negro." *Hearings before the Subcommittee to Investigate the Administration of the Internal Security Act.* 87th Cong., 1st sess. 1961.
_____. Select Committee to Study Government Operations. *Interim Report: Alleged Assassination Plots Involving Foreign Leaders.* Report no. 94–465. 94th Cong., 1st sess. 20 November 1975.
U.S. Information Agency. *Communist Propaganda Activities in Latin America in 1961.* Washington, D.C., 1962.

BOOKS AND ARTICLES

Aguirre, M. "The Persecution in Cuba." *Catholic World* 193 (April 1961): 28–35.
Alexander, Robert J. "Castroism vs. Democracy." *New Leader* 44 (6 February 1961): 3–5.
_____. "Castro's Challenge to America." *New Politics* 1 (Fall 1961): 7–15.
_____. "Communism in Latin America." *New Leader* 44 (30 January 1961): 15–19.
_____. "Cuba and the Sugar Quota." *New Leader* 43 (21 March 1960): 3–5.
_____. "The Inter-American Conference on Freedom." *New Leader* 43 (30 May 1960): 8–10.
_____. *Prophets of the Revolution: Profiles of Latin American Leaders.* New York: Macmillan, 1962.
Allen, James S. *The Lessons of Cuba.* New York: New Century, 1961. Pamphlet.
Alvarez Díaz, José R., ed. *A Study on Cuba.* Miami: University of Miami Press, 1965.
American Friends Service Committee. *Understanding Cuba.* N.p.: Peace Education Program, November 1960. Pamphlet.
Aptheker, Herbert. "The Cuban Revolution Part I and Part II." *Political Affairs* 40 (March 1961; April 1961): 47–52; 34–45.
Aronson, James. *The Press and the Cold War.* Indianapolis: Bobbs-Merrill, 1970.
Baggs, William C. "The Gringo and the Revolution in Latin America." *American Scholar* 30 (Fall 1961): 567–70.
Bailey, Norman A. "Latin America Since the War." *Journal of International Affairs* 14 (1960): 115–25.
Baklanoff, Eric N. *Expropriations of U.S. Investments in Cuba, Mexico and Chile.* New York: Frederick Praeger, 1975.
Baran, Paul A. "Cuba Invaded." *Monthly Review* 13 (July/August 1961): 84–91.

_____. *Reflections on the Cuban Revolution.* New York: Monthly Review Press, 1961. Pamphlet.

Batista, Fulgencio. *Cuba Betrayed.* New York: Vantage Press, 1962.

Beck, Kent M. "Necessary Lies, Hidden Truths: Cuba in the 1960 Campaign." *Diplomatic History* 8 (Winter 1984): 37–59.

Bender, Lynn Darrell. *The Politics of Hostility: Castro's Revolution and United States Policy.* Hato Rey, P.R.: Inter American University Press, 1975.

Benítez, Jaime. *The U.S., Cuba, and Latin America.* Santa Barbara, Calif.: Center for the Study of Democratic Institutions, 1961. Pamphlet.

Berle, Adolf A. *The Cold War in Latin America.* Storrs: University of Connecticut, 1961. Pamphlet.

_____. "The Cuban Crisis: Failure of American Foreign Policy." *Foreign Affairs* 39 (October 1960): 40–55.

_____. *Latin America—Diplomacy and Reality.* New York: Harper & Row, 1962.

Berle, Beatrice Bishop and Jacobs, Travis Beal, eds. *Navigating the Rapids, 1918–1971: From the Papers of Adolf A. Berle.* New York: Harcourt Brace Jovanovich, 1973.

Bernstein, Victor, and Gordon, Jesse. "The Press and the Bay of Pigs." *Columbia University Forum* 10 (Fall 1967): 4–13.

Bethel, Paul D. *The Losers: The Definitive Report, by an eyewitness, of the Communist Conquest of Cuba and the Soviet Penetration in Latin America.* New Rochelle, N.Y.: Arlington House, 1969.

Blasier, S. Cole. "The Elimination of United States Influence." In *Revolutionary Change in Cuba,* edited by Carmelo Mesa-Lago, 43–80. Pittsburgh: University of Pittsburgh Press, 1971.

_____. *The Hovering Giant: U.S. Response to Revolutionary Change in Latin America.* Pittsburgh: University of Pittsburgh Press, 1976.

_____, and Mesa-Lago, Carmelo, eds. *Cuba in the World.* Pittsburgh: University of Pittsburgh Press, 1979.

Bonachea, Ramón L., and San Martín, Marta. *The Cuban Insurrection, 1952–1959.* New Brunswick, N.J.: Transaction Books, 1974.

Bonachea, Ronaldo E., and Valdés, Nelson P., comps. *Cuba in Revolution.* Garden City, N.Y.: Anchor Books, 1972.

_____, eds. *Revolutionary Struggle, 1947–1958.* Cambridge, Mass.: MIT Press, 1972.

Bonsal, Philip W. "Cuba, Castro, and the United States." *Foreign Affairs* 45 (January 1967): 260–76.

_____. *Cuba, Castro, and the United States.* Pittsburgh: University of Pittsburgh Press, 1971.

Bottone, Sam. "Cuba: Socialist or Totalitarian." *New Politics* 1 (Fall 1961): 23–35.

Bowles, Chester. *Promises to Keep.* New York: Harper & Row, 1971.

Brennan, Ray. *Castro, Cuba and Justice.* Garden City, N.Y.: Doubleday, 1959.

Briggs, Ellis O. *The Anatomy of Diplomacy.* New York: David McKay, 1968.

Castro, Fidel. "Why We Fight." *Coronet* (February 1958): 80–86.

Casuso, Teresa. *Cuba and Castro.* New York: Random House, 1961.

CBS News. *Face the Nation—1959.* Vol. 5. New York: Holt Information Systems, 1972.
———. *Face the Nation—1960.* Vol. 6. New York: Holt Information Systems, 1972.
Chapelle, Dickey. "Remember the 26th of July!" *Reader's Digest* 74 (April 1959): 50–56; 233–56.
Cleere, Ford W. "The Intellectual as Change Agent in the Writings of C. Wright Mills." Ph.D. dissertation, University of Colorado, 1971.
Cohen, Bernard C. *The Press and Foreign Policy.* Princeton, N.J.: Princeton University Press, 1963.
Cozean, Jon D. "Profile of U.S. Press Coverage on Cuba: Was Bay of Pigs Necessary?" *Journal of International and Comparative Studies* (Washington, D.C.) 5 (Winter 1972): 18–53.
Davis, Harold Eugene. "Revolutionary Cuba: Something Old and Something New." *World Affairs* 124 (Spring 1961): 7–11.
Dean, Vera Micheles. "U.S. Dilemma on Cuba." *Foreign Policy Bulletin* 40 (15 February 1961): 87–88.
Dellinger, David. "A Pacifist Revolutionary Looks at the Campaign Against Castro." *Liberation* 6 (April 1961): 8–12.
Dewart, Leslie. *Christianity and Revolution: The Lesson of Cuba.* New York: Herder & Herder, 1963.
Domínguez, Jorge I. *Cuba: Order and Revolution.* Cambridge, Mass.: Harvard University Press, 1978.
Dorschner, John and Fabricio, Roberto. *The Winds of December.* New York: Coward, McCann & Geoghegan, 1980.
Draper, Theodore. *Abuses of Power: From Cuba to Vietnam.* New York: Viking Press, 1967.
———. "Castro and Communism." *Reporter* 28 (17 January 1963): 35–48.
———. *Castroism: Theory and Practice.* New York: Frederick Praeger, 1965.
———. "Castro's Cuba: A Revolution Betrayed?" *Encounter* 16 (March 1961): 6–23.
———. "Castro's 'New' Communists." *New Leader* 45 (16 April 1962): 3–7.
———. *Castro's Revolution: Myths and Realities.* New York: Frederick Praeger, 1962.
———. "Cuba and U.S. Policy." *New Leader* 44 (5 June 1961): sect. 2.
———. "Cubans and Americans: A Report from New York." *Encounter* 17 (July 1961): 59–77.
———. "Five Years of Castro's Cuba." *Commentary* 37 (1 January 1964): 25–37.
———. "The Nature of Cuba's Revolution." *New Leader* 43 (4/11 July 1960): 3–4.
———. "New Stage in Cuba." *New Leader* 44 (10 April 1961): 7–9.
———. "The Runaway Revolution." *Reporter* 22 (12 May 1960): 14–20.
———. "The Strange Case of Professor Williams." *New Leader* 46 (29 April 1963): 13–20.
Dreier, John C. "The OAS and the Cuban Crisis." *SAIS Review* 5 (Winter 1961): 3–8.
DuBois, Jules. *Fidel Castro: Rebel, Liberator or Dictator?* Indianapolis: Bobbs-Merrill, 1959.
Eisenhower, Dwight D. *Public Papers of the Presidents of the United States:*

Dwight D. Eisenhower. 8 vols. Washington, D.C.: Government Printing Office, 1958–61.

———. *Waging Peace, 1956–1961.* Garden City, N.Y.: Doubleday, 1965.

Eisenhower, Milton S. *The Wine is Bitter: The United States in Latin America.* Garden City, N.Y.: Doubleday, 1963.

Facts on File, Inc. *Cuba, the U.S. and Russia, 1960–63: A Journalistic Narrative. . . .* New York: Facts on File, Inc., 1964.

Fagen, Richard R. "Calculation and Emotion in Foreign Policy: The Cuban Case." *Journal of Conflict Resolution* 6 (September 1962): 214–21.

———. *The Transformation of Political Culture in Cuba.* Stanford, Calif.: Stanford University Press, 1969.

———. "United States–Cuban Relations." In *Prospects for Latin America,* edited by David S. Smith, 304–25. New York: Columbia University Press, 1970.

———; Brody, Richard A.; and O'Leary, Thomas J. *Cubans in Exile: Disaffection and the Revolution.* Stanford, Calif.: Stanford University Press, 1968.

Farber, Samuel. *Revolution and Reaction in Cuba, 1933–1960: A Political Sociology from Machado to Castro.* Middletown, Conn.: Wesleyan University Press, 1976.

Ferguson, Halero P. "The Cuban Revolution and Latin America." *International Affairs* 37 (July 1961): 285–92.

Ferlinghetti, Lawrence. *One Thousand Fearful Words for Fidel Castro.* San Francisco: A City Lights Publication, February 1961.

Fitzgibbon, Russell H. "The Organization of American States—Time of Ordeal." *Orbis* 5 (Spring 1961): 74–86.

———. "The Revolution Next Door." *Annals of the American Academy of Political and Social Science* 334 (March 1961): 113–22.

Flores, Mark. "Economics of Liberation." *Mainstream* 14 (May 1961): 75–82.

Fort, Gilberto V. *The Cuban Revolution of Fidel Castro Viewed from Abroad.* Lawrence: University of Kansas Libraries, 1969.

Fowler, Robert Booth. *Believing Skeptics: American Political Intellectuals, 1945–1964.* Westport, Conn.: Greenwood Press, 1978.

Francis, Michael J. "The U.S. Press and Castro: A Study of Declining Relations." *Journalism Quarterly* (Urbana, Ill.) 44 (Summer 1967): 257–66.

Frank, Waldo. *Cuba: Prophetic Island.* New York: Marzani & Munsell, 1961.

Frankel, Max. "Journal of Inquiry in Castro's Cuba." *New York Times Magazine,* 22 January 1961.

Franqui, Carlos. *Diary of the Cuban Revolution.* New York: Viking Press, 1980.

Friedenberg, Daniel. "History Will Not Absolve Castro." *New Republic* 143 (10 October 1960): 11–13.

Friedman, Edward, and Kraus, Richard. "The Two Sides of Castro's Cuba." *Dissent* 8 (Winter 1961): 53–65.

Gallup, George H. *The Gallup Poll: Public Opinion, 1935–1971.* 5 vols. New York: Random House, 1972.

Glick, Edward B. "Castro and the Church." *Commonweal* 75 (13 October 1961): 67–69.

Goldenberg, Boris. *The Cuban Revolution and Latin America.* New York: Frederick

Praeger, 1965.

Goldwater, Barry M. *Why Not Victory? A Fresh Look at American Foreign Policy.* New York: McGraw-Hill, 1962.

Gonzalez, Edward. "Castro's Revolution, Cuban Communist Appeals, and the Soviet Response." *World Politics* 21 (October 1968): 39–68.

———. *Cuba under Castro: The Limits of Charisma.* Boston: Houghton Mifflin, 1974.

Halle, Louis J. "Lessons of the Cuban Blunder." *New Republic* 144 (5 June 1961): 13–17.

Halperin, Ernst. *Castro and Latin American Communism.* Cambridge, Mass.: MIT Center for International Studies, 1963.

Halperin, Maurice. *The Rise and Decline of Fidel Castro: An Essay in Contemporary History.* Berkeley: University of California Press, 1972.

Hansen, Joseph. *In Defense of the Cuban Revolution: An Answer to the State Department and Theodore Draper.* New York: Pioneer Publishers, 1961.

———. *The Truth about Cuba.* New York: Pioneer Publishers, 1960.

Hanson, Simon G. "Footnotes to the Castro Story from the Papers of Adolf A. Berle." *Inter-American Economic Affairs* 30 (Summer 1976): 29–44.

Hickey, John. "The Role of Congress in Foreign Policy: Case, the Cuban Disaster." *Inter-American Economic Affairs* 14 (Spring 1961): 67–89.

Hilsman, Roger. *To Move a Nation.* New York: Dell, 1968.

Hilton, Ronald. "The Cuba Trap." *Nation* 192 (29 April 1961): 364–66.

Hobsbawm, E. J. "Cuban Prospects." *New Statesman* 60 (22 October 1960): 596–98.

Horowitz, Irving Louis, ed. *Cuban Communism.* 2d ed. New Brunswick, N.J.: Transaction Books, 1972.

———. , ed. *Power, Politics and People: The Collected Essays of C. Wright Mills.* New York: Oxford University Press, 1963.

Houghton, Neal D. "The Cuban Invasion of 1961 and the U.S. Press, in Retrospect." *Journalism Quarterly* 42 (Summer 1965): 422–32.

Huberman, Leo, and Sweezy, Paul M. *Cuba: Anatomy of a Revolution.* New York: Monthly Review Press, 1960.

———. *Socialism in Cuba.* New York: Monthly Review Press, 1969.

Hulsey, Ramon H. "The Cuban Revolution: Its Influence on American Foreign Policy." *Journal of International Affairs* 19 (July 1960): 158–74.

Jackson, D. Bruce. *Castro, the Kremlin, and Communism in Latin America.* Baltimore: The Johns Hopkins Press, 1969.

James, Daniel. *Cuba: The First Soviet Satellite in the Americas.* New York: Avon Books, 1961.

Johnson, Cecil E. "Cuba: The Domestic Policies of the Castro Regime." In *Case Studies in Latin American Politics,* edited by John M. Claunch, 3–16. Dallas: Southern Methodist University, 1961.

Johnson, Dale. "On the Ideology of the Campus Revolution." *Studies on the Left* 2 (1961): 73–75.

Johnson, Haynes, et al. *The Bay of Pigs: The Leaders' Story of Brigade 2506.* New York: W. W. Norton, 1964.

Johnson, Leland C. "U.S. Business Interests in Cuba and the Rise of Castro." *World Politics* 17 (April 1965): 440–60.

Karol, K. S. *Guerrillas In Power: The Course of the Cuban Revolution.* New York: Hill & Wang, 1970.

Kennedy, John F. "Senator John F. Kennedy on the Cuban Situation: Presidential Campaign of 1960." *Inter-American Economic Affairs* 15 (Winter 1961): 79–95.

―――. *The Strategy of Peace.* Edited by Allan Nevins. New York: Harper and Brothers, 1960.

Kenner, Martin, and Petras, James, eds. *Fidel Castro Speaks.* New York: Grove Press, 1969.

Knudson, Jerry W. *Herbert L. Matthews and the Cuban Story.* Lexington, Ky.: Association for Education in Journalism Monograph no. 54, 1978. Pamphlet.

Landau, Saul, and Hakin, Eleanor. " 'Cuba, Si!': The Eviction of the Yankees." *Studies on the Left* 1 (1960): 86–95.

Langley, Lester D. *The Cuban Policy of the United States: A Brief History.* New York: Wiley, 1968.

―――, ed. *The United States, Cuba, and the Cold War: American Failure or Communist Conspiracy?* Lexington, Mass.: D. C. Heath, 1970.

Lehmann, David. "The Trajectory of the Cuban Revolution." *Journal of Development Studies* 7 (January 1971): 203–13.

Lens, Sidney. "Cuba Revisited." *Liberation* 6 (December 1961): 17–19.

Lévesque, Jacques. *The USSR and the Cuban Revolution: Soviet Ideological and Strategical Perspectives, 1959–1977.* New York: Praeger, 1978.

Light, Robert E., and Marzani, Carl. *Cuba versus the CIA.* New York: Marzani & Munsell, 1961.

Lippmann, Walter. *The Coming Test with Russia.* Boston: Little, Brown, 1961.

Llerena, Mario. *The Unsuspected Revolution: The Birth and Rise of Castroism.* Ithaca, N.Y.: Cornell University Press, 1978.

López-Fresquet, Rufo. *My 14 Months with Castro.* Cleveland: World Publishing Company, 1966.

Lyons, Paul. "The New Left and the Cuban Revolution." In *The New Cuba: Paradoxes and Potentials,* edited by Ronald Radosh, 211–46. New York: William Morrow, 1976.

Macaulay, Neill. "The Cuban Rebel Army: A Numerical Survey." *Hispanic American Historical Review* 58 (May 1978): 284–95.

McGaffin, William, and Knoll, Erwin. *Anything but the Truth.* New York: Putnam, 1968.

Madariaga, Salvador De. *Latin America between the Eagle and the Bear.* New York: Frederick Praeger, 1962.

Margolies, David. "Report from Cuba." *New University Thought* 1 (Spring 1961): 41–46.

Martin, Kingsley. "Fidel Castro's Cuba: Co-existence with Fidelismo." *New Statesman* 61 (5 May 1961): 698–99.

―――. "Fidel Castro's Cuba: Relations with the U.S." *New Statesman* 61 (21 April 1961): 613–16.

Marzani, Carl. "Fidel Castro: A Partisan View." *Mainstream* 14 (May 1961): 23–31.
Matthews, Herbert L. *Castro: A Political Biography*. London: Penguin Press, 1969.
———. "The Cuban Revolution." *Hispanic American Report* 13 (29 August 1960): 1–8.
———. *The Cuban Story*. New York: G. Braziller, 1961.
———. "Dissent over Cuba." *Encounter* 23 (July 1964): 82–90.
———. "Fidel Castro Revisited." *War/Peace Report* (December 1967): 3–5.
———. "The Lessons of Latin America." *Foreign Policy Bulletin* 37 (15 June 1958): 145–46; 152.
———. "Return to Cuba." *Hispanic American Report* Special Issue (1964).
———. "The United States and Latin America." *International Affairs* (London) 37 (January 1961): 9–18.
———. *A World in Revolution: A Newspaperman's Memoir*. New York: Charles Scribner's Sons, 1972.
Matthews, Joseph Brown. "Some Truths about Castro." *American Opinion* (February 1959). Pamphlet reprint.
May, Ernest R. "An American Tradition in Foreign Policy: The Role of Public Opinion." In *Theory and Practice in American Politics*, edited by William H. Helsen, 101–22. Chicago: University of Chicago Press, 1964.
May, Henry F. "In a Time of Unmanifest Destiny." *American Scholar* 30 (Fall 1961): 541–53.
Mesa-Lago, Carmelo, ed. *Revolutionary Change in Cuba*. Pittsburgh: University of Pittsburgh Press, 1971.
Meyer, Karl E., ed. *Fulbright of Arkansas*. Washington, D.C.: Robert B. Luce, Inc., 1963.
Meyer, Karl E., and Szulc, Tad. *The Cuban Invasion: The Chronicle of a Disaster*. New York: Frederick Praeger, 1962.
Miller, Warren. *90 Miles from Home*. New York: Fawcett World Library, 1961.
Mills, C. Wright. *"Listen, Yankee": The Revolution in Cuba*. New York: McGraw-Hill, 1960.
Mintz, Norbert L. "The Cuban 'Episode' and the American Press, April 9–23, 1961." Committee of Correspondence *Newsletter*, 12 May 1961.
Morray, J. P. "Cuba and Communism." *Monthly Review* 13 (July/August 1961): 3–55.
Morton, Ward M. *Castro as Charismatic Hero*. Lawrence: Center of Latin American Studies Occasional Publication no. 4, University of Kansas, 1964.
Murkland, Harry B. "Fidelism for Export." *Current History* 40 (April 1961): 219–24.
Murphy, Charles J. V. "Cuba: The Record Set Straight." *Fortune* 64 (September 1961): 92–97; 223–36.
Neeley, Frances E. "Controversy over Cuba." Staff study prepared for the Friends Committee on National Legislation. Washington, D.C., February 1961.
Nelson, Lowry. *Cuba: The Measure of a Revolution*. Minneapolis: University of Minnesota Press, 1972.
Niebuhr, Reinhold. "Drama on the Cuban Stage." *New Leader* 45 (5 March 1962): 11.
———. *The Irony of American History*. New York: Charles Scribner's Sons, 1952.

_____. "Mistaken Venture." *New Leader* 44 (1 May 1961): 3–4.

Nixon, Richard M. "Cuba, Castro and John F. Kennedy." *Reader's Digest* 85 (November 1964): 283–300.

North, Joseph. *Cuba: Hope of a Hemisphere.* New York: International Publishers, 1961.

O'Connor, James. "Cuba: Its Political Economy." *Studies on the Left* 4 (Fall 1964): 97–117.

_____. "Cuba's Economic Revolution." *Progressive* 25 (January 1961): 19–22.

_____. "Cuba's Foreign Policy and Ours [Part I and Part II]." *Progressive* 24 (December 1960): 8–11; 25 (February 1961): 20–23.

_____. "On Cuban Political Economy." *Political Science Quarterly* 79 (June 1964): 233–47.

_____. "The Organized Working Class in the Cuban Revolution." *Studies on the Left* 6 (March/April 1966): 3–30.

_____. *The Origins of Socialism in Cuba.* Ithaca, New York: Cornell University Press, 1969.

_____. "Patria or Patriarchy: Cuba Comes of Age." *The Second Coming* 2 (June 1962): 43–46.

_____. "Political Change in Cuba, 1959–1965." *Social Research: An International Quarterly* (Summer 1968): 312–47.

Operation Zapata: The "Ultrasensitive" Report and Testimony of the Board of Inquiry on the Bay of Pigs. Frederick, Md.: University Publications of America, Inc., 1981.

Oppenheimer, Joel; and Jones, LeRoi; et al. *January 1st, 1959: Fidel Castro.* New York: Totem, 1959.

Perez, Louis A., Jr. *The Cuban Revolutionary War, 1953–58: A Bibliography.* Metuchen, N.J.: Scarecrow Press, 1973.

Pflaum, Irving Peter. *Tragic Island: How Communism Came to Cuba.* Englewood Cliffs, N.J.: Prentice-Hall, 1961.

Plank, John, ed. *Cuba and the United States: Long-Range Perspectives.* Washington, D.C.: Brookings Institution, 1967.

Radosh, Ronald. "The Cuban Revolution and Western Intellectuals." In *The New Cuba: Paradoxes and Potentials,* edited by Ronald Radosh, 37–55. New York: William Morrow, 1976.

_____, ed. *The New Cuba: Paradoxes and Potentials.* New York: William Morrow, 1976.

Reason, Barbara; et al. *Cuba since Castro: A Bibliography of Relevant Literature.* Washington, D.C.: Research Division, American University, 1962.

Rivero, Nicolás. *Castro's Cuba: An American Dilemma.* Washington, D.C.: Robert B. Luce, Inc., 1962.

Roche, John P. "Confessions of an Interventionist." *New Leader* 44 (15 May 1961): 5–6.

Rubin, Morris H. "The Tragedy of Cuba." *Progressive* 25 (June 1961): 9–26.

Ruiz, Ramón Eduardo. *Cuba: The Making of a Revolution.* New York: W. W. Norton, 1970.

Safford, Jeffrey J. "The Nixon-Castro Meeting of 19 April 1959." *Diplomatic His-*

tory 4 (Fall 1980): 425–31.

St. George, Andrew. "Inside Cuba's Revolution." *Look* 22 (4 February 1958): 34–38.

———. "A Visit with a Revolutionary." *Coronet* (February 1958): 74–76.

Schapsmeier, Edward L., and Schapsmeier, Frederick H. *Walter Lippmann, Philosopher-Journalist.* Washington, D.C.: Public Affairs Press, 1969.

Scheer, Robert, and Zeitlin, Maurice. *Cuba: Tragedy in Our Hemisphere.* New York: Grove Press, 1963.

Schleifer, Marc. "Cuban Notebook." *Monthly Review* 13 (July/August 1961): 72–83.

Schlesinger, Arthur M., Jr. *Robert Kennedy and His Times.* Boston: Houghton Mifflin, 1978.

———. *A Thousand Days.* Boston: Houghton Mifflin, 1965.

Shapiro, Samuel. "Castro's Challenge to America." *New Politics* 1 (Fall 1961): 16–22.

———. "Castro's Cuba Revisited." *New Republic* 144 (6 February 1961): 15–16.

———. "Cuba: A Dissenting Report." *New Republic* 143 (12 September 1960): 8–26.

———. "Doing Good in Latin America." *New Republic* 145 (4 December 1961): 11–14.

Sherrill, Robert. *Gothic Politics in the Deep South: Stars of the New Confederacy.* New York: Grossman, 1968.

Sinclair, Andrew. *Ché Guevara.* New York: Viking, 1970.

Smith, Earl E. T. *The Fourth Floor: An Account of the Castro Communist Revolution.* New York: Random House, 1962.

Smith, Robert Freeman. *The United States and Cuba: Business and Diplomacy, 1917–1960.* New York: Bookman Associates, 1960.

———. "The United States and Latin American Revolutions." *Journal of Inter-American Studies* 4 (January 1962): 89–104.

———, ed. *What Happened in Cuba? A Documentary History.* New York: Twayne Publishers, 1963.

Sorensen, Theodore. *Kennedy.* New York: Harper & Row, 1965.

Stebbins, Richard P. *The United States in World Affairs, 1960.* New York: Harper & Brothers, 1961.

Steel, Ronald. *Walter Lippmann and the American Century.* Boston: Little, Brown, 1980.

Stein, Edwin C. *Cuba, Castro and Communism.* New York: Macfadden-Bartell, 1962.

Stone, R. E. "The Revolution in Cuba." *Political Affairs* 42 (August 1963): 54–65.

Suárez, Andrés. *Cuba: Castroism and Communism, 1959–1966.* Cambridge, Mass.: MIT Press, 1967.

Suchlicki, Jaime. *Cuba: From Columbus to Castro.* New York: Charles Scribner's Sons, 1974.

———. *University Students and Revolution in Cuba, 1920–1968.* Coral Gables, Fla.: University of Miami Press, 1969.

———, ed., *Cuba, Castro, and Revolution.* Coral Gables, Fla.: University of Miami Press, 1972.

Sutherland, Elizabeth. *The Youngest Revolution: A Personal Report on Cuba.* New York: Dial Press, 1969.

Swanberg, W. A. *Luce and His Empire*. New York: Charles Scribner's Sons, 1972.

Syed, Anwar Hussain. *Walter Lippmann's Philosophy of International Politics*. Philadelphia: University of Pennsylvania Press, 1963.

Taber, Robert. *M–26: Biography of a Revolution*. New York: L. Stuart, 1961.

Tannenbaum, Frank. "The Political Dilemma in Latin America." *Foreign Affairs* 28 (April 1960): 497–515.

———. *Ten Keys to Latin America*. New York: Alfred A. Knopf, 1962.

———. "The United States and Latin America." *Political Science Quarterly* 76 (June 1961): 161–80.

Tanner, Hans. *Counter-Revolutionary Agent*. London: G. T. Foulis, 1962.

Te Paske, John J., and Fisher, Sydney Nettleton, eds. *Explosive Forces in Latin America*. Columbus: Ohio State University, 1964.

Tetlow, Edwin. *Eye on Cuba*. New York: Harcourt, Brace & World, 1966.

Thomas, A. J., Jr. "The Organization of American States and Subversive Intervention." *Proceedings* of the American Society of International Law (1961): 19–24.

Thomas, Hugh. *Cuba, or the Pursuit of Freedom*. London: Eyre & Spottiswoode, 1971.

Tierney, Kevin B. "American–Cuban Relations, 1957–1963." Ph.D. dissertation, Syracuse University, 1979.

Tomlinson, Edward. "What We Have Lost in Latin America." *American Legion Magazine* 70 (September 1961): 12–13.

The Truth about Cuba Committee, Inc. *Letter to the International Peace Commission, Organization of American States on the Communist Dictatorship in Cuba*. Miami: 1961. Pamphlet.

Valdés, Nelson P. "Revolution and Institutionalization in Cuba." *Cuban Studies* 6 (July 1976): 1–38.

———, and Lieuwen, Edwin. *The Cuban Revolution: A Research-Study Guide (1959–1969)*. Albuquerque: University of New Mexico Press, 1971.

Vann, Carl R., ed. *American Policy and the Cuban Revolution*. Syracuse, N.Y.: Maxwell Graduate School of Citizenship and Public Affairs at Syracuse University, 1961. Mimeograph.

Walters, Robert S. "Soviet Economic Aid to Cuba, 1959–1964." *International Affairs* (London) 42 (January 1966): 74–86.

Walzer, Michael. "Cuba: The Invasion and the Consequences." *Dissent* 8 (special issue, June 1961): 1–15.

Welch, Richard E., Jr. "Lippmann, Berle, and the U.S. Response to the Cuban Revolution." *Diplomatic History* 6 (Spring 1982): 125–43.

Welch, Robert. *Fidel Castro Communist*. *American Opinion* (April 1959). Pamphlet reprint.

Weyl, Nathaniel. *Red Star over Cuba*. New York: Devin-Adair, 1960.

Whitaker, Arthur P. "Our Reaction to Communist Infiltration in Latin America." *Annals of the American Academy of Political and Social Science* 330 (July 1960): 103–15.

———. "Yankeephobia: The United States and Latin America." *Current History* 42 (January 1962): 15–19.

Wilkerson, Loree A. *Fidel Castro's Political Programs from Reformism to Marxism-*

Leninism. Gainesville: University of Florida Press, 1965.

Williams, William Appleman. "Cuba: Issues and Alternatives." *Annals of the American Academy of Political and Social Science* 351 (January 1964): 72–80.

———. *The Tragedy of American Diplomacy*. Cleveland: World Publishing Co., 1959.

———. *The United States, Cuba, and Castro: An Essay on the Dynamics of Revolution and the Dissolution of Empire*. New York: Monthly Review Press, 1962.

Wright, Quincy. "Intervention and Cuba in 1961." *Proceedings* of the American Society of International Law (1961): 2–19.

Wrong, Dennis H. "The American Left and Cuba." *Commentary* 33 (February 1962): 92–103.

Wyden, Peter. *Bay of Pigs: The Untold Story*. New York: Simon & Schuster, 1979.

Index